Footprints in Time

John Colville

FOOTPRINTS
IN TIME

COLLINS
St James's Place, London

William Collins Sons and Co Ltd
London . Glasgow . Sydney . Auckland
Toronto . Johannesburg

First published 1976
© Harriet Colville 1976
ISBN 0 00 216248 2
Set in Monotype Perpetua
Made and Printed in Great Britain by
William Collins Sons and Co Ltd Glasgow

Contents

Contents

Illustrations

Acknowledgments

I am much indebted to Sir Osbert Lancaster for his kindness
in recapturing for me the likeness of His Beatitude Archbishop Damaskinos, to Miss Josephine Butler for typing the
manuscript impeccably and to the Trustees of the Chartwell
Settlement for not objecting to the reproduction of certain
manuscripts of Sir Winston Churchill's.

John Colville
September, 1976

Demise of a Bright Idea

I thought the idea was a winner. It did not come to me in my bath, or on a long solitary walk, or at the driving wheel or on any of those occasions when inspiration usually strikes. It came in church. As the organ began to play 'Once in Royal David's City', I reflected how widely men, women and children of all denominations, in every English speaking country, church-goers and non church-goers alike, know that hymn. I should have been concentrating on things above; but I began to wonder about the author, Mrs C. F. Alexander, who also wrote 'There is a Green Hill Far Away', 'All Things Bright and Beautiful', and other hymns to which I was much addicted in my childhood.

Who was Mrs C.F. Alexander? I was sure that few could answer that question and as the hymn, which has a lot of verses and was being played so slowly as to be positively lugubrious, went on and on, I had plenty of time to decide to write a best-selling book, not only about her but about others whose end-products were world famous but whose life-stories, and perhaps their very names, were scarcely known. By the time we sang 'Amen', my course was clear.

I pursued the project with zeal. There was, I discovered, a Mr Kirkpatrick Macmillan of Dumfries who invented the bicycle in the 1820s. There was Mr Shillibear, father of the omnibus, Mr William Paterson, founder of the Bank of England, and the inventors of matches, water-closets, hire purchase and countless other boons, or at least facilities, for the human race.

I started with the source of my inspiration, Mrs Alexander. On request Lambeth Palace were helpful. A kind parson in Ulster told me where I could buy an admirably written monograph about her. She was, I discovered, a saintly lady, unselfish, unwordly, poetic and charitable, although as a sop to the egalitarians it has been necessary to omit from 'All Things Bright and Beautiful' the verse about the Rich Man in his Castle and the Poor Man at his Gate. She must have been the embodiment of pious Victorian women at their evangelical best. Her husband rose high in the Church and ended his career as Archbishop of Armagh and Primate of All Ireland.

Turning to the Dictionary of National Biography I read all that is recorded there about Mr Kirkpatrick Macmillan and his bicycle. It seemed that nothing but extensive detective work in Dumfries would be likely to yield more. Mr William Paterson, for his part, turned out to be the subject of several biographies already, and there is a school of heretical opinion which maintains that not he, but Mr Charles Montagu and Mr Michael Godfrey should be canonised, or at least beatified, as the true originators of the Bank of England.

I plodded on until at last the truth was plain. All these admirable men and women, benefactors of the human race, had one thing in common: as the subjects of biographical essays they were deadly dull. It became ever less likely as my researches proceeded that their sales value might be redeemed by the dramatic revelation of vices hidden from posterity by charitable friends, relations and executors.

Should I nevertheless, in the sacred cause of truth and in the interest of historical research, pursue my theme? I remembered a Fellow of Trinity College, Cambridge, an American of polished culture and agreeable hospitality, whose contribution to learning was the history of the County Palatine of Durham during a few mediaeval years. This vast tome sold, I believe, three copies and is never likely to be superseded. If I went ahead I might, assuming I could find a publisher, aspire to be his equal, for it is said that those good-natured institutions, the British Museum, the Bodleian and the Cambridge University Library acquire every book published in the United Kingdom, although they expect to receive their copy free.

Discretion triumphed over valour and unselfishly I decided to renounce my exciting theme and bequeath it to posterity. Instead I wrote this series of autobiographical sketches, though I am uneasily conscious that such exercises should be the preserve of the eminent. I have no eminence whatever nor can I aspire, in this world or the next, to approach the footstools of Mrs C.F. Alexander, Mr Kirkpatrick Macmillan or Mr Shillibear. But I have occasionally found myself in curious situations, sometimes alone and sometimes in the shadow of others. The kaleidoscope revolves with ever increasing speed so that the people and the years to which these sketches

Demise of a Bright Idea

relate will soon be shrouded in historical mist and, no doubt, in historical misrepresentation. I hope, therefore, that I shall not be thought presumptuous in presenting them and in portraying some of the lighter events in my own life as well as a few of the more substantial characteristics of those with whom I have worked and travelled.

Part 1

ECHOES OF THE MORNING

1. World War I in the Nursery

We lived at 53 Cadogan Place. The day-nursery was on the third floor, looking out over the mews where Mr Smith kept his riding school, containing among other weary hacks two small ponies called Monty and Amelia. I used to watch my elder brothers riding them over the cobbles in the direction of Hyde Park until the day came that David fell off Amelia, broke his arm and refused ever again to look at a horse. Indeed, when the Second World War broke out he hastily joined the Navy, confident that he would never come face to face with a horse in one of His Majesty's ships. My other brother, Philip, valiantly persisted with Monty.

There was no such excitement for me; but there were compensations. There were my bricks which my father, who was a skilful carpenter, had made himself and which were admirably designed for building castles. There were my lead soldiers, which included Marshal Joffre on a horse, but which were mostly badly wounded, frequently armless or legless, as a result of the constant storming of the castles and their bombardment by a toy cannon. There was a gramophone, with a vast horn and a picture of a white fox-terrier listening appreciatively to His Master's Voice. On this machine Nanny would play such stirring records as 'Belgium put the Kibosh on the Kaiser', 'Sister Susie Sewing Shirts for Soldiers', and her favourite 'Sussex by the Sea', which unfortunately had a scratch on it and repeated the word 'Sussex' endlessly until Nanny had time to rush across the nursery and move the needle on.

Then there were the air-raids. It was thrilling to be woken up in haste, swathed in an eider-down, carried downstairs and placed in my pram in the basement. While the rest of the household sat apprehensively in the servants' hall, Nanny wheeled me up and down the basement passage and fed me with Air Raid Sweets. They were, I believe, acid drops, but such is the power of psychological persuasion that they tasted quite different from any sweets eaten in daylight and I positively looked forward to air-raids on account of them. The raids, mainly by Zeppelins, were insignificant affairs by comparison with those of a generation later, but there was one exciting night when a bomb fell in Lyall Street, scarcely two hundred yards from where I was contentedly sucking an Air Raid Sweet.

Then there were the gardens of Cadogan Place, quite the best gardens in London, with a swing, a see-saw, large bushes behind which to hide, and frequent views of fire engines, manned by splendid warriors in gold helmets, which emerged from the Fire Station in Basil Street and careered down Sloane Street with a huge brass bell clanging. They were all motor fire engines except for one which was drawn by two galloping grey horses with shaggy manes. We went to Hyde Park every day except Thursdays which were reserved for a visit to the Royal Hospital to buy radishes from the Chelsea Pensioners, one or two of whom were relics of the Crimean War.

In the winter evenings I watched from the night-nursery, with its windows looking over Cadogan Place, lamp-lighters running down the street, placing ladders against each lamp-post in turn, scurrying up to light the gas mantles and illuminating the whole street in a matter of minutes. Sometimes, when the windows were tightly shut against a thick Pea-Soup fog, I could see through the encircling gloom of midday men who carried flaming pitch-pine torches, such as had been used for centuries past, picking their way along the obscured pavements.

Nanny, whom I loved more than anybody or anything except the toy white rabbit which I always took to bed, held strong views. She had a brother called George who was fighting in Flanders and who, she maintained, had frequently been recommended for the DSO and was likely at any moment to win the VC. She shared George's view that the Germans, and the Kaiser in particular, had risen straight out of Hell and must be sent back there at whatever cost. In consequence she disliked dachshunds which we used sometimes to meet in Hyde Park and from which she would avert her eyes in disgust. Her heroes, though not for some reason George's, were the Belgians for whom she exhorted me to pray every night; but she was a bit doubtful of the French who, she believed, frequently claimed the credit for the glorious deeds of George and the rest of the British

Army. She was not quite sure about the Russians either, and her indignation when the Czar was murdered knew no bounds. She kept on the nursery mantelpiece a picture of the unfortunate ex-Emperor digging in the snow, which she had cut out of the *Daily Mirror*, and she used to wax eloquent about the monstrosity of the way he was treated. My early training in foreign affairs was thus somewhat slanted; but I was in no obvious danger of being infected with left-wing views in spite of my mother's strong, Liberal distaste for the Conservative Party.

November the 11th, 1918, dawned, though the dawn was unfortunately obscured by a threatening Pea-Souper. My father was in bed with the Spanish Influenza, my mother was working as a clerk in the Ministry of Pensions and my two brothers were away at school. I was alone with Nanny when at 11 a.m. the maroons sounded to announce the glad news that Armageddon was over. 'Quick', said Nanny, 'there's an air-raid'. And we bustled downstairs to the basement.

2. Lord Rosebery's Lamb

Archibald Primrose, 5th Earl of Rosebery, was a formidable man. He impressed his elders, terrified his contemporaries and was revered by his juniors. He was rich, he was famous as an orator and he wrote as well as he spoke. Queen Victoria sent for him as Prime Minister in preference to Sir William Harcourt; in after years Winston Churchill spoke of him with a respect bordering on adulation. He was spoilt, he was selfish and when he stayed with his favourite sister, Lady Leconfield, he would, according to his niece Margaret Wyndham, carefully survey the assembled company at Petworth with the aim of choosing the most vulnerable on whom to display his wit and exercise his powers of sarcasm.

In my mother's family, the mere mention of his name was all but accompanied by genuflection. His daughter, Lady Crewe, was gifted, witty and astringent; but she spoke of her father, 'my parent', with a deference otherwise reserved for the reigning Sovereign. Rosebery lived for more than thirty years after his retirement from active politics, an idol at whom nobody threw stones, the magnificent late-flowering embodiment of the Whig oligarchy. He was one of the last of the great Whig noblemen, polished, detached and scholarly, as much at home on the race-course as in the library, likely to have read *Das Kapital*, but probably in a rare edition, specially bound in calf.

In the spring of 1921 there was a long, sunny drought. I was six years old and I was staying at Epsom where Lady Crewe had taken a house so as to be near her father at the Durdans. I was there as the friend and playmate of my half-aunt, Mary, also aged six. We spent the days in the hot sunshine, climbing trees, assuaging our thirst in iced water (a delectable novelty) and occasionally escaping from adult eyes in search of adventure.

It was in the course of such an escapade that one morning after breakfast we crept away by ourselves to the Durdans and prowled inquisitively about the stables, where Lord Rosebery's huge bay carriage horses had recently returned from the nightly expedition with their owner, unhappy victim of almost constant insomnia, who had driven himself along the country lanes while others slept.

There was one apparently empty loose-box and this we managed to open. Inside, prostrate on the straw, was a lamb which we instantly concluded to be dead or dying. Having satisfied ourselves that it was still breathing, we conferred about the steps we must take to restore it to health. Mary had heard that brandy was the remedy in such cases; and surely there must be brandy in the Durdans.

I remember the shimmering heat on the lawn and the French windows wide open. There was nobody about, nobody with whom to confirm Mary's conviction about the brandy. So we walked through the French windows into the dining room and after some research discovered a bottle which could well, we thought, be brandy.

Down we ran to the stables, proud of the succour we were bringing to the dying lamb. It did not cross our minds that the lamb might just be prostrate with the heat. It was, after all, rather more thickly clothed than we were. We tore into the loose-box and I held open the lamb's jaws while Mary poured down its throat the entire contents of the bottle. The effect was remarkable. The lamb jumped to its feet, ran three or four times round the box and dropped stone dead.

That evening Lord Rosebery sent for us. He stood in the library, a frightening figure in dark green glasses. He spoke to us with sorrow rather than anger. 'My children', he said, 'you little know what you have done to me'.

What we had done was to pour his last bottle of Napoleon brandy down the throat of a lamb of such quality as to be segregated from the herd. It had been confidently expected to win a Championship at the Royal Show.

We were contrite, but we did not realise that in all probability nobody over six had ever in all his long life so maltreated Lord Rosebery and left him impotent to retaliate.

3. The Loss of a Shirt

When I was twelve I was appointed a Page of Honour to King George V. The service demanded was not an onerous one. It involved three annual appearances, all of them luckily in term time, at two of the royal Courts and at the Opening of Parliament. Although there were only four pages, a special stiff-boarded roster was printed to show in which month we were in waiting and this was solemnly despatched to each of us by the Lord Chamberlain.

My first appearance was all but disastrous. In the summer of 1927 there were to be two Courts held in May and two in June. As I was in waiting in May, I left my preparatory school at Winchester on the morning of the first Court, enraptured at the thought of the Latin verses I was not going to compose and the geometrical problems I was not going to solve. The rest of my form were gratifyingly jealous, especially when I explained with smug satisfaction that the Court would actually begin after lights-out time, and that I should almost certainly not be in bed before midnight. The bruises I sustained in consequence of these and other ill advised remarks were, by good fortune, invisible.

Another beautifully printed missive from the Lord Chamberlain had informed me that a royal carriage would arrive at my father's house at ten minutes before nine o'clock to convey my fellow-Page and me to Buckingham Palace, and that we were to be in the Royal apartments at ten minutes past nine precisely. Presumably the Royal Mews knew exactly how long it would take a brougham to go from Eccleston Square, where we then lived, to the Palace. At least five minutes before the carriage was due I was downstairs in the front hall, dressed in my scarlet Queen Anne uniform, complete with white knee breeches and silk stockings, white and gold satin waistcoat, lace jabot and cuffs and, most important of all to me, a sword with a white and gold handle in a sharkskin scabbard. I was wearing a dark blue cape and carrying a tricorne hat with red feathers. I might indeed have been setting out for the Court of Queen Anne and I much wished the other fellows in my form could have seen me, fearful though the results would unquestionably have been.

Ten to nine came and there was no carriage. At five to nine my parents became a shade anxious, at nine definitely worried and at five past nine desperate. My father set forth to hail a taxi, but there was none in sight. Finally, just before a quarter past, the brougham arrived with my fellow-Page inside. He was Harry Legge-Bourke, a truly honest and delightful person who later became a Member of Parliament and was well known for his punctilious behaviour. However, on this important occasion he had mislaid his white silk shirt. By the time the search had been abandoned and a substitute provided, the coachman had been waiting at his mother's door a full twenty-five minutes.

We had a resourceful coachman. He set off from Eccleston Square at a fast trot and when we reached Buckingham Palace Road he whipped the horse into a canter. Passers-by must have been dumfounded to see a royal carriage careering by at close to a gallop, while within the two youthful passengers were jogged, jolted and flung against each other with irresistible force as the brougham swayed dangerously on its slung springs. At headlong speed we dashed round the corner of the Palace, through the gates into the forecourt and finally pulled up with a jerk at the Grand Entrance. It was 9.25 and the King and Queen were due to enter the ball-room in full state at 9.30.

On the steps of the Grand Entrance stood two figures in the full dress uniform of Privy Councillors, one wearing the pale blue sash of the Order of St Patrick and the other some equally distinguished Order. They were the Lord Steward, Lord Shaftesbury, and the Lord Chamberlain, Lord Cromer. They each carried a white wand of office and their faces were of thunder. There was no time to explain or apologise: headed by an athletic footman, with powdered hair and full State Livery, we ran up the grand staircase, sprinted through countless doors and finally came to rest panting and disordered in the Queen's Sitting Room. Awaiting us were King George V and Queen Mary with the Prince of Wales and the Mistress of the Robes standing anxiously in the background.

Harry Legge-Bourke, who had already been a Page for a whole

year, wasted no time. He went straight up to the King, bowed and said: 'I am extremely sorry, Sir. It is not Jock Colville's fault: it is all mine. You see, Sir, I lost my shirt'. The King looked at the youthful figure in front of him, the anger vanished and he laughed. 'Lost your shirt, did you?' he said. 'Well, that's the only damned thing nobody can see in the rig you're wearing. But you're quite right to take the blame yourself, my boy'. The Queen had a long train and that was why the procession could not move without the Pages. Perhaps it could have done so; the Ladies in Waiting might have carried the train; but it was laid down that this was the Pages' function and nothing, on a State occasion, could be allowed to go wrong. Nor could anything be allowed to start late. The King's Parthian shot, as he moved towards the door, was: 'I was going to see three Indian Princes before the Court started. You have probably wrecked the Empire'.

The Courts, at which young ladies wearing short trains attached to their shoulders and white feathers in their hair were presented to the King and Queen by their mothers, aunts or other eligible relations, ended for ever in 1939. So did the Levées at St James's Palace where young gentlemen were presented to the King. Perhaps they served no useful purpose; perhaps, because of the line of social distinction drawn between those who were eligible to be presented and those who were not, they deepened the valleys of class discrimination; but the Courts were occasions of grandeur, indeed of beauty, which will never recur, and as such they merit description.

King George V wore either the full-dress uniform of an Admiral of the Fleet or the scarlet of the Brigade of Guards. Queen Mary, who loved jewellery and could adorn herself with any amount of it without appearing gaudy, wore a different tiara on every occasion. One evening it might be diamonds only; on another emeralds or rubies or sapphires. There were necklaces, ear-rings, vast brooches and countless bracelets to match whichever tiara she was using. Though never beautiful, as Queen Alexandra had been, she was always magnificent, and it may be doubted whether any more regal figure has ever been associated with the British throne.

The doors from the private apartments were flung open. As the King and Queen emerged, the Lord Steward and the Lord Chamberlain (whose reproving eyes the Pages were anxious to avoid) fell into place facing them and began the difficult feat of walking backwards through a whole series of State Rooms. The Queen's train, which we carried some two feet off the ground, was different each night; but it was invariably embroidered with gold or silver thread and was about eight feet long. Close behind walked the Mistress of the Robes, herself wearing a tiara almost rivalling the Queen's in splendour; then the Prince of Wales, the old Duke of Connaught and other members of the Royal Family; and finally a retinue of the Royal Household in uniforms of varying colours and designs. There were Hussars, Dragoons and Lancers, Guardsmen and Sailors, and officers of the Indian Cavalry Regiments, all emblazoned with gold lace, stars, medals and sashes on their scarlet, dark blue or green tunics.

The procession was long and it advanced slowly, the pace being set by the speed with which the Lords Steward and Chamberlain could walk backwards. It was, however, so timed that except on this occasion (which was assuredly unique in the annals of British ceremonial history) it entered the ball-room precisely at 9.30 p.m.

As the national anthem was played, the King and Queen moved to their two golden thrones, side by side on the crimson carpeted dais, and the Pages performed their only responsible task which was so to spread out the Queen's train that its full beauty, and the detailed work of the patient seamstresses, might be visible to the assembled company.

There was a pause. The King and Queen remained standing while the Marshal of the Diplomatic Corps led in the Doyenne of the Diplomatic Corps, the Marquesa de Mery del Val. When she had made her curtsies, the other Ambassadresses followed; and then came the Ambassadors, still few in number in 1927, followed by the Ministers of those many countries which did not rate an Ambassador at the Court of St James's, and at diplomatic last a few Chargés d'Affaires. The Ambassadors mostly wore dark blue and gold uniforms; one or two were in olive green; the Danish Minister was outstanding in red; and the Ethiopian Chargé d'Affaires wore a leopard skin. He represented the only independent African nation.

Two Ambassadors had no uniform, and for them the proper dress was an evening tail coat, black knee-breeches and black silk stockings. One, General Dawes, represented the United States; and the other, Mr Sokolnikov, the Soviet Union. Each of them provided a protocol problem. General Dawes, wishing to be publicised back home as a fine democrat who stood no old-fashioned nonsense, refused to wear knee-breeches. It was rude to the King, who minded about such things; but nobody would have paid the least attention had the General not insisted on holding in advance a press conference at the American Embassy to explain why no decent American would wear knee-breeches. Nor, for that matter, did any decent European in 1927, except at Court. The British press, short of murders, atrocities, international crises and sea-serpents, made the General's gesture into headline news. 'Back home' it misfired. The American public were not interested, the President was annoyed and the General had to rely for historic fame on the ill-fated Dawes plan which provided American money to set Germany on her feet again.

Mr Sokolnikov presented a more serious problem. His tail coat fitted perfectly; his knee-breeches were immaculate; but he had been personally involved in the arrangements for the cold-blooded murder of the Russian Imperial family. He had recently arrived in London to open an Embassy closed since the Revolution. The King had flatly declined to receive him when he came to present his credentials and had instructed the Prince of Wales to act in his stead. Here, however, was the Soviet Ambassador, properly dressed, exercising his undoubted right and duty to be present at Court; and nothing could prevent him from making his bow.

As the latest arrival among the Ambassadors, Sokolnikov came last in the line. There was total silence as all within range craned their necks to see what would happen. Slim and slavonically handsome, he walked across the room, gazing straight ahead, until he came opposite the Queen. Then turning smartly to his left, he made a perfect bow. The Queen dropped a hint of a curtsy in acknowledgement. Sokolnikov turned to his right, advanced three paces and then, turning to face the King, made an equally smart bow. The King was occupied with something over his left shoulder. He had turned his head away and was looking keenly at one of his family. The Ambassador passed on unacknowledged. The poor man suffered a worse fate a few years later; Stalin had him liquidated.

Echoes of the Morning

After the Diplomatic Corps came the Archbishops, the Lord Chancellor, the Speaker, the Prime Minister and the Cabinet. When they had all made their bows, the King and Queen sat down and the entire assembly followed suit except for the two Pages who had to stand for two long hours beside the Queen's throne while the proceedings lasted. Each lady's card was handed along a line of officials until it reached the Lord Chamberlain who read out her name, prefixed with 'To be presented'. I remember one occasion when an over anxious lady in the queue trod on the train of her immediate predecessor. The train came off. Unable to contemplate the disgrace of being presented without a train, the injured party withdrew; but she had already handed in her card and that proceeded remorselessly from hand to hand until it reached the Lord Chamberlain. He read out the name. The next in turn, indeed the very lady who had caused the injury, declined to be presented under false colours. She stood stock still and the proceedings came to a halt until the Lord Chamberlain, taking a hazardous plunge, read out the name on the next card and the procession continued on its smooth course.

At twelve years of age two hours is a long time to remain standing in tight knee-breeches and close-fitting patent leather pumps. The apparently endless flow of women with feathers in their hair induced dizziness. The only thing to do was to gaze at the ceiling or at the regimental orchestra in the distant gallery. I tried counting the pieces of crystal in the huge chandeliers; I told myself stories; I wished I were in bed. But endured it had to be, and at last the moment would come when the end of the line of feathered ladies could be seen with certainty at the far side of the ballroom, though there were false dawns when a temporary gap in the line, perhaps because a group of two or three had stopped to gossip or seek courage from their husbands, had seemed to herald the end of the Court.

After the final curtsy had been made, the King and Queen rose to their feet, God Save the King was played once more and the scintillating procession moved slowly back the way it had come. Then, after relinquishing the Queen's train, we were dismissed from the royal presence, invariably with kind words from the King, who never failed to congratulate us on not having fainted. It seemed that

29

the other pair of Pages sometimes did. We scampered through the Picture Gallery to the Entrée Supper Room and there, being very young, we were much cosseted by elderly ladies and gentlemen, ablaze with diamonds, ribands and stars, of whose names and eminence we were entirely ignorant. I do, however, remember that on that first night a swarthy man wearing a long silk costume, countless jewels and a golden hat, came up to me and said: 'It is against the rules of my religion to drink champagne, but fortunately I am so sacred that it turns to water in my mouth'. I believe the Aga Khan made a habit of saying this; but at twelve I was at a loss for a suitable reply. I supposed he was telling the truth.

4. Mr Salthouse

Mr Salthouse was a burglar. He was also a friend of my mother. I remember his coming to our house. He was tall and handsome, but with a suspicious mien and ill at ease in unfamiliar company. This was not wholly surprising as my father happened to have invited at the same time several important dignitaries from the Institute of Chartered Accountants.

His friendship with my mother came about because, apart from being a Lady in Waiting, Chairman of a Juvenile Court and President of innumerable societies and associations, she had long had a close connexion with the Borough of Shoreditch. She had worked there tirelessly since well before the First World War, running an Infant Welfare Centre, acting as Secretary to a School for Mothers and co-opted to the Public Health Committee of the unanimously Socialist Borough Council. She travelled eastwards two or three times a week by Underground, spent long hours visiting the poorer slum families and was familiar to many of the impoverished dwellers of a socially derelict square mile in the East End of London. She loved Shoreditch and felt as much at home in its squalid streets as she did at Buckingham Palace. To my mother all human beings were equally interesting and she discoursed in the same genuine unaffected way with the King and Queen as with the citizens of Shoreditch. Thus, without seeking popularity, she was equally popular at both social extremes.

She came to know the Salthouse family in the course of her weekly visits. Mr Salthouse had suffered from a number of disturbing youthful experiences. Now, as well as being an accomplished burglar, he was a dedicated Socialist, unusual, I believe, among Old Lags who generally support the Conservative Party. He also held strong views about matrimonial fidelity and, perhaps partly because he had both a strong temper and a heavy hand, his pretty fair-haired wife conformed to his views. However, his professional activities involved spells in Wormwood Scrubs and during one of these, lasting a full three years, Mrs Salthouse fell from grace. The result was twins, attractive little girls whom my mother welcomed with open arms at the Shoreditch Infant Welfare Centre, where at the age of about twelve I was dragged to see them scrubbed.

As the date of Mr Salthouse's release from prison drew closer, his wife became afraid. She was convinced that when her husband discovered what had happened he would kill her and probably the twins as well. My mother, unwilling to believe her friend capable of any such thing, none the less became affected by Mrs Salthouse's constantly repeated cries of alarm. So, on the day set for the release of the still unsuspecting cuckold, my mother rose early and set off for Wormwood Scrubs. When the prison gates were opened and Mr Salthouse emerged, he was surprised but delighted to find her awaiting him. They travelled to Shoreditch in a tram and on the journey the full story was unfolded. My mother expatiated not only on the abject penitence of Mrs Salthouse and on the glorious quality of forgiveness, but also on the charm, beauty and helplessness of the twins. By the time they reached the family room, where Mrs Salthouse was waiting in fear and trembling, the battle was won. He embraced his wife; he was enchanted by the twins; and, apart from occasional further sojourns in Wormwood Scrubs, he lived happily ever after.

'Thank you, Lady Cynthia', said Mr Salthouse some weeks later. 'I can never repay what you have done for us, but I can promise you one thing. As long as you live, you will never be burgled'.

Years later, after the Second World War, my mother went to live in Chelsea. Every house in the street was burgled, most of them more than once. The solitary exception was hers.

5. Solent Breezes

Between the two world wars the yachting world at Cowes, where my father had been brought up and where, being a skilled and passionate small boat sailor, he still took a house every summer, was filled with echoes of a spacious, leisurely and more formal age. It was an Edwardian fly trapped in the neo-Georgian amber. At the beginning of August a large pleasure fleet would assemble: steam yachts with brass funnels, gilded figure heads and long bowsprits; schooners of two and three hundred tons; and, dominating the scene the Royal Yacht *Victoria and Albert* of 5000 tons, with her graceful schooner bow, two gleaming funnels, and masts from which flew the Royal Standard and the Flag of the Admiralty. She was guarded by a battleship, on which there would be a Cowes Week dance arranged with the faultless entertaining skill of the Royal Navy. There were often one or two destroyers as well, and invariably a minesweeper which escorted the King when he sailed on his great racing cutter, *Britannia*, and which was commonly called '*Britannia's* Nanny'. Sometimes, too, Lord Inchcape, Chairman of the P. & O. Line, would arrive in one of his liners, filled with guests and requisitioned for the week without any protest from the shareholders.

Launches plied between the yachts and the jealously guarded landing-stage of the Royal Yacht Squadron. Brass funnelled pinnaces from the *Victoria and Albert* joined them, and the crowd thronging the sea-front knew that if a pinnace with a glass cabin was seen in Cowes Road, the King or Queen was going ashore, but if there was only a brown leather hood behind the funnel, less important persons were to be expected. On the Squadron Lawn there were wicker arm-chairs in which ladies, usually mature and always wearing pleated white flannel skirts, sat with gentlemen in yachting caps, blue serge jackets and white flannel trousers. Tea was provided in a large marquee out of sight of the crowds, while a military string band played waltzes and light airs.

33

Footprints in Time

The Royal Yacht Squadron was wholly sheltered from the taint and growing pretensions of democracy. The Solent and Spithead had been divinely ordained as a Cordon Sanitaire. In 1907 my father, as a younger son of a modestly rich man, had gone into the City in the worthy, adequately paid but not strikingly lucrative position of Secretary of the Institute of Chartered Accountants, because for matrimonial purposes he needed a larger income. On making his decision he had at once felt obliged to offer his resignation from the Squadron. The Commodore looked grave when the reason was explained to him, but he decreed, after consultation with some of the older members, that as an exceptional case this connexion with the City, and thus indirectly with commerce, might be overlooked because my grandfather had been a much respected member for a great many years. My father was lucky, for two years previously Jack Churchill, Lord Randolph's younger son, had sought membership of the Turf Club and the fact that he was a member of the Stock Exchange meant that he was instantly blackballed, whereas his elder brother, Winston, who was less popular but had no connexion with commerce, was elected without demur.

These Edwardian overtones were loudly audible at Cowes in my childhood. Many of the members were still respectably inactive, but there were already quite a lot who, like my father, earned their living. The familiar figures on the Squadron Lawn provided the flavour. There was the Governor of the Island, Princess Beatrice, who drove over from Carisbrooke Castle every afternoon and sat at a table in front of the tea-tent, eating an occasional greengage and receiving the homage due to Queen Victoria's daughter. The Duke of Leeds, good natured and bearded as a pard, was the Commodore. He was renowned as the holder of a Master Mariner's Certificate, but had now abandoned sail and owned a particularly ugly steam yacht in which he lived alone, since the Duchess found him dull and preferred the Italian Riviera to Cowes. There was Lord Albemarle whose good looks, old world courtesy and skill as an artist were only marred by his insistence on having two of the wicker chairs marked with his name in red leather and, still worse, bringing Lady Hinchingbrooke into the Squadron Garden in trousers.

There were famous helmsmen like Sir Philip Hunloke, who steered *Britannia* for the King; Lord Ailsa, reputed to have done

34

heroic deeds at sea many years before, but under a cloud for having married his nurse; and a cheerful Irishman, Sir Hercules Langrishe. When told by the eminent scientist, Lord Rayleigh, that the earth was in danger of colliding with a comet, Sir Hercules commented: 'Begorrah, I hope we shall be on the Starboard track'. No less romantically named than Sir Hercules was Sir Lancelot Rolleston.

There were Sir Godfrey and Lady Baring, hospitable and undisputed overlords of Cowes Society, who had entertained at Nubia House everybody from the Kaiser to Noel Coward. They owned one of the earliest hard tennis courts ever built and there, after the day's sailing was over, the young played tennis and the elderly assembled to watch them.

There was Captain the Hon. Henry Denison, notorious for his ill-natured comments and for a snobbishness exceptional even by Cowes standards. He sat cross-legged in the Squadron Garden, displaying a large dahlia in his button-hole and lying in wait for prey. He said of one fellow member: 'He lives on his wife's money. I always think it is so affectionate of him'; and he left my mother speechless by saying: 'I think your father is a very great man. I met him at Brooks' the other day. He borrowed my umbrella. I haven't seen it again. Yes, he really is a charming man'. One Cowes week morning it was reported that on opening *The Times* at breakfast, Captain Denison had startled his fellow members by announcing: 'Another smart death, I see'.

There was Colonel John Gretton, the formidable Chairman of Bass and leader of the die-hard Tories in the House of Commons. He owned a house with its own landing stage and two yachts of which one, the 160-ton ketch *Cariad*, won the King's Cup six times. There was the gentle, scholarly Sir William Portal, Squire of Laverstoke and owner of the graceful ketch *Valdora*, who went everywhere with his wife in public but was alleged never to speak to her in private on account of an infidelity twenty years previously. Lady Ormonde, widow of a previous Commodore and still notably handsome in her late seventies, was the owner of Solent Lodge which was only inhabited for one week each year. She flirted playfully with Sir William Portal and tried without success to keep a restraining hand on two beautiful grand-daughters whose innocent high spirits were too much in keeping with modern trends to be accepted as wholly safe and respectable. Another house opened in Cowes week alone was used by Mr Ernest Guinness to lodge over-flow guests who could not be accommodated on his 600-ton square-rigged barque, *Fantôme*. This was a yacht which all hoped to see under full sail, but she caused annual disappointment by puffing into Cowes Road emitting black smoke half way up her main mast from a carefully disguised engine.

There were two elderly and impoverished Ladies Stanhope who emerged, chattering like small crickets, from their castellated Stanhope Lodge which nobody had been invited to enter for at least fifty years. Standing 200 yards back from the sea, and half hidden by rank undergrowth, it would have been the ideal setting for a film of Grimm's Fairy Tales. It was guarded by a vicious pony which never failed to rend a large segment out of the coat of any unwary yacht-watcher foolish enough to lean against the iron railings which separated the unkempt grounds from the sea-front. And among a host of other Edwardians there were two rich ladies, Eleanor, Viscountess Gort (as, although remarried she still insisted on calling herself) and Sir Philip Hunloke's sister, Miss Perceval. Neither was admitted to the Squadron Garden (Lady Gort because of her husband and Miss Perceval because her brother detested her), and so they were driven up and down the front at Cowes, the one in a Victoria and the other in a Barouche, each fiercely proud of her smart top-hatted coachman and splendid horses, and neither deigning to salute the other.

The Squadron Lawn was scarcely a place for children, except for a brief daily visit to gorge on greengages and strawberry ices. We had a number of small boats in which we sailed and we caught lobsters and prawns in quantity, but my brothers and I were exceptionally lucky as far as another side of Cowes life was concerned. This was the age of the 'J' Boats, six or seven large cutters and one schooner which, with vast areas of canvas spread and professional crews of twenty or thirty, raced up and down the Solent providing a nautical sight as beautiful as any within living memory. At the start of each race they would tack close to the shore through the hundreds of yachts moored in Cowes Roads. Often, in order to cheat a foul tide, they would return with their spinnakers set right through the middle of the yachts, a man posted in the bow to shout directions to the helmsman whose view was totally obscured by the sails. How they avoided collisions, particularly when there was a strong breeze and they were travelling at great speed, I have never been able to understand.

We were invited to race on many of the 'J' yachts; on *Britannia*, after the King had left Cowes, on *White Heather*, *Candida* and *Lulworth*; but, above all, on the largest of them all, the 320-ton schooner *Westward*. Her mainmast was 150 feet high; she would sometimes carry as many as ten different sails; and with a strong wind on her beam she would fly through the water at 17 or 18 knots. She could not point as close to the wind as the cutters, so that she only won, and then usually by a wide margin, when the wind blew strongly from the north or south.

The guests on *Westward*, which carried a smaller crew of paid hands than did the cutters, were expected to work. There were no mechanised aids and hauling in the main sheet required the full exertion of every muscle on board. The owner, T.B. Davis, acted as First Mate and drove the guests and the crew to work with loud commands and, often as not, picturesque censure of their laziness or incompetence. He would stand to leeward of the wheel, holding on to a rope and sometimes up to his thighs in water as the great schooner plunged through the sea, heeling well over with her decks awash. He watched the set of the sails and shouted orders to tighten or loosen the jib-topsail sheet or lower the fore-topmast staysail. Racing on *Westward* in a stiff breeze was a thrilling adventure, but it was no sinecure.

T.B. Davis, unlike the owners of the other big yachts, had been born and bred a seaman. His first nautical experience was as cabin-boy on a small trading vessel, hailing from Jersey, which ran ashore on the Goodwin Sands in a heavy sea. The Captain gave order to abandon ship, and placed the cabin-boy with food, water and his top-hat in the long-boat. Before he or the rest of the crew could follow suit, a giant wave heaved the ship clean over the sand-bank into deep waters. Young Davis, left alone in the long-boat, had to keep her head to the gale for three whole days in the North Sea, bailing as best he could with the Captain's top-hat. He was rescued by a fishing boat and returned to Jersey just as his family were going to church for a memorial service. Having survived this ordeal, and journeyed to many parts of the world in big sailing ships, he settled at Durban, started a stevedoring business which soon extended along the whole east coast of Africa, and made a fortune.

He was a remarkable man and an incorrigible tyrant. He treated women as an inferior race and on board *Westward* they were strictly confined to the deck-house. He disapproved of lip-stick and regarded painted finger-nails as the emblem of the whore of Babylon. When, in disregard of his known rules, the daughter of the Vice-Commodore of the RYS came on board with scarlet nails, he seized her by the arm and scraped off the paint with his pocket-knife. He did, however, have an unlimited respect for my mother, who delighted in his straightforward honesty, revelled in his stories of life before the mast in sailing ships and was oblivious of his rough manner. She, alone of women, was allowed to remain on deck throughout the race, whatever the weather, and she much regretted the adamant refusal of the RYS even to consider him for membership. She refuted the belief generally held at Cowes that he used obscene language and would assert against all comers that he never said anything worse than damn or, very occasionally (and only when seriously put-out), bloody. She even persuaded Queen Mary to overcome every objection and invite him to dine on the *Victoria and Albert* where in the event King George V found his company stimulating. There was a good deal of head-shaking over my mother's revolutionary sentiments, which some thought positively dangerous in Court circles.

'T.B.' was the antidote to all that was artificial and out of date at Cowes. Each winter he returned to Durban, dominated his business affairs, terrorised his son (to whom he nominally entrusted them), insisted on his two pretty grand-daughters being home by 10.00 p.m. and, eschewing the richer and rarer foods he could well afford, lived on the salt-pork to which he had grown accustomed as a seaman in the windjammers. I stayed with him twice at Durban in the Second World War and listened with a mixture of awe and fascination as he pronounced, in his stern deep-throated voice, his disapproval of all things modern and his belief that society was destroying itself by renouncing a clean, simple life in favour of ease and luxury.

When King George V died, the new King had *Britannia* towed

into the Channel and sunk. When T.B. Davis died, his son did the same to *Westward*. It would have been unthinkable that those two thoroughbreds should be sold, re-rigged and sent to the Mediterranean as cruising boats, like race-horses condemned to pull hackney-carriages. Such had been the fate of the Kaiser's yacht *Meteor* and the same unhappy end was in store for most of the 'J' Boats. *Britannia* and *Westward* went to Valhalla instead.

6. Lady Chatterley's Lover

When I was a child, the word 'damn' was not used in polite circles, although even well brought up young ladies were allowed to say 'Dash', knowing full well that it replaced the unspeakable word. 'Bloody', of course, was unthinkable except in male society, and its introduction on the stage in Bernard Shaw's *Pygmalion* must have given the Lord Chamberlain, stern censor of theatrical morals, sleepless nights. When I asked my mother, in strict privacy, why it was so dreadful, she said that it was a swear-word derived from the Oath 'By our Lady'; but she admitted that it was much in vogue among her friends in the East End of London who were probably unaware of its blasphemous origin.

Time passed and I heard even wickeder words. Indeed, during my years in the RAF I found myself regularly ascribing a capacity for sexual intercourse to the most unlikely inanimate objects. All the same, at the end of World War II four-letter words were still avoided in respectable mixed society except by former members of the Women's Services who from time to time forgot themselves. There was one well-known work the author of which had brazenly defied the conventions. This was *Lady Chatterley's Lover*, widely considered to be the least good of D.H. Lawrence's novels, but notorious because of the words used by Lady Chatterley's friend the gamekeeper, words which were only printed in the unexpurgated text. Sale of the book in Britain was permitted in a bowdlerised version which was unreadably dull.

There had long been an unexpurgated Tauchnitz edition on sale abroad. On a summer's day in 1933, steaming up the Rhine among German tourists who sang *Die Lorelei* in faultless harmony as we passed the famous Cliff, I espied Lady Chatterley in the steamer's book-stall. For two marks I bought her. By the time I rejoined my family in the Isle of Wight, I had only another forty pages to read. My mother, who was far from being a prig, saw me absorbed in the last chapter, expressed slightly pained surprise and proceeded to borrow the book, explaining somewhat disingenuously that she would just like to see what all the fuss was about.

A day or two later she left for Balmoral, where it was her turn to be in waiting on Queen Mary. During the long train journey to Aberdeen, she somehow contrived to keep the cover of the book hidden from her fellow-travellers. She made no attempt, however, to disguise her guilty secret from Queen Mary to whom she described, with suitable expressions of horror, the fascination combined with revulsion that the book evoked in her. Queen Mary would have been less than human if she had not asked to have a glance at the famous work.

Several days past. One morning after breakfast, the King's Page came into my mother's sitting room and announced that His Majesty wished to see her at once. King George V was in a towering rage. He brandished the offending book. 'Look,' he said, 'what I have found the Queen reading! I am astonished and horrified that you should bring such a disgusting thing into my house. What is more, it has plainly printed inside: *Not to be imported into the United Kingdom of Great Britain and Northern Ireland*. I am indeed amazed at such behaviour'. My mother retired abashed.

A day or two later, Prince George was in high spirits when he saw my mother. 'What *have* you done to Papa?' he cried. 'I went into his room just now and saw him reading a book. He didn't hear me come in. I crept up behind him and found that it was *Lady Chatterley's Lover*. He said it was a disgusting book, which you had produced, but he felt it his duty to study the kind of temptations to which his subjects were exposed. It was a pretty lame excuse and he was so cross with me for laughing that he flung the book into the fire.'

Twenty-five years passed and in a generation which found it increasingly hard to distinguish liberty and licence, otherwise impeccable men like Mr Roy Jenkins and the Bishop of Woolwich, passionately devoted to the abolition of censorship, gave evidence in a Court of Law suggesting that *Lady Chatterley's Lover* was a book of such literary importance that its obscenity was of trivial significance when weighed up against the wickedness of suppressing a sublime work of art. For some inexplicable reason the Judge and jury accepted this testimony and so began the removal of legal bars to the publication of far greater obscenity. By comparison with what has followed Lady Chatterley seems almost decent, though unquestionably dull. She was, however, the Lady invited formally to open the floodgates and those who issued the invitation have some claim to the title: 'Founding Fathers of Permissive Society'. As far as quality is concerned, neither the stage nor literature seem to have profited in the way the Founding Fathers confidently predicted.

The *Times* felt obliged to weigh in after the jury had given their verdict. It published a long, ponderous leading article in the course of which the word copulation was used four times. I seized my pen and wrote to the editor, Sir William Haley, as follows :—

'Sir,

Your leading article about *Lady Chatterley's Lover* will have been admired by many, but not by those like myself who were brought up to believe that monosyllabic words of Anglo–Saxon origin should be preferred to polysyllabic words of Latin origin.'

I received a type-written postcard to say that no space could be found for my letter but that 'the Editor has taken due account of the views which you express'. Shortly afterwards I sat next to Sir William at dinner. I asked him why he had refused to publish my letter. He said he had seen it, but had not understood what it meant. I explained. I deduced that the editor of *The Times* had not heard of the four-letter word in question.

7. False Accusation

When I was at Harrow the only sport at which I was at all above the average was fencing, and in due course I became Captain of the school team. At the end of my last term, the Public Schools Fencing Competition was held at the London Fencing Club and I entered with enthusiasm. It was the first time I had ventured into a Club by myself, and as there were no other Harrovian competitors I found myself, with a degree of alarm, alone among total strangers. However, the Secretary of the Club welcomed me with friendliness and led me to a changing room where some other boys were already encasing themselves in canvas tunics, fingering foils and sabres and clutching their masks and gauntlets. I took off my clothes and prepared for battle. In the inside pocket of my coat, which I hung on a convenient peg, was my wallet. It contained three one-pound notes, all the money I possessed in the world.

The contest took place and to my great satisfaction I came third in the foil competition. On returning to the changing room I found that my wallet had gone. I told the Secretary of the Club and he told the police. Some weeks later I received a Summons to attend at Great Marlborough Street Magistrates Court. The thief had been caught and the wallet, but not the £3, had been recovered.

On the appointed morning I arrived at the Court in good time. Having been told to be there at 10 a.m. I assumed, in my ignorance, that the case in which I was to be a witness would be heard punctually at that hour. Sitting on a long bench inside the Court Room were twenty young ladies whom I supposed to be witnesses also. I took my place next to the last in the line and thought it polite to make conversation. So I started to talk about the weather. Before she could reply, the Magistrates made a ceremonial entry and we all rose to our feet.

'Susan Jones', said the Clerk. The first young lady stepped into the box and the Chairman of the Bench informed her that she was charged with being a Common Prostitute and with soliciting in Piccadilly Circus. Had she anything to say? 'No, Sir', replied Miss Jones.

'Fined ten shillings', said the Magistrate and Miss Jones stepped down from the box.

At great speed the other nineteen young ladies were similarly dealt with, and the Chairman of the Bench did not even look up from the list in front of him as he read out their names and imposed the fines. Presently the bench was empty as my neighbour, last of the line, stepped up to receive her due punishment. Now, I thought, my case is coming up. Accordingly, as soon as the twentieth prostitute had left the box and the Court, I replaced her.

Evidently there should have been twenty-one young ladies. Perhaps the twenty-first was ill or was late. At any rate, the Chairman of the Bench, without raising his eyes from his list, began to accuse me of being a Common Prostitute. I coughed discreetly and the Chairman looked up. He was evidently amazed and enquired who I was and what I was doing. I explained that I had come to bear witness against a miscreant who had stolen my wallet. 'All in good time ; all in good time', he said ; and so I returned to my deserted bench.

When an hour or two later the case of the stolen wallet came to be heard, I was at long last invited to take my stand in the witness box. I gave an account of what had happened and, much to my surprise and gratification, the Chairman twice intervened to congratulate me on the way I was giving evidence. Seldom, he said, had he heard such a lucid exposition. I was flattered by his kind words, but it was explained to me afterwards that his courtesy might have been designed to lessen the risk of my seeking damages for slander. I was, of course, too young and inexperienced to know what a chance I was missing.

8. Two Faces

When I left school in the spring of 1933, I went to Germany for three months in order to improve my meagre acquaintance with the language and to learn something of the outside world before going to Cambridge.

The train crawled along the Rhine valley and deposited me on the platform at Karlsruhe, capital of the former Grand Duchy of Baden and esteemed for its opera house, on which the musical Grand Duke had been wont to spend most of his Civil List, but not for much else. Thence a vehicle, apparently bred by a train out of a tram, chugged up the twisting valley of the River Alp, called the Alptal, and after penetrating deep into the Black Forest stopped at the village of Marxzell. One of the larger houses in this village was Albion Haus, home of Herr Professor Nohe, a small man with twinkling eyes and a pointed white beard who taught German to half a dozen young Englishmen, invariably including one naval officer working for an interpretership. To help him in this task he had his large, competent wife who was good-natured and laughed pleasantly, but had firm old-fashioned ideas about morals, manners and politics. As her daughter had recently married one of the British Naval officers, she had imported a 'Haustochter' whose function was to help the Frau Professor run the house and also talk German to the English pupils. In the event the young lady's ample bust and fluttering lids distracted them fatally from their study of the irregular verbs.

Three months before my arrival at Marxzell, President Hindenburg had appointed Adolf Hitler Chancellor of the German Reich. To those owning no crystal ball this was not particularly alarming, though Dr Cyril Norwood, the Headmaster of Harrow, told me he thought it a disaster for Europe, and my mother said that everything she read about Hitler and his National Socialist party filled her with revulsion. After I had been in the Black Forest for a week or two, I

45

concluded that these prejudiced views showed a total misunderstanding of the youthful and infectious spirit sweeping across
Germany. Much as I respected Dr Norwood, and deeply though I
loved my energetic, fearless and liberal-minded mother, I now
perceived that the older generation at home were, and doubtless
always had been, hopelessly biased and out of touch with the
modern world.

It was an idyllic summer. The young Englishmen in the house
were gay, friendly and good company. Every kind of German beer,
light or dark, flowed freely. We went for long walks in the un-
spoiled forest, passing through enchanted villages of painted wooden
houses. Sometimes two or three of us would stay in small spotlessly
clean inns where a night's lodging cost 2 marks (and there were 25
marks to the pound). We made excursions to Munich, Stuttgart and
Heidelberg, and went on foot through the forest to Baden-Baden.
There was a personable young lady called Mitzi who lived in
Karlsruhe and felt she had a mission, on payment of five marks, to
make the young Englishmen less inhibited. In the evenings, after a
bath at Albion Haus (for which the Frau Professor charged one
mark, because it entailed the carrying of huge brown cans of hot
water by two brawny peasant girls), some of us accompanied the
Professor to the local inn to play poker. The gamblers included the
butcher, the school-master, the inn-keeper's wife and the head
forester of the district. The play was low but keen, encouraged by
glasses of the local white wine laced with soda-water and, as the
evening progressed, by the singing of German folk-songs and an
occasional recital of heroic verse by the Professor if he happened to
be winning.

All was welcoming, all was cheerful. Politics were a rare topic of
conversation and none of the local inhabitants, except for the head
forester, were at all favourably inclined towards the National Socialists. They did, however, think that Germany needed cleansing and
revitalising after a crushing and, of course, unmerited defeat in war,
an inflation that had wiped out all savings, and the establishment of a
permissive society which was, we were told, particularly scandalous
in Berlin and shocked the puritanical susceptibilities of every decent
German. At any rate the Frau Professor said it did. The Professor
was no puritan; he had even supplied me, quite spontaneously, with

Mitzi's address; but he and the poker-players at the inn drew the line at excesses that were, they asserted, entirely the fault of the Weimar Republic.

This attitude, which seemed to be shared far and wide, was accompanied by visible determination to put the country soundly on its feet again. The Black Forest was invaded each week-end by troops of boys and girls, all dressed in brown and singing cheerfully as they marched, with picks and shovels on their shoulders, to perform some voluntary labour service for the Fatherland. In the towns and villages, festooned with Nazi flags and with the old black, white and red ensign of Imperial Germany, there was an atmosphere of purpose and alert contentment. It was a little disturbing that fat middle-aged Storm-Troopers, dressed like boy-scouts, shook collection-boxes rather menacingly at every passer-by, for it was well known that the funds, nominally to be devoted to the welfare of the poor in the winter, were actually earmarked to build an air-force which the vicious, punitive and inequitable Treaty of Versailles forbade Germany to possess. All the same, my generation, brought up on talk about the Great War and long since bored to tears by the subject, thought it high time the past was forgotten and Germany was treated like any other self-respecting, independent state. There would never be another war : our generation would see to that. In the meanwhile the Germans were courteous to foreigners, efficiency reigned, and whether at concerts, beer-halls or outdoor performances of plays by Schiller and Goethe, I found it impossible not to be infected by the unflagging enthusiasm. In 1933 the Nazi slogan, 'Strength through Joy', had an evident reality.

In July, a week before I was due to go home, Terence Rattigan arrived at Marxzell. I thought him a man of immense significance, for he had been one of the opening batsmen in the Harrow Eleven and, more remarkable still, had organised single-handed a mutiny in the Officers Training Corps. He had informed the *Daily Express* of this successful revolutionary manoeuvre and Dr Norwood had therefore been the more incensed, especially when a telegram arrived from the Eton College OTC offering to march to his assistance. This heroic character had come to Marxzell to write a play. He did so and it had a long, strikingly successful run. It was called *French Without Tears* and its *dramatis personae* included most of the

Footprints in Time

occupants of Albion Haus, notably the current Naval officer and the seductive 'Haustochter'. Fortunately I left before there was time for my follies, foibles and caricaturable defects to be impressed on the playwright's imagination.

I returned to England speaking and writing German with a measure of fluency and prepared to argue against all comers that even though the National Socialist spirit was not what we needed at home, it was mean and unrealistic to deny the benefits it offered Germany. I was opposed to anti-semitic sentiments, sometimes expressed with emphasis even in the Marxzell inn; and I thought a group of German students with whom I had spent a week-end at Tübingen University went altogether too far when they insisted that Britain was governed by the Jews, as a glance at the names of British Cabinet Ministers made clear. Sir John Simon and Sir Samuel Hoare were Jews, they said: their names proved it. I had seen no evidence of active persecution, and all men were entitled to their opinions, however difficult it was to believe that every ill which had befallen Germany must be ascribed to cunning plots contrived by the Children of Israel.

I, like the Tübingen students, went altogether too far when I expressed these views forcibly to a close friend of my family, Mr Lionel de Rothschild. 'Your son', he subsequently complained to my mother, 'comes to stay in my house, shoots my pheasants, drinks my champagne, smokes my cigars and then tells me there is a lot to be said for Hitler'. All the same he often asked me again.

Four years passed. Some of the keen, ill-judged but not un-generous enthusiasms of a boy of eighteen were blunted, and new discoveries jostled with beliefs less firmly anchored than I had supposed. At Cambridge I studied the history of political thought and attended discussion groups at Professor Ernest Barker's house, where *The Theory of the Modern State* was debated by a number of bespectacled undergraduates most of whom were members of the Communist Party. I waded through *Das Kapital*; I made an un-availing effort to read *Problems of Leninism*. Plato and Aristotle seemed to me not only easier to understand and infinitely less turgid, but also gentler, more humane and intellectually more convincing. My Marxist fellow-students might excoriate Hitler; but their un-diluted praise of Stalin failed to move me. Fascism was obscene;

48

Communism was incontrovertible. To dispute this self-evident fact was to court abuse, and on one occasion when I read a paper to Professor Barker's discussion group, arguing that the values of Christianity and the Greek Philosophers were eternal while those both of Fascism and Marxism were transitory, I was laughed to scorn as an out-of-date, reactionary, Imperialist and mentally subnormal enemy of the people; and the cloth cap which I habitually wore was seen to be the emblem of the Pitt Club rather than of Keir Hardie.

I travelled in Italy, where Mussolini's legions were marshalling against Abyssinia and the Sons of the She Wolf in their black shirts were as drenched in patriotic fervour as the Hitler Jugend in their brown shirts. Now, however, it was war with bombs and mustard-gas against ill-equipped Africans that lit the fire in those youthful eyes and not, as I had firmly believed in Germany, a selfless enthusiasm for national regeneration. I went to Russia, too, in the hot July of 1936, arriving on the day the Civil War began in Spain. Although there was a welcome absence of coloured shirts, and just a lot of grubby white ones against the background of flaking palaces in Leningrad, marble underground stations in Moscow and concrete blocks in Kharkov, the old Bolsheviks were being liquidated and the Kulaks deported to prison camps in Siberia while we jaded tourists, moving from deconsecrated churches to People's Culture centres, were subjected to earnest propagandist discourses by our Intourist Guide. I had no hesitation in admitting that I found the old things in Russia – the Hermitage, Peterhof and the great monastery at Kiev – more exciting than the new.

Yet it was not till the following year that my eyes were opened to the truth about police states and my surviving illusions dispelled. I had taken my degree and decided to sit for the exacting Foreign Office entrance examination. This consisted of eighteen three-hour papers and several interviews. Like Holy Matrimony, it was not by any to be enterprised, nor taken in hand, unadvisedly, lightly or wantonly, but reverently, discreetly, advisedly and soberly. It was necessary, amongst other things, to write and speak French well and to be only slightly less polished in German. So I spent the last part of 1936 and the first part of 1937 in Paris working under the redoubtable diplomatic coach, Monsieur Martin, whose establishment was, I later discovered, also incorporated in Terence Rattigan's *French Without Tears*. Realising that my German was further from the requisite standard than my French, I resolved to return for a final three months to the village of Marxzell, hoping that by diligent attention to Professor Nohe's lessons I should make the necessary improvement.

Thus after four years' absence, I took the train through the Rhineland, which Hitler had recently occupied without opposition in flat defiance of the Treaty of Versailles, and alighting from the Rheingold express at Karlsruhe, I climbed once more into the egregious machine which was peculiar to the Alptal. Old President Hindenburg was dead and Adolf Hitler was now not only head of the Government, but also Head of the State and officially acclaimed throughout the land as Führer of the German Reich. Outwardly there was little change at Marxzell. The Professor's eyes still twinkled mischievously, Albion Haus was still inhabited by young Englishmen studying the language with varying degrees of zeal and the Frau Professor was as jolly, outspoken and welcoming as ever. There was still a naval officer working for an interpretership, but the flighty 'Haustochter' had been replaced by the Frau Professor's own sensitive and intelligent daughter, Hilla Carlill, whose British naval husband was away at sea. It was Hilla, with whom I went for a walk in the forest the day after my arrival, who spoke with sad foreboding of the changes I should find and the dangers lying ahead.

There was also in the house a German boy called Max. He was 19, tough, noisy and opinionated. As he spoke no English, whereas most of the young Englishmen found it less strenuous to converse in their own language, I spent much time practising my German on Max. The only thing that made a man of one, he said, was war. Germany having first rooted out all the poison in her own system – Jews, Gypsies and other lesser breeds – would soon dominate the world; for the Germans were real men, not decadent, pleasure-loving lounge-lizards like the Latins or money-grabbing Jewish financiers like the Americans. There was, he thought, some hope for England, if she accepted the hand of friendship which the Führer offered and put her own corrupted house in order. 'Strength through Joy' was no longer much in evidence, but Max was sure that the current slogan, endorsed by the Führer, reflected the future.

Echoes of the Morning

It was *'Heute gehört uns Deutschland, morgen die ganze Welt'* – 'Today, Germany is ours; tomorrow the whole world'. I was distressed that the kindly Frau Professor, who constantly reprimanded Max for his bad table-manners and loud voice, said that all the same he spoke the truth: he represented what young Germany, enthused 'by our Leader', believed; and her one prayer was that England, too, would see the light. The Professor, I thought, was only in partial agreement, and Hilla not at all. But they kept silent and left the arguing to me.

As the weeks went by, the new face of Germany became known to me. Mendelssohn's music was banned on account of his racial origin, and because even Hitler could not stop the Germans singing *Die Lorelei*, by the Jewish poet Heine, its authorship was given in the new song-books as Anonymous. At the evening poker-sessions in the inn, there was little laughter and if there was singing, the songs were new and unfamiliar. The head forester, now holding official rank and wearing a swastika arm-band, ended a political argument (which he had started) by saying: 'Well, I suppose you picked up those ideas in Russia'.

'How did you know I have been to Russia?' I asked, for I had thought it inadvisable to mention the fact to anybody on German soil. He looked flustered. Presumably the Soviet Visa in my passport had been noted by the immigration official at the frontier and reported, as a precaution, to the responsible Nazi official in the district to which I was travelling.

In Karlsruhe and in Munich I saw shops with broken windows and in Stuttgart I walked behind a frightened, cringing man wearing the Star of David. I was warned again and again by the Professor not to air my views in restaurants or indeed anywhere in public. I heard, for the first time, of a place called Dachau and another called Buchenwald to which people who spoke out of turn might be sent for reformatory purposes. In Baden-Baden I stood beside a large bonfire into which the citizens were hurling books. I picked up a singed one: it was a calf-bound edition of *Buddenbrooks* by Thomas Mann. 'Throw it back into the fire', said a stern Storm Trooper who strode towards me when he saw me pick it up. This was no occasion for argument: I did as I was told.

A few days later I went on a walking expedition to Wildbad. We arrived in the evening to find a crowd of many thousands assembled and I stood on the edge of it. The Führer, the glorious, magical Führer, was coming in person to speak. The houses in the town were scarcely visible, so numerous were the flags, and in addition to the usual throng of brown-shirted SA men, there were groups of tall, unsmiling SS in black uniforms and stiff military caps. I had never before, and have never since, seen an exhibition of mass-hysteria so universal in its scope. When, after the ecstatic preliminaries, the Führer started to speak, I was too far away to hear his words distinctly, nor can they have been audible to any of the crowd near me. But there was a look of glazed adoration on every face as the people stood in dead silence while a distant sound of ranting carried across the still summer night. 'Tomorrow the whole world', I thought; and a deep uneasiness possessed me.

I left Marxzell on a dismal, rainy morning which matched my thoughts. Two of the high spirited young Englishmen, recently expelled from their Public Schools for reasons tactfully shrouded in mystery, but entirely likeable and overbrimming with high spirits, saluted my departure by tying a chamber-pot and a tin-bath to the rear axle of the Alptal train-tram. After we had gone a few hundred yards to the sound of clattering tin and breaking china, combined with merry English laughter from the Marxzell platform, the driver stopped the machine and the guard descended to untie the noisy impedimenta. It was the same guard who four years previously would have clenched his fist in mock anger, twirled his waxed moustache, shouted a few words of cheerful abuse at the adolescent practical jokers on the platform and roared with laughter as he climbed back into the train. Now there was no smile on his face. He muttered a few ill-tempered words about decadent young Englishmen who deserved a good hiding and scribbled furiously in his note-book what I took to be an official report of the unseemly incident. There was no room for practical jokers in the new Germany. There was increasing Strength matched by diminishing Joy.

Back in England the sun was shining. Events in Germany were of small consequence. Prosperity was returning,. the figures of unemployment were falling sharply and the people were thinking about their summer holidays. I, too, was so heavily preoccupied with the approaching Foreign Office exam that I had no time to reflect at length on what I had seen and heard in the Black Forest. I had, however, realised the physical strength and grim purpose of the German people. Of one thing I was sure as 1937 gave way to 1938 and first Austria, then Czechoslovakia, were aligned in the Führer's sights. We were not in the mood to confront a Germany united in purpose and design. Nor could we possibly be assumed to possess the physical and material strength required to do so. Only time, energy and luck could supply our deficiencies. Luck seemed to be the best bet, and the belief, to which so many of my compatriots firmly subscribed, that God is an Englishman.

9. The Holy Mountain

I have only once been to an inhabited place where it was impossible, except by looking at one's own clothes, to find any visible proof that the 20th century had arrived. It was Mount Athos, a monastic republic then consisting of some twenty monasteries, mainly Byzantine in origin, and containing in its community, which was jealously guarded from the outside world and totally barred to women visitors, about 5000 monks, hermits and lay brothers.

I went there partly as an economy. It was 1934 and the Long Vacation. With two close friends from Cambridge I had been travelling cheaply down the Danube, but by the time we reached Istanbul our finances were straitened and we were reduced to sleeping on straw palliasses in the Sailors' Rest, an institution intended for indigent seamen. Luckily one of my companions remembered that the British Ambassador was his cousin by marriage and so we went to call. The Ambassador, among other courtesies and indeed hospitality (for we moved from the Sailors' Rest to the imposing mid-nineteenth-century palace designed by Barry) suggested that we should visit Mount Athos to the advantage of our pockets, since the monks provided board and lodging free to those who contrived to get there, and also of our education. He accordingly sent us to the Phanar, seat of the Orthodox Oecumenical Patriarch, and with such august backing – for in 1934 the British Ambassador was considered a mighty potentate – we received from His Beatitude a magnificent scroll, embellished with seals and inscribed in copper plate handwriting, which enjoined the Blessed Community on Mount Athos to offer us every civility in their power.

Clutching this invaluable document, we set off by train across Asia Minor with 3rd class tickets, boarded an Italian boat at Smyrna and after many vicissitudes arrived at Mount Athos in a cargo boat from Salonica. We were at once arrested by the only non-clerical character in the entire Holy Peninsula, because we had not

54

had our passports endorsed by the Salonica police and he did not care a fig for the Patriarch's missive.

So back we had to go to Salonica, sleeping on deck with a herd of sheep, to have our passports stamped. Then, at long last, we were able to return to the Holy Mountain, to pass the last secular barrier and to start the long walk from Daphni, the solitary port on the peninsula, to the monastery where we planned to spend the first night.

We were translated into a new world or rather into a very ancient one, where time was of no account and neither machines nor roads nor electricity existed. The width of the peninsula varies from four to seven miles and its length of thirty miles is dominated by a ridge which culminates in the shining white peak of Mount Athos, rising 6000 feet above the sea. The monasteries are dotted among the wooded slopes on either side of the ridge, where paths are few and narrow. The monks arrived from Constantinople at the end of the 10th century, long preceded by hermits who were much offended by the community life which the invading monks established.

We decided to spend the first night at the great monastery of Vatopedi which was built in AD 980. We picked our way there along a narrow path through almost virgin forest, climbing hills from which we could gaze on the deep blue Aegean, descending into valleys where there were butterflies of every shape and colour, sometimes pausing to drink at the springs and fountains by the way. We met an occasional monk, with high black hat and flowing robes, who would salute us gravely, and once we stood aside to let pass a Russian bishop with an auburn beard and hair. His robes were a rich purple and on his chest was a large cross of amethysts. He rode on a mule and behind him marched a retinue of attendants. He blessed us as he passed.

Vatopedi, like most of the Byzantine foundation in the Community, is surrounded by a high wall to keep out the pirates and the Saracens. Within the wall is a village of painted houses and ten or more separate chapels. We were received with the ceremony of drinking Turkish coffee, eating rose-leaf jam with a teaspoon and then drinking water out of a glass in which the jammy teaspoon must first be placed. This was found to be the standard reception practice.

We went from monastery to monastery, admiring the ancient manuscripts and the jewelled treasures, embarrassed by the quality of relics (St Chrysostom, for instance, seemed to have more pre-served limbs than any one saint had any right to possess) and feeding off fish, fruit and vegetables, either with the monks in the refectories or in our own cells. The only reasonable cause for complaint was the sanitary arrangements which were as Byzantine as every-thing else.

One ancient monastery where we were entertained is called Iveron. Among its numerous chapels is one containing a sacred Ikon of the Virgin Mary. The ornaments with which it was adorned ranged from a gold necklace given by the Byzantine Empress Pul-cheria to a ribbon of the Legion d'Honneur. The Ikon is said to have hung at Constantinople above the altar of St Sophia. In the 8th century an iconoclast Emperor called Leo, anticipating Oliver Crom-well, had all the images and relics in Constantinople cast into the Bosphorus. The lesser ones perished; but this Ikon, so the Abbot told me, floated down the Dardanelles into the Aegean. The keen-sighted hermits of Mount Athos, beholding it from afar and scenting its importance, waited for it to be washed ashore. But it declined to be profaned by their touch. Every time they stretched out their hands to seize it, it retired back into the sea. Finally it came ashore of its own volition and in due course Iveron was founded to enshrine it. It certainly looked as if it had been battered by the elements.

A monk rowed us from Iveron to the landing beach below the Grand Lavra, the most important monastery of them all, which stands on the slopes of Mount Athos itself. A kindly hermit had taken the document from the Oecumenical Patriarch on ahead and so we were expected. As we climbed laboriously up the stony path leading from the little landing cove to the cloud-capped towers above us, the doors of the Grand Lavra swung open. The Abbot appeared, tall and dignified, with a long snow-white beard. He wore on his head a mitre of no ordinary quality, and behind him followed a score of black-robed monks. He was coming to meet those whom the Patriarch had seen fit to honour and when he was ten yards from us, he raised his hand in blessing. We were acutely self-conscious, for we were dressed like any hikers, with ruck-sacks on our backs, and we had not the least idea how to behave when blessed on a mountain side by an Orthodox Abbot. Besides there were bound to be linguistic problems. So we knelt on the path, our bare knees suffering acutely from the jagged stones. Then the Abbot approached. He signalled to us to rise, held out his hand to the nearest and said in an unmistakable Illinois accent, 'Well, boys, I hope your journey around the place has been OK so far'. He was an American.

The mediaeval illusions vanished and we thought we were part of a Hollywood film; but it was only momentary. The Abbot was a learned and a saintly man. He led us along a path gay with wild flowers and through a portico consisting of a dome supported by four porphyry columns. The roofs of high wooden houses could be seen above the walls and several rooms projected over the battlements presenting an effect similar, I imagine, to that of old London Bridge. We walked back into the middle ages as we were ushered into a spacious courtyard surrounded by white domes and shaded by tall cypress trees, which were said to have been planted by Athanasius of Trebizond himself when he built the monastery in AD 962. There were fifteen chapels within the walls and another nineteen close by; and the library held two thousand precious Greek manuscripts and palimpsests.

The Treasure Chamber was the finest in the peninsula and the principal church was adorned with 14th-century frescoes. I never fail to be enthralled by the imaginative powers of mediaeval fresco-painters. The largest was a representation of the Last Judgment in which the principal figure was the Devil, contentedly munching sinners as if they were whitebait. Down below him was a lake of blood where hundreds of diminutive devils, armed with pitchforks, were playing hide and seek with some tadpoles which, on closer inspection, turned out to be more sinners. The small devils and their elusive prey were having such a jolly game that it was quite depressing to turn to the heavenly part of the fresco where a score of priggish saints, with worn or second-hand haloes, were gazing down on the scene below and, I thought, probably wishing they were allowed just half an hour's frolic in the sinners' lake.

In the huge refectory there are other frescoes. Androcles whispers to the Lion on one wall, and on another the Apostles, in gilded haloes, are listening to Christ's words at the Last Supper. Meanwhile the only halo-less character, Judas, seeing that nobody is watching him, has seized the opportunity to steal a large boiled cod. With a dastardly smile, he is slinking away with the fish and is sure to be out of the door before anybody notices. Perhaps, I thought, this represented a historic misdemeanour by one of the monks in days gone by.

We went on from monastery to monastery and stayed at the great Russian foundation of St Panteleimon where there were still four hundred pre-Revolutionary monks who sang for hours, with their miraculous range of voices, in celebration of St Vladimir's day. On our last night, I stood in a courtyard under the full moon which cast its silvery light on the white buildings and the cypress trees. A black cowled figure passed, so ghostly in appearance that a shiver ran down my spine. The silence was complete. Leaning against the wall of an ancient chapel I reflected once again that this was a place where historic time was of no significance. It did not matter to a monk of Mount Athos if he were living in the 14th, 17th or 20th century. Life was the same for him in 1934 as it was for his predecessors when the Battles of Agincourt, Blenheim, Waterloo and Passchendaele were being fought in northern lands. Passions, changes and inventions elsewhere had no influence on the unalterable sea and sky nor on scenery with which no man had tampered. The monks' clothes and conventions had remained the same; their objective was still prayer and a life of simplicity and holiness.

We returned to Salonica still under the influence of our sojourn in a community which was entirely cut off from the world outside. 'Dollfuss murdered', were the headlines. Italian troops were said to be moving to the Austrian frontier. War, said the Greek newspapers, was imminent. It was not, at least for a few more years; but the vision and the dream vanished, never to return.

10. Introduction to Diplomacy

In the Diplomatic Service, which I entered in 1937, it was the policy to train newly recruited Third Secretaries in London for two years before despatching them abroad. The Foreign Office was efficient, but it still retained some characteristics dating from an already distant past. The day's work began at 11.00 a.m.; letters, even to foreign Embassies and Legations in London, had to be written in impeccable French, the universally accepted diplomatic language; and time was spent in learning the correct methods of procedure. For instance, it was vital not to address Roman Catholic bishops by territorial designations, such as Westminster or Liverpool, which were reserved for the Established Church; and whereas it was proper that a despatch to an Ambassador be signed: 'I am, Sir, with great Truth and Respect, your Excellency's humble, obedient servant', a Minister received Regard instead of Respect and a mere Chargé d'Affaires nothing but Truth.

An admirable tradition of the system was that junior members of the service were at once given responsibility. Every despatch, every letter and all but the most urgent telegrams began their progress through the machine on the desk of a Third Secretary who had to decide whether to take action himself, whether to submit the document to higher authority, with or without his own proposals attached, or whether to write 'No Action' and cast the document into the outer darkness of the Registry archives. In addition to this written work, it was thought wholesome that Third Secretaries should handle affairs of a different kind, either by speaking for the Foreign Office at interdepartmental meetings or by assuming tasks which required diplomatic handling outside the Office. One of these soon came my way.

On arrival in the Department it fell to my lot to deal with the affairs of two countries, Turkey and Persia. The Persians were, incidentally, already showing a regrettable tendency to call their

59

country Iran and to express a wish that others should do the same. This was clearly unacceptable for, after all, the Italians did not expect us to call Florence Firenze, nor did we demand that the French call Angleterre England. We had, by some illogical decision, agreed to change Angora to Ankara; but there were good political reasons for being obsequious to the Turks in view of the unremitting but largely unsuccessful German pressure on Kemal Ataturk.

The Shah of Persia, Reza Pahlevi, was a sensitive monarch. He had done much to restore order and the power of the Central Government, which the previous dynasty had brought close to dissolution, and he laid the foundations on which his abler and better educated son built so well. However, in all matters relating to foreign relations, his touchiness knew no bounds. Thus he had withdrawn his Minister from Washington on account of some imagined slight; and when the newspaper *Paris Soir* published an account of a Cat Show, with a superimposed photograph of a Persian cat and the caption: 'Sa Majesté le Chat reçoit', diplomatic relations between France and Persia were severed by Imperial decree. For Britain, with a vital interest in Persian oil and a huge fleet to be fuelled, good relations with Persia were still more important than for France and the United States. The Anglo–Persian Oil Company had already sought favour by changing its name to Anglo–Iranian.

Meanwhile a new Third Secretary arrived at the Persian Legation in London. His English was imperfect and he was lonely. One evening he was afflicted by a strong feeling. To cater for it is, according to the *Book of Common Prayer*, one of the causes for which matrimony was ordained. Not having the benefit of that honourable estate, he walked down Curzon Street in pursuit of consolation. He found it easily enough; but when, some half an hour later, he emerged into the street, his wallet, containing a large sum of money which belonged to the Legation, was missing. He accosted a policeman to whom he explained with the utmost linguistic difficulty that he had been robbed, and he was invited to lead the constable to the scene of the theft. Unfortunately in his distress and confusion he went to the wrong flat, and the wrong girl was arrested. The next day she instituted proceedings for defamation of character. She might be a prostitute but she was not, she protested, a thief.

Echoes of the Morning

The Persian Minister called at the Foreign Office. He said that if the young man claimed Diplomatic Immunity, which was of doubtful wisdom in such a case, the fact would be reported in the press and he would certainly have to send a report to Tehran. The young man would be recalled and some horrible punishment, perhaps even Capital, would be imposed. If, on the other hand, the case went to Court, there would be garish headlines and possibly some tasteless references to the Shah with results too regrettable to contemplate. The Foreign Office must find a solution. 'There', said the Head of my Department when the Minister had left. 'Go and see what you can do'.

I made my way to the Home Office where I was received by an official who seemed to me immensely ancient and dignified. I explained the problem and suggested that the case be settled out of Court or, better still, quashed. I should have known better. The important official said he was astonished. Was the Secretary of State for Foreign Affairs really proposing that the Home Secretary should seek to interfere with the administration of justice? Then, taking pity on my youth and embarrassment, he melted. After a short and not too severe lecture on the immunity of British justice from political pressure, he sat for a minute or two in reflective silence. 'I will see', he said, 'if there is any way in which we can be helpful'.

On the following day he telephoned. The case would be heard in one of two adjacent courts. By some lucky chance – and he carefully avoided saying who had thrown the dice – there would be in the other Court, at the same hour, a case of rape more horrifying than any which had hitherto been recorded in the 20th century.

It worked like magic. The reporters one and all flocked to the adjoining Court. The Persian Third Secretary apologised to the lady and agreed to pay her substantial damages. Not a word appeared in the papers; the Shah remained unperturbed; and the Third Secretary's punishment consisted of a long series of deductions from his monthly salary to repay the Legation for the sum stolen, to compensate the maligned prostitute and to recompense the Minister for his kindness in not reporting the affair home.

11. Peace with Honour

Dressed in his sailor suit, which was the attire worn on Sundays and best occasions by many small boys when Britannia still ruled the waves, my father was smuggled on to the steps of the throne in the House of Lords to hear Lord Beaconsfield make an important speech. The steps of the throne were reserved for Privy Councillors and the Elder Sons of Peers and my father was neither. However, as he was a son of the Master of the Buckhounds, an office which combined the duties both of hunting the royal buckhounds in Windsor Forest and being Chief Government Whip in the Lords, he got away with it.

The occasion induced in him a deep reverence for Dizzy. One always spoke, he explained, of 'Dizzy', but one never referred to his rival as anything but *Mr* Gladstone. And although several years later, in 1878, my father was doubtless at school rather than on the pavement at Downing Street when Dizzy and Lord Salisbury returned triumphant from the Congress of Berlin, he used to tell me how all Britain thrilled to Dizzy's announcement, made from a first floor window at 10 Downing Street, that he had brought back Peace with Honour.

Exactly sixty years later, Neville Chamberlain came back in triumph from Munich. The Foreign Office, in which I was now a Third Secretary of one year's standing, was unenthusiastic and indeed, within the bounds of propriety, positively hostile. So for some minutes I stood alone on the first floor balcony facing No. 10, while my colleagues buried their recalcitrant heads in their work. Down in the street there was no sign of recalcitrance. The crowd cheered themselves hoarse and sang patriotic songs in the most cacophonous tones imaginable. Unlike my colleagues I shared the crowds' enthusiasm, for it seemed to me that world war had at least been postponed by Chamberlain's initiative and a war postponed might well be a war averted.

Echoes of the Morning

While the returning Prime Minister's car was surging through hysterical crowds, a French window opened beside me and the Deputy Under Secretary, Sir Orme Sargent, stepped on to the balcony. He surveyed the scene below with dislike and disdain. 'You might think', he said to me, 'that we had won a major victory instead of betraying a minor country'. Then, after a pause, as the window opposite opened and it was clear that Chamberlain was expected to say a few words, Sargent added: 'I can bear almost anything provided he doesn't say it is Peace with Honour'.

Meanwhile, as I subsequently learned, Chamberlain was greeted by his loyal and elated staff at the end of the long red-carpeted passage which runs from the front door of No. 10 to the Cabinet Room, and he said that in response to the clamour outside he must go up to the first floor window – Dizzy's bedroom – and say a few words. It was then that Mrs Chamberlain put the words into his mouth : 'Tell them', she said, 'that you have brought back peace, but not just peace – peace with honour'. Tell them he did, and as the crowd roared in applause Sir Orme Sargent turned on his heel, closed the French window behind him and left me alone on the balcony.

Two years passed and I was myself a Private Secretary at No. 10. Disliking the unfresh air of the Central War Room, where a bedroom deep under ground was available to me, I contrived to have a bed provided in the large and now empty room from which first Disraeli and then Neville Chamberlain had sent their words echoing round the country and the world. Honour we still had, in abundance; but Peace was only a memory and night after night the bombs in their hundreds devastated London. Early in 1941 the blast from one of them shattered the famous window as I pushed my head under the bed clothes to avoid the shower of glass.

Part 2

HIGH SUMMER

12. Diaries

By the diaries they wrote, some have made their reputation and others have come close to destroying what reputation they had. Because a diarist writes without the falsification which memory so readily provides; because his thoughts and observations are unsullied by that wisdom after the event which distorts the judgment of historians; because he writes in keeping with the views, knowledge and conventions of contemporary opinion, unaffected by the different moral attitudes of a later generation: for all these reasons a diary should be living history. Estimates of people or of policy may be written hastily, under the stress of emotion, and criticism of an individual is sometimes based on passing irritation or a lack of understanding which later, mature experience would contradict. A diarist is seldom objective and his views may be so biased in favour of one party, one creed or one social conviction that he is far from painting a true picture of contemporary opinion. It is unlikely that he will reflect in his mirror anything but the views and activities of a small and, more often than not, unrepresentative sector of society. It would, for instance, be wrong to suppose that Lady Cunard's *obiter dicta*, reported by Chips Channon, represent the opinion of informed and influential opinion in the London of the 1930s. However that may be, in what relates to fact rather than opinion the diarist describes what he actually heard or saw that selfsame day.

I kept a diary during the war years. I shall not publish it because it contains opinions of people and views of events which in the light of subsequent knowledge I believe to be unjust. Nevertheless, by keeping this diary I have learned three lessons. First I have discovered how fallacious is memory. I have sought from time to time to check a fact which I remembered, as I thought, with entire clarity, only to find that according to what I had written at the time my memory was both inaccurate and inadequate. I once contradicted Lord Beaverbrook flatly, which was a rash act. He was describing events at Chequers on 22 June 1941, the day that Hitler invaded Russia. Those present that day had been unanimous in believing Russian resistance would scarcely last six weeks, though Churchill was adamant that all the support and supplies we could spare, and even more than we could spare, should be rushed to the aid of our new allies. I remembered the scene vividly; I recalled who had been there; I denied with emphasis that Beaverbrook had been present, thus implying that what he had said was a figment of his imagination. The next day I referred to my diary which indeed recorded his presence; and so I wrote a letter of profound apology. Yet, by memory alone, I should have betted a large sum he was not there.

Secondly, I have found that if several people write an account of the same event, those accounts, though perfectly truthful, often bear little relation to each other; for every man sees and describes what he records through his own blinkers. At least twice I described an event and a discussion at which other diarists were present. The first occasion was in the evening of 10 May 1940, when Lord Dunglass, Parliamentary Private Secretary to Neville Chamberlain, suggested to me that we should walk over to the Foreign Office to tell R.A. Butler, Parliamentary Under Secretary for Foreign Affairs, and his P.P.S., Chips Channon, that Mr Chamberlain had been to Buckingham Palace to resign and that the King had sent for Winston Churchill. The Germans had begun their offensive against France. A national coalition was an obvious necessity and just before 5.00 p.m. Mr Attlee had telephoned from Bournemouth to say that the Labour Party would not serve under Neville Chamberlain. Lord Halifax had steadfastly refused to enter the lists and it had thus become inevitable that Winston Churchill, of whom we all had the strongest doubts, should be the new Prime Minister. I wrote an account of what we all said: how we expressed dire political forebodings and drank to 'The King over the Water' (by which we meant Chamberlain) from a bottle of champagne produced by Channon out of a filing cabinet. The provider of champagne also wrote an account of this lugubrious gathering. His account and mine only bear a superficial resemblance to each other; but both were recorded in diaries and both in their subjective ways are accurate.

Again, at the end of December 1944, I was flying above the Isthmus of Corinth on our journey back from the Conference in Athens between Churchill and the ELAS rebels. Anthony Eden's Secretary, Sir Pierson Dixon, and the Prime Minister's doctor, Lord Moran, were also in the aeroplane. The melodrama of the meeting at the Ministry of Foreign Affairs had made a deep impression on us all. I said I had written a description of it. Lord Moran admitted that he had too. So had Dixon. We read aloud the passages from our diaries. All were true, but each was written from a different angle. Indeed, had the names of the participants been omitted, we might have been reading descriptions of three distinct events. Together they presented a picture painted in detail; separately they recorded an episode seen through one pair of eyes. This is, I suppose, true of many, perhaps most, of the events recorded in history.

A third advantage of keeping a diary is that it can be used to affirm or deny some of the assertions made by commentators a generation later. It may be a surer way of so doing than by reference to some of the official papers preserved in the Public Records Office, for it was often the case that briefs laboriously drafted in a government department, and duly filed in the archives, were not even read, let alone acted on, by the Minister for whom they were prepared. There is, moreover, no shortage of claimants to special relationship and influence whose suspect pretensions can be checked by reference to a contemporary account. Did the advice of Admiral of the Fleet Sir Roger Keyes carry weight in the conduct of military or political affairs in the summer of 1940? Was Churchill unappreciative of Lord Dowding's achievements as Commander in Chief, Fighter Command? Did the Prime Minister deliberately sacrifice Coventry in November 1940, so as to preserve the secret that we had broken the official German cipher? Did he even know that Coventry was the target of the operation, 'Moonlight Sonata', to which the decoded German signals referred? Was Sir William Stephenson (called by his biographer 'Intrepid') in close personal relationship with Churchill and did he act as the Prime Minister's liaison with Roosevelt? According to my diary the answer to all these questions is 'No'.

There are diaries of many kinds and some might, with advantage, have been suppressed. To me the most readable are those which, be the writer Pepys, Greville, Creevey or Chips Channon, are social diaries with strong political overtones. Looking back on the men and women I remember, I can think of several who might have left supremely important records of their times. There are people who were widely known in their own generation, who sparkled when they talked, who were concerned with the important events of their day but whose names, because they left nothing behind in writing, are destined to be mere footnotes in the memoirs and histories of their times. Brendan Bracken was one, Lady Desborough another, Lord Normanbrook a third. The list is long but near the top of it I place Sir Philip Sassoon, a man who employed his wealth with impeccable taste, who entertained lavishly but not with vulgarity, who pined for royal favour but yet had time for all men, and who deliberately invited totally unlike people to meet each other at Trent, Lympne or his house in Park Lane, to their mutual pleasure and advantage.

He had been Private Secretary to Haig before becoming Parliamentary Private Secretary to Lloyd George. This was no mean achievement since the two men were irreconcilable. He entertained everybody of political, literary and social importance. Friend and benefactor of the Royal Air Force, and for a short but fruitful span First Commissioner of Works under Neville Chamberlain, he soared like a shooting star through the political and social skies, brilliant and considerate as a host, a tolerant perfectionist, satisfied only with the best for others as well as for himself. His wit was original and even his casual remarks were amusing because of his effective use of stress and accentuation.

Skilful entertaining and exquisite taste are transitory. Good conversation and original wit are scarcely less so. Redecorating Government offices and arranging splendid exhibitions are no claim to immortality. Philip Sassoon achieved all these things. For a generation his name was famous and his witticisms were quoted. If he had kept a diary he would have become part of history just as, in contradistinction, the names of Pepys and Evelyn would, but for their diaries, be known today only to the more erudite historians of the reign of Charles II; and nobody would have heard of Boswell.

13. Serving Three Masters

Early in October 1939 I was seconded from the Foreign Office to become an Assistant Private Secretary to the Prime Minister, Mr Neville Chamberlain. 'I hope we shall get on', he said with a shy and rather frosty smile; 'I have not always seen eye to eye with your Department'. This was an understatement. Although the Foreign Secretary, Lord Halifax, was Chamberlain's loyal lieutenant and was at the same time liked and respected by the Foreign Office, there had been little attempt to disguise the frigidity of the Department towards Chamberlain's activities before, during and after the Munich crisis; nor was there anything but resentment at his determination to conduct foreign policy himself, especially as he was held, with some justice, to know nothing at all about it. It was a good many years since anybody from the Foreign Office had served at 10 Downing Street.

We had been at war for a month, but the office was still conducted as in peace time. The Prime Minister worked in the Cabinet Room which was adjoined by two rooms. In the smaller sat Sir Horace Wilson, Chamberlain's *alter ego*, against whose influence the venom of the Foreign Office, and of those Conservative MPs who were not wholly dedicated to the Chamberlain mystique, was principally directed. The larger adjoining room was occupied by the two senior Private Secretaries, Arthur Rucker and Cecil Syers, and beyond that was another large room with three writing tables. These belonged to the Parliamentary Private Secretary, Lord Dunglass; to Miss Edith Watson, a time-honoured resident of No. 10, who had served under Lloyd George, Bonar Law and every subsequent Prime Minister; and myself. There was a staff of a dozen brisk and efficient young and middle-aged ladies, who held responsibilities ranging from typing and filing to the accumulation of knowledge and background information about the Honours List, Civil List Pensions, Lords Lieutenant and the Ecclesiastical Patronage; and there were four dignified messengers who would have made excellent butlers in any large country house. Coal fires blazed in every grate and there was no touch of that bleakness associated with Government offices. I felt I was working in a comfortable, well run private house.

There was no unseemly hurrying. Everything was done with smooth efficiency in accordance with established routine. At 9.30 a.m. precisely the Prime Minister and Mrs Chamberlain set off, with a detective walking twenty yards behind them, to circumnavigate the lake in St James's Park. At 9.50 they returned. At 11.00 the Chief Whip, Captain David Margesson, entered the Cabinet Room, emerging in due course to inform the Private Secretaries what was in the wind. Cabinets began and ended punctually, so that nobody was ever late for luncheon; and the Prime Minister was always at the House well in advance of the time to answer his Parliamentary Questions. At 7.30 p.m. he went upstairs to dress for dinner and the Private Secretary on duty returned at 9.30 to place a limited number of papers in a shallow flat black box which was then deposited on the writing-table in the Prime Minister's study upstairs. Chamberlain went dutifully through them before going to bed, but he required no secretarial assistance after dinner. On Friday evenings he and Mrs Chamberlain retired to Chequers whence no murmur was heard. There was a telephone at Chequers, but it was in the pantry and only to be used in the event of dire emergency.

Chamberlain was aloof to his staff, but polite and considerate. He relied much on Sir Horace Wilson who relieved him of many burdens, was the overseer of all Civil Service appointments, was ready with advice on all matters but did not proffer his views on party political questions unless invited to do so. When I took in some paper requiring a decision, Chamberlain would often say: 'I think that is all right, but go and ask Horace if he agrees'. Horace seemed to view most matters dispassionately, except when he thought the Foreign Office were pursuing some policy on their own, and he was a man for whom all who worked at No. 10 developed an admiration. He was kind; he was considerate; and he was an excellent administrator. He rarely lent his ear to extravagant ideas, but on one occasion I remember his doing so. The Chancellor of the Exchequer, Sir John Simon, had a powerful intellect; but he was widely disliked and distrusted. An uncharitable legal colleague had said: 'There'll be no moaning at the Bar when he puts out to sea'. Nobody surpassed the Governor of the Bank of England, Montagu Norman, in hostility to Sir John and he persuaded Horace Wilson that the Chancellor might be fruitfully replaced by the former Sir Josiah Stamp, a man of outstanding ability who had recently been ennobled. The difficulty was that a peer could not be at the Exchequer, and so in January, 1940, Montagu Norman took to arriving after dark at the garden entrance wearing a black cloak and, with his short beard, closely resembling Mephistopheles. It was usually my job to let him in, because even our respectable messengers must not be allowed to see him, and his purpose in coming was to discuss with Horace Wilson how best Lord Stamp might be de-nobled. I think the Prime Minister was dubious and the scheme, never disclosed to the King or the Cabinet, came to nothing.

It had a curious sequel. In 1941 Lord Stamp was killed by a bomb which scattered his belongings into the street. Among them was an envelope containing a full account of this abortive plot. An Air Raid Warden found it and brought it to No. 10, where I happened to be on duty at the time. Churchill had known nothing of the affair and so I took the envelope to the Treasury, to which Horace Wilson had been exiled on the fall of the Chamberlain Government, and handed it to him. Montagu Norman's unsuccessful initiative remained an undisclosed secret.

Wilson lived on for a full thirty years after his fall from grace and favour. He was abused and attacked from many quarters. Almost all the complaints related to functions performed at the express wish of Chamberlain, whom he had served so conscientiously. This could have been his answer to the accusers; but he made no attempt to defend himself at his master's expense, for he was an honourable man.

Much power was exercised by Captain David Margesson, the Chief Whip, whom many feared but few disliked. He was the ideal Adjutant. He could be counted on to maintain iron control over the parliamentary ranks, to report any breach of discipline or good order, to soothe by his charm the discontented and the disaffected and to arrange parliamentary business to the entire satisfaction of the Prime Minister. He was one of those people to whom others automatically edged nearer: his arrival in the Private Secretaries' room was the signal for all pens to be dropped and on the darkest day the sun was shining while David was in the room. He made no pretension to intellectual ability, but he had some wisdom and much experience: and he was a dedicated servant of his country as well as of the Conservative Party.

Lord Dunglass meant much to Chamberlain, as he has meant much to others since. One November afternoon in 1939, when he was down at the House with the Prime Minister, Miss Watson and I were working away at our tasks. Hers was the preparation of replies to Parliamentary Questions. She suddenly said to me: 'You know, Mr Colville' (Christian names were never used between the sexes in office life), 'there is hardly anybody here nowadays who understands the House of Commons. The PM doesn't and Sir Horace certainly doesn't. I sometimes think Captain Margesson and Captain Dugdale don't either. The only one who does is Lord Dunglass. He will be Prime Minister one day'.

I replied: 'Of course you have much more experience of these things than I have, Miss Watson; but long before the time comes that Lord Dunglass could be Prime Minister, he will be Lord Home; and I cannot believe that a peer could ever again be Prime Minister'.

'Well, say what you will, I shall be dead before it happens, but on the day Lord Dunglass becomes Prime Minister I hope you will remember what Miss Watson said.' I did, and I wrote to tell him.

Lastly, there was Chamberlain himself. His sin was vanity, much enhanced by the hysterical adulation that Munich brought and his belief that he had a mission which none but he could fulfil. This sin was as nothing to his totally unselfseeking ambition to serve his country, increase the welfare of his fellow-men and banish the threat of war. Certainly by the time I knew him, he was incapable of mean thoughts and although it took long to penetrate the cold, unforthcoming defences of an essentially shy man, it was a rewarding exercise. Neville Chamberlain was long derided and lampooned. Perhaps he was too easily deluded by apparent success and popularity;

perhaps he dived into waters that were deeper than he knew; perhaps he was too prone to reject advice which conflicted with his hopes; but he was at heart an unselfish idealist who, when things went wrong, was given all too little credit by his contemporaries for the valiant efforts he had made on their behalf.

I knew him for less than a year; but when I went to say good-bye and for the first time he spoke to me, straight from his heart, of what he had tried and failed to do, I was in the presence of a man whose residual vanity had been destroyed by the Norwegian disaster, but whose courage was unimpaired. There was much that was sad, but nothing that was undignified, in the faith which he had placed in unworthy men and in the failure of hopes that had seemed to him so bright.

2. WINSTON CHURCHILL

Churchill arrived on the scene like a jet-propelled rocket. That scene, for a month, was Admiralty House for the greater part of the twenty-four hours, and No. 10 in the middle of the day. The even tenor of our life was rudely disrupted; that is to say of mine, for many of the familiar faces vanished and I, being the least important, was taken over with the furniture. The admirable ladies remained, although the new Prime Minister brought several of his own. He took months to realise that others existed and then annexed some of them to reinforce his over-worked personal staff. The no less admirable messengers quickly adapted themselves to the changing scene. The press officer retired to a distant cubby-hole because Churchill, styling himself a journalist by profession, would trust none but himself to handle the press. He brought two of his own Private Secretaries, Eric Seal and John Peck, from the Admiralty. The alarming unknown quantities, all of whom had to be accommodated, were his three extra-mural myrmidons, Brendan Bracken, Desmond Morton and Professor F.A. Lindemann.

The pace became frantic and totally unfamiliar methods had to be adopted. The Private Secretaries became known as the Private Office, which was an Admiralty expression foreign to 10 Downing Street. The hours expanded from early morning till long after midnight. Telephones of various hues were installed in every nook and cranny, even at Chequers. There was no longer a shallow flat black box, but at least two large, thick and bulging ones. Labels marked 'Action This Day' or 'Report in Three Days' were attached to the ceaseless flow of minutes, dictated straight on to a typewriter, which poured out of the Prime Minister's bedroom, the Cabinet Room or even the Bath Room. The Chiefs of Staff, the Secretary to the Cabinet, Ministers of all kinds and dozens of almost un-identifiable characters came and went with bewildering speed. Replies were expected within minutes of questions being asked, staid officials actually took to running and bells rang continuously. Whitehall was galvanised and the office at No. 10 was pandemonium. We realised we were at war.

There was no respite at Chequers, where night and day merged into one and business was conducted over the dining-room table until well after midnight. The hospitality of the Churchills to their staff as well as to their guests was munificent and the Prime Minister's view that his own contribution to the war effort called for self-expression rather than self-denial was extended, at least as far as absence of self-denial was concerned, to all in his immediate circle. He treated his Private Secretaries as part of his family without the slightest touch of that aloofness which had characterised Chamberlain. When he was in a relaxed mood, he also had the engaging habit of talking to those years younger than himself as if they were contemporaries and of holding nothing back. Reticence was as foreign to his nature as was pomposity; and he contrived to be at once self-centred and immune from personal vanity.

Yet there were times when some of the features of the previous Administration would have been welcome. There was nothing which could be described as orderly in Churchill's method of work. The car would be standing outside No. 10, with its engine running, when there were only three minutes to go before the Prime Minister's Questions were due at the House, and no Prime Minister had emerged. He would still be in bed, correcting a speech, when he ought to have been on the Front Bench preparing to deliver it. On Monday mornings, with the Cabinet due to meet in London at 11.00, he would still be at Chequers at 10.00; and the cars would be forced to tear up to London – police bells ringing, shooting red lights, going the wrong side of islands, while Churchill sat unconcerned within. The windows were tight shut, he was smoking a cigar and he was dictating to a stifled, long-suffering stenographer who sometimes had to be revived with brandy on arrival. The Cabinet usually dragged on till 1.30 p.m. or even 2.00 so that in days when food was soon off the menu, many a Cabinet Minister would find nothing but meagre scraps available at a club or restaurant. Churchill would say that he intended to leave at a certain time and then postpone the departure hour by hour, or sometimes till the next day. Trains and aeroplanes would be ordered, but not used. Cabinets and Chiefs of Staff meetings would be summoned at short notice and at inconvenient times. Exhausted Ministers, Civil Servants and leaders of the Armed Forces, long abed, would be required at No. 10 in the early hours of the morning. There was a lot of rhyme, especially at meals, but very little reason. Yet the machine worked and though people grumbled, they never rebelled. What is more, with a few exceptions such as Sir John Reith, they loved Churchill as much as they respected his energy and his abilities.

The Prime Minister's Office became peripatetic. Unlike Chamberlain, who rarely travelled anywhere but Chequers or the House of Commons, Churchill was constantly on the move, visiting defences, new weapon displays, bombed cities and military formations or, as the war expanded, Washington, Moscow and the theatres of war. Wherever he might be, he expected to carry on his normal business precisely as if he were sitting in the Cabinet Room in Downing Street. So there had to be front echelons and rear echelons, and groups of WREN or WAAF cipherers available to travel by sea or air at short notice. Moreover, since there was no hour of the night or day at which service might not be required or action taken, the Private Office soon doubled in size, with a proportionate increase in clerks, typists, filing staff and messengers. By the end of the war 10 Downing Street was scarcely recognisable to those who had known it at the beginning; but it reflected the dynamism of its master. At the same time, those who worked there had of necessity to supply the administrative skills which Churchill, contributing none himself, took for granted. It had been the same with the Elder Pitt who led the country, not perhaps at its finest hour, but certainly at a climax of its military and imperial grandeur. Nobody complained, because in war it is drive and inspiration which are needed at the top, and good administrators are much more readily found than outstanding leaders. All the same, without the unruffled competence of the Cabinet Office which became, under Sir Edward Bridges, the powerful organisation it has ever since remained, and the patient diplomacy of General Ismay's Office of the Minister of Defence, the machinery of Government would have broken under the strain.

For me those war years at Downing Street were interspersed with refreshing excursions into the field of active war, while some of my colleagues bore a different and more exhausting heat and burden at home. It was sometimes wearisome and sometimes exasperating; but it was the most exhilarating of all experiences to serve, at close quarters and in war, that wayward, romantic, expansive and explosive genius, with the inspirational qualities of an Old Testament Prophet, Winston Spencer Churchill.

3. CLEMENT ATTLEE

Attlee, who was as much a conservative by temperament as Churchill was a radical, accepted the staff, the systems and the physical appurtenances of 10 Downing Street without change or demur. Indeed, in July 1945, he astonished the Russians and the Americans by returning to the Potsdam Conference, which had been adjourned for a few days while the results of the British General Election were declared, with precisely the same staff as Churchill had taken home with him. He even had the same valet, thoughtfully provided by Churchill when Attlee had first travelled to Potsdam, at Churchill's suggestion, as Leader of the Opposition. Our allies had expected a largely new team: the same military and diplomatic advisers perhaps, for the sake of temporary continuity; but Churchill's Private Secretaries, Churchill's typists, Churchill's chauffeur and a valet provided by Churchill, that surely proved that the British were even more wilfully idiosyncratic than was commonly supposed. Meanwhile Attlee, for his part, lent Churchill Chequers, his aeroplane and me.

I thus had a curious start as one of Mr Attlee's Private Secretaries. Churchill tried to make political capital out of an ill-judged letter

Doodles – by Winston Churchill *(left) and* Clement Attlee.

written by Professor Harold Laski during the recent Election Campaign. He and Attlee exchanged angry letters on the subject for publication. It became my duty to go to Claridges, where Churchill had temporarily established his headquarters, and help him draft a Joshua-like blast of the trumpet to Attlee. I delivered it to Attlee and helped him draft a withering reply. This enjoyable and totally ineffective exercise lasted several days. Each knew that I was assisting the other.

It was not only the Russians and the Americans who failed to understand that Prime Ministers are temporary, but their civil servants are permanent. In the days immediately following the change of Government, letters of congratulation poured into Downing Street and we drafted replies to the more important for the Prime Minister to sign. One came from a General who owed his high promotion to Churchill alone and had never ceased to express his loyalty and devotion. He told Attlee how overjoyed he was, both on political and personal grounds, by the Election results. Another, in the same vein, came from a man who had actually served as a Minister in Churchill's Government. Obviously I could not sneak; but the temptation to do so was heavy, especially when I saw them both at a cocktail party which Duncan and Diana Sandys gave for the outgoing Administration.

Churchill, who liked and respected Attlee, felt it his duty as Leader of the Opposition to attack the Government with vigour and, having started with the Laski-letter squib, he was in constant search of sticks with which to beat the Government. Yet having a loyal and affectionate nature, he could never bring himself to lambast either Attlee or Ernest Bevin with his full strength. The feeling was reciprocal. During the week-end after the Election, when I was on loan to Churchill at Chequers ('Now I am out of office, I wish you would stop calling me Sir and call me Winston'), he opened a rehoboam of champagne at dinner and announced: first, one must never give way to self-pity; secondly, the new Government had a clear mandate which the Opposition had no right to deny or attack in principle; thirdly, no Government in modern times would have a more difficult task than this one and it was the duty of everybody to support them on matters of national, as opposed to Party, interest.

A fortnight later I went to Chequers with the Attlees. One contrast was the greater formality. Whereas Churchill, except on grand occasions, wore a siren suit over a soft silk shirt for dinner, Attlee put on a dinner jacket and a stiff collar. Another was the Old School Tie. Geoffrey De Freitas came down to be inspected as a potential Parliamentary Private Secretary. Being highly intelligent and no less highly likeable, he won immediate approval. The Prime Minister asked me what I thought of him and I echoed the general sentiment. 'Yes', said Attlee, 'and another advantage is that he was at my old school, Haileybury'. I recollected that Churchill, when he wished to say something friendly about me, sometimes mentioned that I had been a fighter pilot; but he never suggested that my having been at Harrow was a special recommendation.

Attlee was endearing in his simplicity. He may well have been the only British Prime Minister in all history without a touch either of vanity or of conceit. Service was his motive as an undergraduate for social work in the East End of London; service was the basis of his gallantry at Gallipoli; service was his reason for going into politics and the mainspring of his effort as Prime Minister. Personal ambition played no part and he cared nothing for money or position. He might occasionally be the dupe of those whose motives he believed, in his uncomplicated calculations, to be as disinterested as his own; but when it came to handling his colleagues, his party and those who worked for him, nobody could have been either fairer or firmer. He was a competent administrator and a Chairman who stood no nonsense from great or small.

I remained on his staff but a few months, for the time had come for me to return, after six years' absence, to the Foreign Office. I left No. 10 glad to have served, for however short a period, a man whom I could not perhaps love, admire, laugh with and be uplifted by to the extent that I could feel and do all those things with Churchill; but one for whose integrity and competence I have an imperishable respect.

'They that have power to hurt and will do none' are, according to Shakespeare, the people 'who rightly do inherit heaven's graces'. These three men all had power to hurt. Churchill in particular, at the summit of his war-time power and popularity, could have acted as a dictator. It is to their abiding glory that they never used their power to hurt and that all three looked on themselves as the servants of the House of Commons.

14. *Preux Chevalier*

Faces young and old brightened in the presence of Major-General J.E.B. Seely. He was vain and egotistic, but unfailingly good-natured and open-handed. At the age of six or seven I could count on the immediate gift of half-a-crown every time he saw me. As a result of still more lavish extravagances, the fortune he had inherited from a rich, industrialist father had shrunk to an extent which created some alarm and despondency among the tradesmen who supplied his everyday needs in the Isle of Wight. His gallantry in war was famous and undoubted. He made no effort to disguise the fact because he thought modesty an unnecessary and overrated virtue. He was reputed to have recommended his soldier servant for the VC, 'Standing, as he was, never less than twenty yards behind me throughout the engagement'; and it was said that his readable book of memories, *Fear and Be Slain*, had been delayed beyond the expected date of publication because the printer ran out of capital I's. He carried on an unceasing war, until personally rebuked by King George V, in order to assert his precedence as Lord Lieutenant of Hampshire over Queen Victoria's daughter, Princess Beatrice, who was Governor of the Isle of Wight. When he was created a peer and assumed the title of Lord Mottistone, the wags at once hailed him as Lord Modest One. Yet none of the stories told against him was repeated with anything but amused affection. His charm and good nature were proof against all malice; and if it be true that the genuinely brave are normally the most reticent about their deeds, Jack Seely was indulgently admitted to be the exception who proved the rule.

Winston Churchill had gone to Harrow when Seely was at the top of the School, a 'blood' as the successful, swashbuckling older boys were described by their admiring juniors. Some fifteen years later Churchill, in his capacity as a newspaper correspondent in the Boer War, was riding his jaded pony across the veldt when he saw a column of British Cavalry approaching. Alone, twenty yards ahead of his men, mounted upon a black horse and resplendent against the rising sun was Colonel Seely. He seemed to Churchill to represent all that was magnificent in British Imperial power and virtuously bold in the conduct of war. They exchanged greetings and went their respective ways.

Another ten years passed and Churchill, by then First Lord of the Admiralty, entertained the Prime Minister, Mr Asquith, in the Admiralty yacht, *Enchantress*, for a summer cruise in the Mediterranean. Having the Prime Minister trapped for a whole fortnight on board a yacht was enormously satisfactory to Churchill. How could the great man possibly avoid discussing all the affairs of State on which Churchill was longing to express his views and exert some influence? But the great man somehow managed it. Day after day went by and every time Churchill tried to bring the conversation round to foreign affairs, or finance, or an Irish Settlement, Asquith would launch into an erudite discussion about the classical antiquities they had been visiting or suggest a game of bridge.

Only on the last evening of the cruise, as *Enchantress* steamed in a calm sea towards Marseilles, was Churchill given the opening for which he longed. The ladies had gone below to dress for dinner. Asquith and Churchill were sitting on deck in basket chairs. Suddenly Asquith said that he felt it essential to make a change at the War Office and was totally unable to decide who the new Secretary of State for War should be. Had Churchill any ideas? The enquiry was unexpected; Churchill had abandoned all hope of serious political conversation, and he was temporarily at a loss. Suddenly there floated before his eyes the 'blood' whom he had so admired at Harrow and the splendid cavalry officer leading his men to war in South Africa. 'What about Jack Seely?', he impetuously volunteered. 'Hm', said Asquith; 'We should, I think, go and dress for dinner'.

No more was said, but a fortnight later Churchill read in the newspapers that Major-General J.E.B. Seely had been appointed Secretary of State for War.

There followed the Curragh Incident. The British Officers stationed in Ireland came close to mutiny in their opposition to the Government's proposal to include Ulster in the plan for Irish Home

Rule. Fairly or unfairly, much of the blame fell on the Secretary of State for War, and so after a short, inglorious tenure of office Seely returned to the back benches. Churchill felt that his contribution to Cabinet-making had, to say the least, been of doubtful value; but he never lost his affection for Jack Seely. Indeed, he thought Duff Cooper's wit went too far when, accused across the dining room table of being the worst Secretary of State for War in the present century, he swelled with pretended rage and replied: 'How dare you say that in the presence of Jack Seely.'

One June morning in 1940 I was at my desk at 10 Downing Street, immersed in the frantic activities of those anxious days, when a messenger informed me that Lord Mottistone was at the front door, demanding to see me. 'Bring him in, of course', I said. The messenger said he had indeed invited him in, but His Lordship had declined. So I went to the front door and there, resplendent in the full dress uniform of a Lord Lieutenant, stood the seventy-year-old General.

'Winston', he said to me, 'is one of my oldest friends. But I don't wish to disturb him at this moment when the future of the world rests on his shoulders'. He fumbled in his pocket and I thought for one moment that he might be going to give me half-a-crown. Instead he brought out a piece of paper on which were written the words: 'Hampshire is behind you.' 'Give that to Winston from me', he said, and with a gallant smile turned to walk back to Waterloo Station. I gave the Prime Minister the message. He shook with laughter as he read it and then, quite suddenly, he wept.

15. A Grand Design

An impetuous, potentially far-reaching and actually insignificant event in modern history was the proposal in June, 1940, to unite France and Great Britain. It happened, or nearly happened, with breath-taking speed. The early part of the story, as recounted to me on 16 June that year by Captain David Margesson, the Government Chief Whip, and Major Desmond Morton is as follows.

On Friday, 14 June, the Churchills were moving into 10 Downing Street. They had hitherto remained at Admiralty House since the day Churchill became Prime Minister. That evening one of the Whips asked Margesson to see Monsieur René Pleven, of whom he had never heard. Pleven unfolded to him the idea of a political union between the two countries, combined with the evacuation of as many French troops as possible from the West of France to Britain. Margesson consulted Morton, to whom Major Jean Monnet had been speaking on similar lines, and Morton welcomed the proposal. So Margesson, whose personal links with Neville Chamberlain, now Lord President of the Council, were then closer than with Churchill, made his way to 11 Downing Street where he found the Chamberlains entertaining Lord and Lady Halifax to dinner. He told me that he advocated the French suggestion with as much eloquence as he could muster, but his audience was not enthusiastic. He discovered, however, that Sir Horace Wilson, now Secretary to the Treasury and still close to Chamberlain, though far indeed from Churchill, had also embraced the Pleven–Monnet idea with great warmth, and he had found a well-disposed listener in Brendan Bracken. Thus when Churchill arrived at No. 10. after dinner Bracken persuaded him to see Pleven in the Cabinet Room. Churchill was interested in the idea of bringing French troops across the Channel so as 'to make the island stiff with soldiers' and increase the defences against invasion. He was less interested in the grandiose idea of a Franco–British union. Indeed, according to

85

Margesson, he was 'bored and critical', although he did finally walk through to No. 11 to talk the matter over with Chamberlain. Certainly for the next thirty-six hours the suggestion was far from Churchill's thoughts: his mind was concentrated on the importance of keeping the French Fleet out of German hands if France should capitulate.

It was on Sunday, 16 June, that in the course of a few hours the affair became a matter of supreme, if transitory, political importance. I can best illustrate what happened by extracts from my diary for 15 and 16 June:

'Saturday, 15 June

After tea Winston dictated long telegrams to Roosevelt and to the Dominions (whose premiers had all sent the most touching and encouraging messages) pointing out that we had now got to face the trying ordeal of heavy bombing and saying to all that he personally was convinced that the carnage and destruction in this country would bring the United States into the war. He said that the French condition for carrying on had been a promise of active US support: the promise of redoubled supplies which had been received was not sufficient, and though France might fight on from her Colonies, her resistance at home would now almost certainly come to an end. "If words counted, we should win this war", he said as a comment on his own telegraphic efforts.

'We arrived at Chequers in time to dine at 9.30. The party consisted of Winston, Duncan and Diana Sandys, Lindemann and myself. It was a dramatic and fantastic evening. Before going into the dining-room, I learned by telephone that the position was deteriorating fast and the request to be allowed to make a separate peace was being put in a more brutal form. I imparted this to Winston who was immediately very depressed. Dinner began lugubriously, the PM every now and then firing some technical question at Lindemann, who was quietly consuming his vegetarian diet. The Sandys' and I sat silent, because our sporadic efforts at conversation were not well received. However, champagne, brandy and cigars did their work and we soon became talkative, even garrulous. Winston, in order to cheer himself and us up, read aloud the messages he had received from the Dominions and the replies he had sent to them and to Roosevelt. "The war is bound to become a bloody one for us now", he said, "but I hope our people will stand up to bombing and the Huns aren't liking what we are giving them. But what a tragedy that our victory in the last war should have been snatched from us by a lot of softies!"

'Winston and Duncan Sandys paced up and down the rose-garden in the moonlight while Diana, Lindemann and I walked on the other side of the house. It was light and deliciously warm, but the sentries with tin helmets and fixed bayonets, who were placed all round the house, kept us alive to the horrors of reality. I spent much of the time telephoning, searching for Winston among the rose-bushes and listening to his comments on the war. I told him that fuller information had been received about the French attitude, which appeared to be slipping. "Tell them", he said, "that if they let us have their Fleet we shall never forget, but that if they surrender without consulting us, we shall never forgive. We shall blacken their name for a thousand years!" Then, half afraid I might take him seriously, he added: "Don't, of course, do that just yet". He was in high spirits, repeating poetry, dilating on the drama of the present situation, maintaining that he and Hitler only had one thing in common – a horror of whistling – , offering everybody cigars and spasmodically murmuring: "Bang, bang, bang, goes the farmer's gun; run rabbit, run rabbit, run, run, run".

'Kennedy telephoned and Winston, becoming serious for a minute, poured into his ears a flood of eloquence about the part that America could and should play in saving civilisation. Referring to promises of industrial and financial support, he said such an offer "would be a laughing-stock on the stage of history", and he begged that we should not let President Roosevelt's efforts "peter out in grimaces and futility".'

'*Sunday 16 June*
'Woken at 6.30 by the telephone and shortly afterwards by a despatch rider who brought the full facts about the French from London. When I heard that the PM was awake, about 7.30, I took them to his room and found him lying in bed, looking just like a rather nice pig clad in a silk vest. He ruminated for some time and then decided to call the Cabinet in London at 10.15, abandoning

his project of having the French General de Gaulle, together with Eden and the CIGS to luncheon at Chequers. So I hurried back to my room, ate a hasty breakfast and was ready to leave by 8.30. I had to wait till after 9.00 before we started, being called from time to time to Winston's room, where he was wasting time with Duncan Sandys, to receive orders. Finally we drove back to London in pouring rain, disregarding traffic lights and speeding down the Mall, to arrive just as the Cabinet assembled.'

There had been no word spoken of Franco–British union at Chequers and Churchill, who seldom kept anything of importance entirely to himself, had evidently forgotten all about it or dismissed it from his mind as a fantasy.

At the Cabinet a telegram to Reynaud was drafted, saying in effect: 'Ask for an armistice but let us have your Fleet.' Then Churchill lunched at the Carlton Club with Corbin (the French Ambassador), Eden, de Gaulle and Sir John Dill. It was at this luncheon that de Gaulle reminded Churchill of the project for a political union of the two countries and begged him to consider it seriously.

The Cabinet met again at 3.00 p.m. and I ushered Corbin and de Gaulle into a room adjoining the Cabinet Room to wait until they were summoned. They told me that Reynaud had already been sounded about this stupendous proposal and had said that in such circumstances France would fight on, for there was now 'a ray of light at the end of the tunnel'.

Sir Edward Bridges, the Secretary of the Cabinet, came out of the Cabinet to dictate the proposed wording of the Declaration of Union. My diary continues:

'Desmond Morton tells me that Horace Wilson has been working hard on the proposal, that Vansittart, one of its principal sponsors, has suddenly returned into the limelight, and that Monnet is the man to whom the chief credit for the idea should be given. Apparently most of the day has been spent telephoning to Reynaud and Mandel, persuading them to hold fast and not give in to the defeatist pressure of their colleagues. De Gaulle has been strutting about in the Cabinet Room, with Corbin too: the Cabinet meeting turned into a sort of promenade, Winston beginning a speech in the Cabinet Room and finishing it in some other room; and everybody has been slapping de Gaulle on the back and telling him he shall be Commander in Chief (Winston muttering: "Je l'arrangerai"). Is he to be a new Napoleon? From what I hear, it seems that a lot of people think so. He treats Reynaud (whom he called "ce poisson gelé" at one point) like dirt and discourses familiarly on what he will do in France: yet he is only a major-general just recently discovered.

'Meanwhile the King does not know what is being done to his Empire. The Lord President is going to see him and will break the news. We may yet see the Fleur de Lys restored to the Royal Standard.'

I am sure that Churchill was not carried away for long by this Grand Design, which he regarded less as a dramatic change in the map of Europe than a means to the highly desirable end of keeping the French Colonial Empire and Fleet at war with Germany. His own account of the affair, written seven years later in his *History of the Second World War*, is incorrect as far as the chronology is concerned; for the official Diary which his staff meticulously and laboriously maintained throughout the war had mysteriously vanished by the time he came to write and it has never been found. His account does, however, portray correctly his own initial lack of interest in the proposal and the degree to which he was swept along by the enthusiasm of his Cabinet colleagues and of General de Gaulle. He did think it warranted one last diplomatic effort on his own part and he proposed to leave that very night by sea for Bordeaux, taking Mr Attlee, Sir Archibald Sinclair and the Chiefs of Staff with him. I was to go too. A special train for Portsmouth was awaiting us at Waterloo Station when a telegram arrived to say that the meeting was cancelled. Reynaud's colleagues had suspected that this was a plan to turn France into a British Dominion. My flippant thought about restoring the Fleur de Lys to the Royal Standard had evidently occurred to others too, but with a more sinister interpretation. Reynaud resigned and as Pétain and Laval stepped into his place, a long, dark night fell on France.

16. Counsellors

It is wrong to assume that great men necessarily, or indeed normally, have good judgment. Napoleon allowed his strength to be sapped in Spain and destroyed himself by invading Russia. Churchill, brilliant though his imagination and many of his projects undoubtedly were, can scarcely be credited with good judgment in his White Russian adventure after the First World War, his rampant opposition to Mr Baldwin's Government of India Bill, his restoration of the Gold Standard in 1925 or his support of Edward VIII at the time of the Abdication. However he possessed, and provided for others, the inspiration normally associated with the Old Testament Prophets. I am not a sufficiently erudite biblical scholar to pronounce whether Isaiah, Ezekiel, Amos and the others had good judgment. Jeremiah seems to have erred a little on the 'bearish' side and I suspect that if he were reincarnated, it would be as a meteorologist or perhaps as a Cambridge economist, comforted by the knowledge that should his prophecies be wrong, they would soon be forgotten in the sunshine of returning prosperity. Nor, on reincarnation, would he be so rash as to record his predictions again.

Churchill was no Jeremiah. Indeed he was at his energetic, pugnacious and unconquerable best when the clouds were darkening for an approaching storm, and though he was wise enough to offer blood, sweat and tears rather than manna from heaven, he never lost faith in his conviction that all would be well in the end. Like Isaiah, he prophesied salvation.

He did need restraining and one of his virtues was that pertinaciously though he might contest an issue, tirelessly though he might probe, he did not reject restraint once he had convinced himself that the arguments for caution were neither craven nor bureaucratic. Unless he was so convinced, he was not susceptible to influence even by his closest friends and advisers. There was no man or woman to whom a suitor could go in the expectation that through

High Summer

such a favoured intermediary Churchill would be persuaded to promote a plan or further an objective.

It was thus that those with whom Churchill was intimate differed in their scope and authority from the members of some of the other Garden Suburbs and Kitchen Cabinets established by Prime Ministers throughout the ages. Nevertheless they played their part, sometimes with substantial force; for however much Churchill was determined to make up his mind, he seldom refused to listen and he was always prepared to weigh a good argument from whatever source it came. The sole proviso was that both the man and his motives deserved respect.

In seeking to describe a body of friends and advisers, whom Churchill called 'The Secret Circle', I omit his family and his Private Secretaries, although none of them was discouraged from expressing their opinions; and I restrict my observations to the Second World War. His close associates can be divided into two groups, the Official Advisers and the Grey Eminences.

The Official Advisers
Two of these were outstanding: General Sir Hastings Ismay, universally known as Pug, and Sir Edward Bridges.

Ismay took charge of the 'Office of the Minister of Defence', established by Churchill in May, 1940, when on becoming Prime Minister he created for himself the new title of Minister of Defence. Unlike Chamberlain Churchill proposed to assume direct responsibility for the conduct of military operations. Ismay had not known Churchill before the war, although he was a dedicated admirer of his writings and could repeat by heart extracts from the World Crisis, in particular his tribute to the Army of the Somme. When Churchill was First Lord of the Admiralty, Ismay had been exasperated by his constant interference in all military matters, by no means only those relating to the Navy. He was prominent among the many soldiers and Civil Servants who in the spring of 1940 hoped against hope that Churchill would not become Prime Minister; but once the die was cast, there was none whose loyalty, patience, unflagging energy and wise discrimination surpassed Ismay's. Nor, as the months went by, did Churchill have a more devoted admirer, even though the General used often to mutter: 'The PM is superb

91

in a Test Match, but he is no good at all at Village cricket'. He was the buffer, and a stalwart one, between the Prime Minister and the Chiefs of Staff. When Churchill demanded something which the Chiefs of Staff found unreasonable, Ismay advised them how to handle the situation. When the Chiefs of Staff dug their toes in, Ismay sat at Churchill's bedside, never flatly contradicting him but putting the counter arguments so skilfully and so soothingly that all animosities were avoided. His sugaring of unpalatable pills was masterly and his diplomatic gifts were outstanding. He contrived not only to retain for himself the deep affection and total confidence of both the Prime Minister and the Chiefs of Staff, but he deserves more credit than any other man for the absence in World War II of the suspicion and the strife which so bedevilled the relationship of the soldiers and the politicians in World War I. He was supported by a small, exceptionally able staff, two of whom, General Ian Jacob and General Joe Hollis, became so acceptable to Churchill that he took them on his travels and treated them as his own.

Ismay seldom took even a day's holiday and was in continuous demand. When, as often happened, Churchill was concentrating his thoughts with undivided energy on a particular problem, such as the Battle of the Atlantic or the inadequacy of the tank supply, his black box would soon be overbrimming with minutes and tele-grams on military matters. We used to ring up Ismay who would come over to No. 10, remove those papers which he judged in-essential, shorten those that were indigestible and ensure that only a manageable residue of the genuinely urgent and interesting re-mained for us to force on the Prime Minister's attention.

He was, incidentally, the only man I ever heard predict, before the enemy attack in May, 1940, that the French Armies would collapse before the German onslaught.

Perhaps in the war years Ismay was nearer to being indispensable to Churchill than any other man, but Sir Edward Bridges, Secretary to the Cabinet, followed close behind. What Ismay was in the military sphere, Bridges was in the civil, and they galloped side by side, in perfectly matching harness, without a whisper of jealousy, antagonism or indeed disagreement. Much as Churchill disliked Committees, it became necessary to decentralise the conduct of total war by creating them. Bridges advised on their establishment, their composition and, as time passed, on their effectiveness, and he expanded his office to provide a ubiquitous secretariat. The son of a Poet Laureate, himself a scholar at Eton and a man of profound learning, he retained a boyish approach to life (which usually took the form of punching one playfully in the tummy), possessed an infectious sense of humour and became one of the most powerful men in the land without ever losing either his humility or his sense of the ludicrous. His predecessor, Hankey, had made himself a great name: under Bridges not only the Secretary of the Cabinet, but the Cabinet Office itself acquired the influence and assumed the power of overriding importance in the Government of the country which it has retained ever since.

There was a third official, later to become a Secretary of State, who sometimes, and on specific matters, had Churchill's ear. This was P.J. Grigg, Permanent Under Secretary at the War Office. He had been Churchill's Principal Private Secretary at the Treasury fifteen years before. He had a brilliant mind and a sharp tongue, a total inability to suffer fools gladly and a positively Churchillian passion for trespassing on other people's preserves. If he disagreed with a Minister, including his own political chief, he said so with asperity and he saw no point at all in being loyal to anything or anybody except his King and Country, for either of which he would gladly have died. Perhaps Churchill found in him some resemblance to Admiral Jackie Fisher, who had alternatively fascinated and infuriated him at the Admiralty in years gone by. He did not really like Grigg, but he respected his dynamic ability and he invited him to Chequers frequently, listened attentively to his views, however explosive they might be, and charged him with the duty of reading all the telegrams between Delhi and Whitehall so as to ensure that neither the Viceroy nor the Secretary of State, Mr Leopold Amery, strayed from the straight and narrow path of firm resistance to Indian Nationalist pretensions.

On one occasion Churchill, alerted by Grigg about some Vice-regal tendency of which he disapproved, instructed me to send a telegram to the Viceroy in his own private cipher. I pointed out that he had no private cipher. He was aghast.

'Do you mean to say that all those telegrams I send to the President and the Dominions' Prime Ministers go in some common cipher which is handled by Foreign Office clerks?'

I explained that there were specially trained, utterly reliable cipher officers.

'Procure me a personal cipher at once,' he demanded; 'and use it to send this message to the Viceroy without letting Leo Amery see it.'

It was no use explaining or expostulating. I took the message over to the India Office, swore the senior cipher officer to secrecy, insisted that no copy be retained for the India Office and worked for an hour or two, not without a great measure of help from the senior cipher officer, in order to despatch the telegram. When the reply came it was deciphered at the India Office without my unprofitable intervention.

After the fall of Singapore it became necessary to make a ritual sacrifice to appease the House of Commons. Captain David Margesson, who had been an efficient Secretary of State for War, well liked by the Generals, was chosen for slaughter and although he could scarcely be held responsible for the disaster, he readily agreed to be the victim. He was less pleased when P.J. Grigg, immediately on his return from Chequers, where he had been making one of his frequent Sunday visits to go through a batch of India Office telegrams, put his head round the door of his Secretary of State's room and announced that he, Grigg, was his successor. Churchill did sometimes act impetuously, and he was convinced of Grigg's ability; but Margesson thought with some justice that the affair might have been handled more graciously. Curiously enough, once Grigg had been promoted so high, he ceased to have much personal contact with Churchill or to be the Prime Minister's adviser on Indian affairs.

The Grey Eminences

When Churchill came to Downing Street in May, 1940, he brought with him three men of striking dissimilarity. They were Brendan Bracken, Member of Parliament for Paddington, Professor F.A. Lindeman, Student of Christ Church, Oxford, and Major Desmond Morton, formerly member of the Industrial Intelligence Centre, a secret Government agency which had been responsible for collecting information about German armaments and manufacturing capacity. Exaggerated rumours and allegations about this fearsome triumvirate had reached 10 Downing Street during the winter of 1939–40 and I viewed their arrival with alarm. This was rapidly dissipated and they became convivial members of a Mess which Bracken established (providing an admirable Swedish cook at his own expense) for the Private Secretaries and Advisers to the Prime Minister. He presided over this gathering every night, with ready wit and inexhaustible gossip, while the bombs fell down on London.

Almost as loquacious as Bracken, and the source of countless amusing if improbable stories, was Desmond Morton. He had miraculously survived being shot through the heart in the First War and on recovery had been appointed ADC to Haig. He had a house at Edenbridge, close to Chartwell, and in the years immediately before the Second War he was a constant visitor there, supplying Churchill with facts and figures about German rearmament which Churchill, who was accorded this privilege because he was a Senior Privy Councillor and a member of the Committee of Imperial Defence, used to great effect in attacking the Government for the tardiness of its rearmament measures. Why the Government allowed one of its servants to supply ammunition to its principal critic and gadfly, I have never understood; and I suspect that Morton gave Churchill more detailed and secret information than Neville Chamberlain or the Foreign Office would have approved. After the war I asked Churchill this question direct and he gave what was for him an uncharacteristically evasive answer. In fact all he said was: 'Have another drop of brandy.' Whatever the truth, by 3 September 1939, Morton had become a Chartwell habitué and when Churchill went to the Admiralty, he attached him to his staff.

During the summer of 1940, Desmond Morton played a prominent role as Churchill's liaison officer with the Free French and the other dispossessed allied governments established in London. He was also made Chairman of a Foreign Office Committee responsible for the support and encouragement of these distinguished but largely powerless foreigners and he rapidly succeeded in antagonising the Foreign Secretary and irritating his Department. This was a pity because Morton's zeal was boundless, he took endless pains to serve and conciliate the exiled governments and the kindness of his nature was matched by deep religious faith and fervent patriotism. There was soon no worthwhile job for him to perform, because in due course SOE and other such organisations assumed responsibility for the European Resistance Movements, and unfortunately Morton was unable to resist pretending in the dining rooms of London to an importance and an influence on the Prime Minister far greater than he in fact enjoyed. He kept a room and a secretary at the wartime Annexe to 10 Downing Street until 1945; but Churchill saw less and less of him and from the end of 1940 onwards he was little but an agreeable and amusing member of the Downing Street Mess who wrote occasional minutes to the Prime Minister about Free French dissensions or Free Yugoslav ambitions; nor, as the war drew towards its close, was he given a significant part to play in guiding and encouraging the emergent European freedom fighters. He deserved better, for he was a good and honest man; and he was deeply hurt that Churchill, who was not in the habit of dropping old friends, and indeed always spoke of Morton with affection when his name cropped up, gradually forgot about him.

No such fate befell Bracken and Lindemann. They were both men of mystery. The first with his crop of wavy red hair, outspoken views and natural friendliness was easy to approach and an entertaining, quick-witted companion. Lindemann, on the other hand, was an acquired taste. Bracken delighted in making a secret of his origin which even his close friend, Lord Beaverbrook, failed to unravel and which has only recently been disclosed by his painstaking biographer, Andrew Boyle. He enjoyed the fictitious rumour that he was Churchill's illegitimate son. Indeed he was quite capable of having invented it. He declined the formal appointment of Parliamentary Private Secretary, although he was never far away from Churchill in the House of Commons, within or without the Chamber, and had his ear pressed close to the parliamentary ground.

Bracken was reluctant to become Minister of Information, an office which had not enhanced the reputations of Lord Macmillan, Sir John Reith and Duff Cooper; but he filled the post for four years with tact and success. This did nothing to diminish his attention to the affairs of 10 Downing Street, where he continued to exercise a well-informed and unprejudiced influence on appointments in the Church and the Universities, on the choice of Lords Lieutenant, on recommendations for Honours and on changes in the Administration. The remarkable thing was that nobody objected, neither the Chief Whip, James Stuart, who had been deeply suspicious oı Bracken in the pre-war parliament, nor the leaders of the Labour and Liberal Parties. There were three reasons for this. The first was that the warmth of his personality, his pretended ruthlessness (which all took pleasure in discovering to be a façade) and his readiness to take endless pains to help others endeared him to politicians, soldiers and Civil Servants alike. The second was that he was totally ungrasping and until, with victory in sight, party politics reasserted their sway and disinterested patriotism faded, he exercised his undoubted influence for the general good rather than for that of the Party or his friends.

Thirdly, he recommended and acted with indisputable knowledge. If the name of a man or woman in the official, parliamentary, professional or social world was mentioned, there was no need to refer to a book of reference if Bracken was in hailing distance. With the precision of a computer, and no risk of faulty programming, his brain held the *curriculum vitae* of a vast array of personalities, whether or not he knew them personally or had even met them. The See of Bath and Wells might fall vacant, a Regius Professorship of Civil Law, the Lord Lieutenancy of Stirling and Clackmannan, or the Parliamentary Under Secretaryship at the Board of Education. Bracken seldom failed to have an admirable suggestion for the new incumbent.

His knowledge of architecture was no less encyclopaedic. I remember that one sunny evening in the spring of 1941 he walked into my office, fatally interrupted my labours and insisted on taking me for a walk through the squares and side streets of Westminster. He would stop in front of a house in Cowley Street or Smith Square, recite the names of its occupants during the last 200 years, complain that Lady So-and-So had removed the Regency sashes in 1854 and give me a totally unpretentious lecture on the comparative merits of Hawksmoor and Vanburgh. His knowledge of books, though less comprehensive, could not fail to impress and he was justly proud of his library.

I doubt whether Brendan Bracken on the way up had as attractive a personality as when he had arrived. This is by no means unusual. The ambition which had driven him all the way from a humble house in County Tipperary to the Privy Council and the Cabinet was soon replete; his almost canine devotion to Winston Churchill became, when the war ended, the distant worship of a hero on a pedestal from whom he withdrew himself in public as in private life; he re-established himself in the City as Chairman of Union Corporation, but tired of fame and fortune; he accepted a Viscountcy and never went inside the House of Lords; he became increasingly interested in political gossip and decreasingly active in the realities of politics; and because he, who in his youth had asserted himself so vigorously and, as some thought, so pushingly, ended by hiding his light under a bushel, it is possible that his contribution to victory in the all important post of Minister of Information will be overlooked by historians, however much his unswerving loyalty, habit of doing good by stealth, and genuine, if sometimes weird, moral integrity may be remembered by his surviving friends. His post in Britain was that held by Dr Goebbels in Germany; but the two men had nothing at all in common and Bracken was by comparison a knight in shining armour.

If Lindemann was an acquired taste, it was one to which I person-ally became an addict. He had, as Churchill repeatedly said, 'a beautiful brain' and he also had a distinctive sense of humour. How-ever, unlike Bracken's host of friends and admirers, Lindemann's were an eclectic band and his capacity for making enemies was surpassed by few. This was because he pursued his dislikes, whether of the Germans, of Sir Henry Tizard or of a number of other scientists, air-marshals, statisticians, economists, dons and Mini-sters, with unflagging zest. Against those who had ever thwarted him, or otherwise aroused his antagonism, he placed his personal black mark and refused to allow that they might have any virtue at all.

Churchill abhorred what he called 'faddists' and could never see much advantage in mortifying the flesh. Indeed, in seeking to restrain Lord Woolton from imposing too severe rationing on the people, he wrote: 'Almost all the food faddists I have ever known, nut-eaters and the like, have died young after a long period of senile decay. . . . The way to lose the war is to try to force the British public into a diet of milk, oatmeal, potatoes, etc., washed down on gala occa-sions with a little lime-juice'. He made an exception in favour of the vegetarian, non-smoking, teetotal Professor. In return Lindemann, when dining with the Prime Minister, consented to drink a glass of brandy carefully measured, as Churchill affected to believe, in cubic centimetres. Nobody was more fastidious in his personal habits, method of work and use of language; and yet, before or after his cubic centimetres of brandy, he could be the life and soul of a dinner party. With solemn countenance, and without a trace of affectation, he adopted unusual ways of illustrating a point. On one occasion I remember his opening a serious discussion with the words: 'In 1912 I was told by a Russian waiter in Los Angeles . . .'

Originating from Strasbourg, where his family had made a fortune out of the Waterworks, he had studied science at Berlin University. Perhaps the other students had mocked him, or perhaps during the German occupation of Alsace–Lorraine some harm had befallen the Strasbourg Waterworks. Whatever the reason, his hatred of the Germans was obsessive and unlike Churchill, who detested the Nazis but refused to condemn the German people, and who even at the worst time of the war was accustomed to discourse on how best they might be brought back into the comity of nations, Lindemann took active pleasure in hearing of the devastation wrought by our air-raids on German towns. He was quite sorry that owing to the time-factor the Atom Bomb had to be reserved for the Japanese.

I think that, like the protoplasm, he was sexless; but in other respects his knowledge and experience were wide. Not even his enemies denied his eminence as a scientist. He was, at the same time, an economist of ability, was remarkably well read in European history, was impossible to fault on biblical facts and quotations and possessed a distinguished literary style. On top of all this he had been a tennis player who would not have disgraced himself at Wimbledon and did, for some obscure reason, become the Singles Champion of Sweden. When it was still a rare accomplishment to be a qualified pilot, he learned to fly so as the better to conduct some of his scientific experiments. He boasted of nothing and I never heard him tell a story redounding to his own credit. He left that task to others. But he did not deny or even qualify the story Churchill used to tell in his presence that he worked out mathematically the method of recovering from a spin and went up alone, before the days of parachutes, in order to put a plane into a spin and prove that his theory was valid.

His principal value to Churchill was as an interpreter. Better than any man I have known, he could simplify the most opaque problem, scientific, mechanical or economic, in language which provided a lucid explanation and sacrificed nothing of importance. He performed this task with infallible skill and punctuality so that the Prime Minister, who had scarcely been inside a laboratory and detested economic jargon, was enabled to grasp essential facts precisely when he required them without being obliged to deflect his concentration for too long from the major considerations of military strategy, allied relationships and national government. Every week Lindemann produced charts showing clearly and accurately the state of aircraft production, the losses and new building of ships, the output of tanks and guns, the availability of coal stocks and other statistics which saved the reading of long and complex documents. These useful functions more than compensated, at least in Churchill's eyes, for Lindemann's vendettas against Service Departments and other Ministries, and for a number of unsuccessful time-wasting experiments which gave rise to exasperation in Whitehall.

Almost everywhere that Churchill went, 'the Prof' was sure to go. He was never without his bowler hat, which he even wore on battleships at sea, nor his admirable Secretary-cum-Valet, Harvey, who dressed identically, coped imperturbably with all unforeseen problems and drove the Prof's cumbersome limousine. His charts were in daily, sometimes hourly demand, and were held to be indispensable on transatlantic journeys and at major allied conferences. They enabled Churchill to impress and to floor foreign experts with unexpected facts and figures. The Americans were fascinated by the Prof, on sartorial as well as intellectual grounds, and since he genuinely loved the United States he restricted the scope of his more serious vendettas to the British Isles. He believed, as sincerely as Churchill, that the future hopes of humanity must lie in the unity of the English-speaking peoples and that Britain could not survive economically without the United States. Some years after the war he told me he was convinced that if President Roosevelt had survived, and Churchill had been returned to office in 1945, they would have persuaded the two nations to accept a common citizenship. I doubt if he was right; but that was what his intellect dictated and where his heart lay.

17. The Mastership of Trinity

Professor F.A. Lindemann had his defects, but his qualities included unwavering loyalty to Oxford University. He was rich and he had already reached the height of his ambition; but he was suspected far and wide, and particularly by those who did not know him, of scheming to obtain a post of high preferment.

It fell to my lot, as the junior Private Secretary at 10 Downing Street, to look after the Ecclesiastical patronage of the Crown. The Prime Minister submitted to the King the names of Bishops, Deans, Canons and new incumbents for a large number of ordinary parishes where the advowson belonged to the Crown. It was an agreeable relief from the rest of my work. I might be writing a précis of some complicated official report, or wearily sifting through mounds of Foreign Office telegrams and Naval signals, when Dean Arabin would call to recommend a canon, or Mr Quiverful or Mr Crawley would come in urgent search of a Crown Living. All the characters in Trollope's Barchester novels came to visit me by turns and I was frequently to be seen striding along the Embankment to ask the advice of the Archbishop of Canterbury and his resourceful Chaplain, Canon Alan Don. Without their approval no submissions went to Buckingham Palace.

The frontiers of the Ecclesiastical patronage were as irregular as those of an English county. Bishops were chosen by the Crown, but Suffragan Bishops were not. Most Deans and some Canons were our responsibility; others reached their stalls by different routes. Regius Professors at Oxford and Cambridge were within the Downing Street demesne, and so amongst others were the Provost of Eton, the Dean of Christ Church Oxford, and the Master of Trinity College, Cambridge. It took quite a long time to learn which offices were Crown appointments and which were not.

For a full year this was my ploy and, added to my other tasks, it was no light burden. I filled scores of Crown livings; I submitted

Footprints in Time

recommendations for a bishopric or two; I had trouble with a man who thought he should be a Regius Professor. Then suddenly, in August, 1940, the Master of Trinity died. He was the eminent physicist, Sir J.J. Thomson, who with Lord Rutherford had first split the atom; and as he had been Master when I was an undergraduate in the College, I felt a sense of personal loss. I set out for Cambridge to enquire who the College would recommend as his successor.

The Vice-Master of Trinity, D.A. Winstanley, was a historian of eighteenth-century English politics, held in great affection by men of all generations. He greeted me with the news that in expectation of enquiries from Downing Street, the Governing Body of the College had already held long discussions. They had ascertained that the obvious candidate for the Mastership, Professor G.M. Trevelyan, would flatly refuse to let his name go forward. Nothing, said Winstanley, would move him. Therefore the College proposed that the Mastership be left vacant for the duration of the war and the Master's functions be assumed by a small body of Fellows whom the College would select.

Since this was what the Fellows wished, I wrote a short memorandum recommending acceptance of their views and placed it in the large black box containing papers for submission to the Prime Minister. It never reached him, because Brendan Bracken extracted it. This was, he told me, an intolerable suggestion. Prime Ministers were judged in informed circles by the wisdom of their appointments and the quality of the men they promoted to high office. The Mastership of Trinity was an office of exceptional importance. Had not the late Master just been buried in Westminster Abbey? What other College could rival that? If George Trevelyan would not serve and if Trinity could suggest no comparable substitute, then he himself would put forward a name and persuade Mr Churchill to submit it to the King. Bracken's encyclopaedic knowledge of country houses, churches and every kind of building of architectural or historic importance was matched by his equally large fund of information about distinguished men in all walks of life. He carried in his head the details of their careers. I asked him who he had in mind and he replied, after a minute's thought: 'Lord

Justice Wright, formerly Master of the Rolls and an Honorary Fellow of Trinity'.

Trinity might or might not be pleased to have the Lord Justice as their Master. They would certainly be indignant to have His Lordship or anybody else imposed on them by 10 Downing Street, and their indignation would spread like a forest fire through what Brendan Bracken called 'informed circles'. So I decided that some counter-strategy was necessary and I went in search of that pillar of Trinity College, Professor J.R.M. Butler, son of a former Master, classicist and historian of wide repute, my own former Director of Studies and now, disguised as a Colonel, working in the Cabinet Offices. I unfolded my strategic concept, won his approval and set forth once again for Cambridge.

The Prime Minister was, I told Winstanley, unlikely to accept the College's recommendation. Should the Fellows be unable themselves to propose a suitable candidate, Mr Churchill had one in mind. I made every effort to look grave and to imply, by my words and my demeanour, that as a loyal son of Trinity I was distraught by the message I brought. Winstanley blanched. Was it, he asked, somebody very close to the Prime Minister – a member of his entourage? I hesitated before indicating that I could answer no questions. The College must draw their own conclusions and decide.

As soon as I had gone, Winstanley summoned the Governing Body. They concluded, as he had, that it could only be the dreaded Lindemann whom the Prime Minister had in mind. Mass horror and hysteria seized them. In a body they left for Grange Road where Professor Trevelyan lived. On bended knee they begged him to save the College. Would he not sacrifice his own scholarly tranquillity to stave off the threat of a disaster such as Trinity had never suffered in all its long history? The Professor, aghast and stifled by emotion, gave way.

I was thus able to submit a new memorandum to the Prime Minister, approved by Brendan Bracken, stating that the Fellows of Trinity would like Professor George Trevelyan as their new Master. Mr Churchill, who had no idea at all of what had been going on, expressed delight. Was not the Professor an Old Harrovian, whose literary style was above reproach and who, even if he had lapsed from grace by endorsing Macaulay's pernicious opinions about

Marlborough, was nevertheless an expert historian of Mr Churchill's own favourite period, the reign of Queen Anne? An enthusiastic letter of offer went from 10 Downing Street and Trevelyan accepted in no less felicitous terms. Professor Lindemann, to whom I mentioned the matter, remarked that although Oxford was the only university where such affairs interested him, it was certainly fitting that the changes should be rung and that a great historian should succeed a great physicist. He remained ignorant of the part he had played.

Eighteen months after the war ended, I was invited to luncheon at the Master's Lodge in Trinity Great Court. I confessed to the Master the trick that had been played on him. It was, he said, an utterly disgraceful piece of intrigue by Brendan Bracken and myself. It was, he added, one for which he was profoundly grateful because, contrary to all his expectations, the last six years had been the pleasantest of his whole life.

18. A Gift from Cuba

The Battle of Britain had been won, but the Battle of the Atlantic hung in the balance. Convoys were being attacked and supply ships were going down by the score. So food, clothing, cigarettes and petrol were rationed and imported luxuries were but memories. Cigars were not held to be necessities, except by the Prime Minister.

His pre-war stock was all but exhausted and since he smoked, or rather consumed, between ten and fifteen a day, as well as being generous in his offers to guests, even the boxes which were frequently sent as presents by friends and admirers were totally inadequate to meet the demand. The situation was approaching the desperate, when one afternoon late in 1940 the Cuban Minister came to Downing Street in a tall-bodied taxi accompanied by a huge cedar-wood cabinet which contained five thousand of the best Havana cigars. It was, he informed a joyful Mr Churchill, a token of the admiration which the Government and people of Cuba felt for the saviour of western civilisation. The sun broke through the clouds.

The next day an official called with the vexatious information that the Prime Minister owed HM Customs and Excise the sum of nearly £10,000 in payment of Customs duty and Purchase Tax. I happened to be on duty and it fell to me to receive this bird of ill-omen. I pointed out that the Prime Ministerial salary was only £10,000 a year. The British public would be disappointed, perhaps even disaffected, if they saw Mr Churchill without a cigar. The official was granite-faced and adamant. The King alone, he said, was exempt from Customs duty: not the Queen or the Queen Mother, and certainly not the Prime Minister.

With trepidation I broke the news. Churchill merely said: 'It is up to you to find a satisfactory solution.'

In such circumstances a man normally turns to God or to his

Mother. With the greatest reverence for both, I nevertheless felt that neither could be of immediate assistance, and so I fell back upon my Alma Mater, the Foreign Office. I spoke to the Foreign Secretary's Private Secretary. The Prime Minister would, I explained, obviously have to return the cigars and refuse the gift. I supposed this would only lead to a total breakdown of goodwill between the British Empire and Cuba – not perhaps a matter of vital consequence and one must, of course, have one's priorities. But did I not remember seeing in the Foreign Office telegrams a report that the American Government were perturbed about the possible use of Cuban bases by German U-Boats? America was not a belligerent and if we did not mind, perhaps we should not worry if they did.

It had the desired effect. That very day an official letter went from the Foreign Office, written on behalf of Mr Secretary Eden, to inform the Lord Commissioners of the Treasury that it was of the greatest importance, on political grounds, not to give offence to the Government of Cuba in this matter. The Lord Commissioners gave way with good grace; the requisite instructions were sent to the Customs: Churchill kept his cigars; and I kept my job. Moreover, a happy precedent was established. Every succeeding year until the war ended, a beautiful cedar-wood box was delivered to No. 10 by the Cuban Minister as continued evidence of the admiration his Government and people felt for Churchill; and every year it was admitted duty free. The Chancellor of the Exchequer and the Foreign Secretary had to pay duty on gifts they received from abroad; but then the sums in question would not have consumed their entire Ministerial salaries, nor were they national monuments.

19. Jet Engines

The unquenchable desire of the public to write letters to the Prime Minister provided his Private Secretaries with a dreary, daily task of reading and answering them. There were aggrieved council tenants, political enthusiasts, grateful admirers, autograph collectors, violent antagonists and above all inventors. The Second World War encouraged the inventors to give full rein to their ingenuity and a high proportion of them coincided with another class of inveterate correspondents, the maniacs.

One morning I was sitting at my desk in the Annexe to No. 10 Downing Street, established on the relatively solid ground floor of the block of Government offices in Storey's Gate. The Prime Minister and his staff had moved there during the 'blitz' on London because No. 10 itself was such a fragile building. I plodded with resignation through my share of the daily post. Some I marked for the Government Department concerned; some I laid aside to answer. On those from the lunatics and elementary inventors I wrote 'Ack' which meant that a formal acknowledgement would be sent by an unprotesting girl along the corridor.

I was about to join the RAF and had developed an anticipatory respect for Group Captains. I therefore paused over a letter from an inventor who said he had discovered a way of making aeroplanes travel by blowing gases out behind instead of using the, to me, obviously essential device of propellers in front. The letter was signed 'F. Whittle (Group Captain)' and though clearly only a crank could have such absurd ideas, his style differed notably from that of most lunatics. Besides he was a Group Captain.

I was hesitating whether to scribble 'MAP' on the letter, which would have resulted in its being forwarded to the Ministry of Aircraft Production with an official slip attached, and no doubt consigned to oblivion, when into my room walked Colonel Moore Brabazon, the Minister of Aircraft Production, who had arrived for an appointment with the Prime Minister. 'Brab' was one of the pioneers of flying and an encyclopaedia on all things relating to it. 'Have you', I asked, 'ever heard of a man called Group Captain F. Whittle?' To my surprise he said he had. The Group Captain was a genius, but such an awkward one that he fell out with the very people who were trying to develop the product of his inventive efforts. 'The Prime Minister has', I said, 'had a letter from him and I don't know how to answer it. Would you read it and advise me?'

Brab read it. He asked if he might take it away with him and he promised to deal with it personally. He put it in his pocket.

Years passed. The jet engine was universally accepted and the name of Whittle became famous. He had in fact written papers on the theory of jet propulsion in the nineteen twenties, papers which the Germans had doubtless read and from which, as in the better known instance of General Fuller and his original ideas on tank warfare, they had drawn their own profitable deductions. He had worked on the project at Cambridge University in the nineteen thirties and it had been saved from extinction by the timely provision of £5000 by Lord Cowdray's Whitehall Securities; for the Government had not learned its lesson from an earlier episode when only Lady Houston's gift of £1 million, in the face of governmental parsimony, had enabled Great Britain to take part in the Schneider Trophy and, as a war-winning by-product, to develop the Spitfire.

This remarkable genius, Frank Whittle, should already have been assured of his eminence among the great British inventors; but his engine was not being developed in the way he wished and no doubt largely because of his own difficult personality, he had fallen out with the Ministry of Aircraft Production and was a prisoner in the cave of Giant Despair, from which he might never have emerged.

I do not know what Colonel Moore Brabazon did with the letter; but since he was himself a pioneer by inclination, and a man who loved inventiveness, I have little doubt that he delved into the recesses of his Ministry where this most secret invention lay. It had certainly not been forgotten, but it may well have been the victim of slow and vacillating administrative processes. After the war he remembered the incident of the Group Captain's letter and sent me

a copy of his autobiography in which he facetiously wrote this
inscription:

The Author and John Colville,
Winners of the War! !

Neither Brab, nor I, nor even jet engines won the war; but it may
be that the coincidence of the appropriate Minister entering the
Private Secretaries' room at No. 10 Annexe one dismal wartime
morning helped to revive hope and a sense of purpose in Group
Captain Whittle. It may even, for all I know, have done something
to accelerate the production of our first jet engines.

The British sometimes reward with high distinction people who
have contributed little to their country's welfare while they come
near to forgetting those to whom they are genuinely in debt. The
two classic examples from the Second World War are Sir Robert
Watson Watt, without whose invention of radar the Battle of
Britain would assuredly have been lost, and Sir Frank Whittle, the
inventor of the jet engine. They were both knighted, and Whittle
was given a pecuniary award, but neither of them received the full
expression of public gratitude which was their due.

The Americans are more generous. It is said that some years after
the war Whittle bought a ticket to fly to America on a Pan American
aircraft. He was met at the airport by an official who returned the
cost of his ticket and told him that whenever he chose to fly with
them, he would be welcome to do so free of charge since, but for
him, they would not have the magnificent aeroplanes in which they
could now invite him to be a passenger at their expense.

20. *Flying Visit*

This was the name of an ingenious and entertaining fantasy published by Peter Fleming early in the Second World War. In it Hitler made an inadvertent forced-landing in Britain and the story retailed the embarrassment to which this event gave rise. I read it early in 1940, and forgot about it.

The great 'blitz' struck London in September. Night after night the air-raid sirens moaned their warning as darkness fell and night after night up to a thousand Londoners died. The last and perhaps the heaviest raid took place on 10–11 May 1941, and thereafter, because the Nazis had other preoccupations, there was peace in the skies over Britain until sporadic attacks began again in the early months of 1944, followed shortly afterwards by the final assault of the V Bombs.

On 10 May I was alone at 10 Downing Street. One of my colleagues had gone with the Prime Minister to Ditchley since the moon was full and at such times Chequers was believed to be vulnerable. The other two were profiting from a much needed week-end off duty. It was a warm early summer's evening and there was no immediate crisis; but the air-raid sirens sounded and I went to bed in a bunk in the somewhat rickety shelter which had been hastily constructed near the kitchen just before war broke out and which was certainly not bomb-proof.

The bombs fell; several on the Horse Guards Parade and one in Whitehall. For some inexplicable reason I awoke a few seconds before each explosion, all of them shaking the house and the shelter in which I slept. Tired and, by this time, hardened to air-raids I invariably fell asleep again immediately. Before 6.00 a.m. the noise of bombs and anti-aircraft fire slackened. As I lay, half awake, in my uncomfortable bunk and the foetid, badly air-conditioned atmosphere, my dozing thoughts turned to Peter Fleming's book. I remembered, too, the report I had seen in an Air Ministry Intelli-

gence Digest that Goering was believed to fly over from time to
time in a German bomber in order to gloat over the destruction
which the Luftwaffe was wreaking on London. What fun it would
be if he had to escape from a burning bomber by parachute! My
half-waking day-dreams ambled on and always they kept returning
to Peter Fleming's book.

At 7.30 on that Sunday morning I dressed and went out. It was,
or should have been, a perfect May morning; but a low cloud of
smoke hung over the town and because a warehouse full of paper
had been among the night's casualties, small flakes of paper were
falling from heaven for all the world as if it were snowing. The
House of Commons was a ruin; flames were bursting from the roof,
William Rufus's roof, of Westminster Hall; and Westminster Abbey
had received its only direct hit of the war. The Horse Guards Parade
was pitted with craters; water from a ruptured main was pouring
in a torrent down Whitehall. Why 10 and 11 Downing Street,
fragile remnants of Sir George Downing's 17th-century jerry-
building, had not collapsed like a pack of cards, I do not know.

I went to a service in St Faith's Chapel, crowded by those who
like myself wanted to thank God for their survival through such a
night. Back at No. 10 I rang up Ditchley, spoke to the Prime
Minister and described the scene. 'At least,' he said, 'we shot down
thirty-three of the swine' (for he had been talking to the Air
Ministry). The cloud of smoke evaporated; the fire engines and the
ambulances proceeded with their familiar, daily duties; life returned
to wartime London-Blitz normal.

At about 11 o'clock I walked over to the Foreign Office. There
might perhaps be some news and, anyhow, it would be pleasant to
gossip with Nicholas Lawford, an amusing and stimulating Private
Secretary to Anthony Eden whom I knew to be on duty there.

When I opened the door of the large Private Secretaries' room,
adjacent to that of the Secretary of State, Lawford was talking on
the telephone. He saw me and said to the other party: 'Here is the
man you had better speak to. Hold on a minute'. Then, placing his
hand over the receiver, he whispered to me: 'This may be a
lunatic. He says he is the Duke of Hamilton, that something extra-
ordinary has happened, that he is about to fly down from Scotland
to Northolt and that he wants to be met there by Alec Cadogan and

the Prime Minister's Secretary. Alec is having his first day off for months and I refuse to ruin it. And he won't say what it is all about, except that it is like an E. Phillips Oppenheim thriller. Yes, I think he's a lunatic'. He handed me the receiver and the alleged Duke repeated his message. Suddenly, my waking day-dream came back to me. 'Has somebody arrived?' I asked. There was a long pause. 'Yes', he said. 'Please be at Northolt to meet me'. He rang off.

I could scarcely leave No. 10 unmanned, and so I rang up Ditchley and asked for instructions.

'Well, *who* has arrived?' asked the Prime Minister.

'I don't know', I repeated for about the fourth time; 'He wouldn't say'.

'It can't be Hitler?'

'I imagine not'.

'Well, stop imagining and have the Duke, if it is the Duke, sent straight here from Northolt'.

Thus it was that later that day Churchill learned from the Duke of Hamilton, who turned out to be neither an impostor nor a lunatic, that Rudolf Hess had arrived in Scotland. As for me, I make no pretence to psychic powers; but I think it strange that Peter Fleming's story, which I had read many months before and had long since forgotten, should have come flooding into my half-conscious brain that Sunday morning.

21. *Entente Cordiale*

In the spring and summer of 1941 General de Gaulle's behaviour in the Middle East induced an epidemic of apoplexy among British statesmen and soldiers. He was suspicious by nature and he suffered from an illusion that the British would take advantage of France's misfortunes to acquire a lasting hold of Syria and the Lebanon. The flame which burned within him at the time of the abortive proposals for Franco–British union was extinguished and he felt it his duty, even though he had rallied but a few thousand men to the banner of Free France, to insist that his Government be treated as that of a Great Power. Since the exigencies of war meant that there was little time for soothing tactics and none for play acting, and since among our allies the Poles, the Greeks and the Yugoslavs all had more men under arms than the Free French, the British authorities were less attentive and accommodating than the General thought appropriate. So he resorted to nuisance tactics in order to ensure that he was constantly remembered in British Government circles.

On this occasion he had overdone it. The telegrams from Cairo told of a mixture of intrigue, interference and devious behaviour which had diverted everybody, including the Minister of State and the Commander in Chief, from their endeavours to win the war in North Africa. The Prime Minister, who had been impressed by de Gaulle in the early summer of 1940, and had established his authority in spite of American hostility, was deeply incensed. No sooner had the General returned to England than he was summoned to 10 Downing Street. He was to come at 3.00 p.m.

At five to three the bell from the Cabinet Room rang and I went in. Mr Churchill informed me that when de Gaulle arrived he would rise and bow slightly but would not shake hands with him. He would indicate by a gesture that the General was to sit opposite him, on the other side of the Cabinet table. No doubt as a supreme mark of disapproval, he announced that he would not speak to him in French, but would converse through an interpreter. 'And you', he said, 'will be the interpreter'.

Punctually at 3.00 p.m. the General arrived. Churchill rose from his chair in the middle of the long Cabinet table, inclined his head slightly and gestured to the selected seat opposite him. De Gaulle seemed quite unabashed. He walked to his chair, sat down, gazed at the Prime Minister and said nothing.

'General de Gaulle, I have asked you to come here this afternoon'. Churchill stopped and looked fiercely at me. 'Mon Général', I said, 'je vous ai invité de venir cet après-midi'.

'I didn't say *Mon Général*,' interrupted the Prime Minister, 'and I did not say I had *invited* him'. Somehow I stumbled, with frequent interruptions, through the next few sentences.

Then it was de Gaulle's turn. After the first sentence he turned to me and I interpreted. 'Non, non', he interjected, 'ce n'est pas du tout le sens de ce que je disais'. But it was.

Churchill said it was clear to both of them that if I could not do better than that I had better find somebody who could. So I escaped from the room with shame and telephoned to Nicholas Lawford at the Foreign Office. His French was immaculate. He arrived at the double and I showed him into the Cabinet Room where no word had been spoken in the intervening minutes. It seemed no time at all before he emerged, red in the face and protesting that they must be mad: they had said he could not speak French properly and they would have to manage without an interpreter. He had lasted no longer than I had.

An hour slipped away and I began to fear violence. I tried to eavesdrop, but because the Prime Minister alleged that the noise from the Private Secretaries' room interrupted the deliberations of the Cabinet, double doors had recently been installed. I could hear nothing. I walked out into the hall and tried on General de Gaulle's cap, registering surprise at the remarkable smallness of his head. I did my best to concentrate on the papers on my desk. I had decided it was my duty to burst in, perhaps with a bogus message, in case some dire act had been committed. Perhaps they had strangled each other? Just then the bell rang and I went in to find the two of them sitting side by side with amiable expressions on their faces. De

Gaulle, no doubt for tactical purposes, was smoking one of the Prime Minister's cigars. They were talking French, an exercise Churchill could never resist and one which his audience, even when they spoke with the purity of de Gaulle, invariably found fascinating.

The Entente was Cordiale again, at least temporarily.

22. Escape Route

Though less hazardous, escaping from the Diplomatic Service in order to take a more belligerent part in the war was scarcely less difficult than getting away from Colditz. A few succeeded. Robin Hooper had been a pilot so highly esteemed by the Oxford University Air Squadron that none could resist his determination to join the RAF, where he won countless DSO's and DFC's. Fitzroy Maclean, thwarted in his plan to join a Highland regiment, had the bright idea of standing for Parliament, which meant he could no longer serve in the Foreign Office, and he ended his military career as the leader of the British Military Mission to Marshal Tito. I, whose subsequent career on active service was jejune by comparison with that of Hooper or Maclean, owed my escape to Prince Bismarck and to the Prime Minister's black cat, Nelson.

Years before, in the recesses of the Black Forest, I had read Bismarck's *Gedanken und Erinnerungen*. In this book of memoirs he related that a courtier at Potsdam dabbled in painting and thought himself an expert on coal-mining. Among artists, wrote Bismarck, he was esteemed as a coal expert; among coal-miners he was revered as an artist. I decided there was a practical lesson to be learned from this and I took unscrupulous advantage of it.

I went to Adastral House in The Strand and said I should like to be accepted for training as an operational pilot. This idea had symmetric charm because one of my brothers was in the Navy and the other in the Army. I also calculated that it had the best chance of success since a few days before the Prime Minister had waxed eloquent to me about the pilots of the RAF and had declared that the Air Force was 'the cavalry of modern war'. There was no higher praise he could, by his own standards, bestow.

It seemed to me, with Bismarck's reminiscence in mind, that in the Air Ministry I might be revered as the Prime Minister's Secretary and that Churchill would esteem me as an airman. At that

time, early in 1941, the name of Churchill roused undiluted
admiration, but this did not prevent the fear of thwarting his wishes
being deeply implanted in Government Departments. I did not go so
far as to assert that I had come to join up with Churchill's strong
support; but I saw no reason to suggest anything to the contrary.
Without so much as half an hour's delay I was given the requisite
educational test which included my being able to show I knew the
square root of four and the name of the capital of France. Having
survived that ordeal, I was at once examined medically and found to
be totally fit except that I was too short-sighted for aircrew. The
Air Commodore responsible for optical matters looked rueful.
What would Churchill say if I were failed? He was a resourceful
man and suggested that I had some contact lenses made at my own
expense. They were a fairly recent invention, and it might well be
that they would make hundreds of young men with imperfect eye-
sight capable of becoming Pilots, Observers or Rear Gunners. The
Navy, which was old-fashioned, would never contemplate such a
device, but the RAF was modern, the reverse of hidebound and
proud to be experimental in outlook. Would I care to be a guinea-
pig?

The second part of my Bismarckian Strategy was not such plain-
sailing. I told the Prime Minister that I was having contact lenses
most painfully fitted at my own expense and that the Air Ministry
scarcely had any priority so high as that of finding somebody thus
equipped whom they could train as an operational pilot. Churchill
was not impressed. He said he thought it mean of the Air Ministry
not to pay for the contact lenses; he added that he had never thought
me noticeably short-sighted; but finished by pointing out that in his
view I was contributing more to the war effort by staying in a job
for which I was trained than by starting from scratch as an unquali-
fied airman. No, he would not agree that I should go.

Fortunately I had taken Mrs Churchill into my confidence and
had found her entirely sympathetic. I knew that nobody else in the
world had anything like the same influence on the Prime Minister,
except in party political matters on which her views, being strongly
and sometimes combatantly Liberal, had to be discounted. She
advised me to put my request in writing, a method of approach she
had long since found to be the most effective. I did so with all the

persuasion I could muster. The paper came back marked 'RWE' meaning 'return to me at the week-end'. It was about as negative a formula as 'Le Roy S'avisera' which Kings used to write on Parliamentary Bills if they intended to veto them. Mrs Churchill promised to exert gentle pressure whenever an opportunity arose, and she was as good as her word; but I feared my Bismarckian formula was a failure.

Then, one afternoon, there was an air-raid. The Prime Minister was having his usual afternoon sleep in a downstairs bedroom shored-up with a few extra wooden beams, which looked impressive but would certainly not have borne the weight of a collapsing 10 Downing Street. There were strict, oft-repeated orders that he was never in any circumstances to be awoken unless there was an invasion. All the same a bomb or two dropped, there was a clatter of anti-aircraft fire and the Air Ministry said the raid looked like being a fairly heavy one. I was alone on duty. The Prime Minister's valet, the detective and the No. 10 office keeper all appeared in my room and suggested I should wake Churchill and insist on his repairing to the Air Raid Shelter (which was, in fact, scarcely more bomb-proof than the downstairs bedroom). None of them volunteered personally for the task.

I was ruminating whether to disobey orders when a girl came in with a telegram marked Most Urgent. It was addressed to 'Former Naval Person' from President Roosevelt. On reading it I thought it was not so urgent that it could not wait half an hour; but it provided an excuse. I took it in my hand, walked downstairs and knocked loudly on the bedroom door.

There was no reply and so I went in. Churchill, clad in nothing but a silk vest, was on all fours peering under a massive chest of drawers. It was evident that his favourite cat, Nelson, alarmed by the noise of anti-aircraft fire, had chosen its own Air Raid Shelter. He paid no attention to me. 'You should,' he said to Nelson, 'be ashamed of yourself, with a name like yours, skulking under that chest of drawers while all those brave young men in the RAF are up there fighting gallantly to save their country.' Then he turned to me and said: 'That is where I should be if I were your age.' I pointed out that for several weeks I had been asking for nothing more. 'All right', he said, 'you shall go'.

The Foreign Office was indignant. A Minute from Mr Eden arrived, addressed to the Prime Minister and stating that as I was a member of the Diplomatic Service, he and not the Prime Minister had the ultimate responsibility in such matters. My departure to the wars would give rise to grave difficulties in the Service. If I went, how could he argue that others of my age who had been applying to be released for months past should not be given similar treatment? Churchill wrote on it in red ink. 'Foreign Secretary. When I give my word, I stand by it. WSC'.

Thus while Bismarck certainly helped, it was Nelson who held in his black paws the key to the escape-hatch.

23. In the Mess Decks

Acute discomfort may or may not be good for the soul, but to have experienced it at least enables those who normally lead a sheltered life to feel fewer qualms about continuing to do so. The satisfaction for all but the monastic and the masochistic is, however, retrospective.

My discomfort, which was mild indeed by comparison with those who spent years in Prisoner of War camps, sailed in convoys to Russia or were in one way or another victims of war's selective hazards, lasted a mere six weeks. It was suffered in travelling from Liverpool to Durban, with the rank of Leading Aircraftsman, in an overcrowded troopship and in a slow convoy.

There was a depressing embarkation camp at Padgate, near Warrington. I arrived there on a cold January afternoon in 1942, laden with three oblong, white canvas kitbags inscribed in smudged black print 'No. 1395006 LAC Colville'. I was bound for South Africa, to be trained as a pilot, and I did not know a single man in the camp. After ten dismal days, sleeping on a top tier bunk in an evil-smelling Nissen hut, where the solitary oil stove struggled, often unavailingly, to keep the indoor temperature above zero, I paraded one morning with six hundred other airmen. They were all finding their heavy oblong kitbags, to be carried in addition to full packs, as unmanageable as I was. The local Padgate brass band did its best to cheer us up by blowing away merrily on the railway platform and it broke into *Auld Lang Syne* as the train began to puff its way towards Liverpool.

We boarded the former Orient liner *Otranto*. In peace time her complement was one thousand passengers and crew. On this voyage, painted grey and armed with a Bofors gun at her bow, she carried 3000 troops as well as us airmen and 100 merchant seamen bound for Durban to join the *Aquitania*. Our quarters were well below decks: a long, low saloon in which we were to eat and sleep.

Eighteen of us were allocated to each narrow mess-table, which might have held twelve with bearable comfort; and we slung our hammocks above the tables. There were not enough hammocks to go round and those too slow to procure one had to sleep on the tables or on the floor. We were not allowed to undress in case we were torpedoed in the night and we used our cork life-belts as pillows. To move about the ship without a life-belt was a disciplinary offence; but I failed to understand the rule against undressing. It would be easier to swim in pyjamas than in uniform.

When the hammocks were slung, they were so close together that every time one of their occupants turned in his sleep, an entire row of hammocks began to swing. In order to wash and shave it was necessary to leave the Mess Deck, climb a companion way to the deck above and queue for the limited number of wash-basins. As the water was only turned on for an hour twice a day, there was no certainty of reaching a tap before it ceased to flow. Our mugs, tin plates, knives, spoons and forks, with all of which we had been issued as personal attributes, had to be washed in salt water and carefully guarded against theft. By the time we reached Durban I had succeeded in retaining only my fork and my tin mug. Conditions, including the food, the smells and the head-room available, were not far removed from those in the living quarters of HMS *Victory* and before we had been at sea many days I found it easy to imagine myself back in the days of Trafalgar. One might be grateful that, while discipline was strict, the cat-o'-nine-tails was no longer in use; but equally the daily tot of rum was missing.

There were endless guard duties and as I did not suffer from sea-sickness, more than my due share fell to my lot. Several days out from Liverpool the sentry post allotted to me was in the cells which were far down in the ship's hold and exceedingly insalubrious. The prisoners consisted of two Irish privates in the 'Yorks and Lancs', bound with the rest of their battalion for Singapore. Their crime was to have smoked on deck in the blackout and, by displaying lighted cigarette-ends to any supernaturally endowed Focker-Wulf pilot or U-Boat commander, to have endangered the convoy. For a full hour they ranted against all things British, from the King downwards. Sentries were forbidden to talk to prisoners, but finally I could not resist asking them why, if they felt the way they did, they had taken the trouble to come the whole way from County Cork and join the British Army? There was a short silence and then one of them replied: 'Well, begorrah, if there's a scrap on, you wouldn't be expecting us to miss it, would you now? And how was we, without any money, to get over to Germany and join Hitler?' With the rest of their battalion they were destined to reach Singapore just in time to spend the rest of the war in Japanese Prisoner of War camps.

My only enjoyable guard duty was outside the Sergeants' Mess, from which a companion way ascended to the galley. It was staggeringly hot and I was there, on and off, for eight clammy hours. But there were compensations. During my final two-hour tour of sentry-go, one of the Mess Orderlies fell down the companion way with a tray full of fried liver. Every time he tried to get up in the slippery wreckage, he fell flat on his face again; and when he at last succeeded in dragging himself away, a succession of Sergeants, arriving late for their meal, slipped on the greasy liver and fell flat too. I much disliked Sergeants, who tended to treat LAC's like dirt, and so I stood stiffly at ease, clasping my rifle with fixed bayonet, and offered no assistance at all. The final pleasure was the arrival of the Orderly Officer who, having first fallen down on the liver, proceeded to deliver a severe rebuke to those Sergeants who arrived late for their meal and, to the delight of the sentry and other humbler creatures in the vicinity, to send a number of them empty away.

Even being on guard was a welcome contrast to the crowding and stuffiness of the Mess Deck. Shortly after the convoy, which contained some fifty large transports, escorted by a battleship, a light cruiser and half a dozen destroyers, had turned on a southerly course, a Focker-Wulf Condor was sighted. Every gun in the convoy and in the escort vessels opened up, but the aircraft was unscathed. It would, of course, have signalled our position to one of the U-Boat wolf packs. So the vast concourse of ships altered course to the westwards and we sailed for days further and further towards the coast of America. Nobody ever told us where we were or what was happening; but at night we could tell our course by the Pole Star.

One of the airmen in our Mess Deck, a boy of scarcely 19, was smitten by Spotted Fever and we paraded on deck two days later to see his body committed to the deep. By some miracle the fever did not spread in the foetid atmosphere below decks, but we were thenceforward allowed, indeed obliged, to sleep on deck. We were ordered to change into tropical khaki, which was a hygienic improvement after fourteen days and nights in our blue uniforms, but the order came while it was still cold on deck. So spending the night on deck was a limited consolation until we reached the tropics, and sleeping on the hard teak planks, with a life-belt for a pillow, left every bone in the body aching. Yet it seemed to us that anything was better than life in our allotted quarters and finally we found ways of slinging our hammocks on deck.

The two upper decks were reserved for officers and a few WAAFS and nurses. They had a five-course dinner every night, whereas our 'Tea' at 6.00 p.m. consisted of tinned tripe or other almost equally inedible victuals with slabs of bread and margarine. The Officers Mess menus used to be procured and handed round the tables in the Mess Deck by a number of politically conscious airmen. Their objective was furthered after dinner when, on a warm tropical night, serried masses of soldiers and airmen, packed so tight on 'C', 'D' and 'E' decks that they could scarcely lie down, would gaze upwards to 'A' deck and see officers leaning over the bulwarks, deep in conversation with a pretty WAAF or nurse in the intervals of dancing to the ship's orchestra. The music floated downwards to an increasingly disgruntled audience of sardines below. A small number of left-wing enthusiasts found fertile soil in which to sow. Discontent grew even stronger when the drinking water was contaminated with salt water and the food became daily more inadequate.

After a fortnight's slow plod, the convoy, unmolested by the U-Boats which were exacting such a heavy toll of shipping in those days, arrived at Freetown. The sharks swam behind us as we entered the bay, but this did not deter the local boys who arrived in shoals to dive for sixpences. Their elders followed more sedately in 'bum-boats' with every kind of merchandise and livestock to sell. The strictest orders were issued against making any purchases and armed Marines were posted all round the ship to ensure obedience.

I had come to an arrangement. Worn out by nights on guard, constantly awoken by colliding hammocks, stiff from sleeping on the teak planks, I paid 2 5s to a merchant seaman called Luke for the

use of his bunk for two hours every afternoon. The merchant seamen, more pampered than the Army or the RAF, had cabins; and
there were only two in each. Moreover, the cabins had wash-
basins so that my daily cleansing problems were greatly eased.

I made this advantageous deal as we lay in Freetown. Luke and his
cabin-mate, Joe, were friendly Liverpudlians of Irish descent with
a libertarian disregard for orders from the OC Troops or any other
military authority. Thus they and the other merchant seamen, who
from time to time came close to mutiny, were a source of constant
exasperation to the Military Police and the smart, stern-faced
company of Marines who, when necessary, were called upon to
impose discipline and restore order. To show his independence
Luke, in defiance of the regulations, acquired a monkey after dark
from one of the 'bum-boats' which continually edged alongside the
ship in the expectation of custom. The monkey was called Rosie.

I was normally left alone with Rosie for my afternoon nap until at
4 o'clock the obliging Joe would awake me with a cup of tea from
the Merchant Seamen's Mess. I had to put up with Rosie's unflagging energy, which included jumping on to my stomach
whenever she saw that I had dropped off; but I did have suspicions
of her cleanliness and had nagging doubts about the diseases she
might be carrying. Luke, however, said that he had made a wonderful bargain. He had swapped her for an old pair of trousers. He
proposed to 'get her organised' by the time we reached Durban
and to sell her there for a respectable sum of money.

Three days out of Freetown disaster occurred. I was sunk in
slumber when Rosie, scenting another illicitly owned monkey,
climbed out of the porthole on an amorous excursion. Losing her
way, she emerged on the deck above and was arrested by a steward,
surrendered to the authorities just before Luke arrived for the
rescue and mercilessly destroyed by a lethal injection. Luke, whose
affection for Rosie was only partly inspired by the lucrative prospects at Durban, hung about all day in search of the wisely elusive
steward. Finally he knocked down and severely damaged the wrong
steward and was removed to the cells by several burly Marines. He
managed to break out of gaol for just long enough to tell Joe and me
the details of the vengeance he would wreak on the real villain
when at last we went ashore at Durban. Joe and I felt sorry for Luke

in a cell in the tropics, but we agreed in welcoming the flea-infested Rosie's departure from the scene.

There were three weeks more at sea. The cloudy equatorial weather retreated before clear skies and a refreshing breeze. Flying fish, glinting silver in the sunlight, rose in shoals like partridges from a root-field and skimmed the bow wave as we steamed at a steady eight knots through the smooth sea. But the monotony and the dreary, irritating routine seemed endless. It was only at night, under the Southern Cross, that some soldier would start playing a harmonium and several thousand men, temporarily forgetful of their accumulated misery, would sing sentimental songs in chorus, drowning the music of the officers' band on 'A' deck. As we neared the Cape of Good Hope, the Trade Winds blew, chilling us to the marrow, and an albatross fell into formation in our wake. At night I shivered in my hammock which did not lend itself to the sagacious arrangement of blankets in the dark. One of the older merchant seamen, who had served in troopships in the First World War, told me as we sipped almost undrinkable tea tasting of salt water, that of all the ships he had ever sailed in, this was the worst. Yet the merchant seamen lived in greater comfort than did we.

The seas got bigger and the cold became more intense. I was not the only one who sat huddled on deck dreaming of the carefree life and secure family happiness we had left behind so long, it seemed, ago. Suddenly, bringing me back to the grim reality of the present, the bows of HMS *Resolution*, and then her whole length, surged forward into the empty sea space between two lifeboats at which I had been gazing in home-sick reverie. That grey camouflaged hull and the 15″ guns represented a wide gulf between present dejection and the times of quiet plenty when change was so gradual, small personal problems were the only complications of my life and a delicious chocolate soufflé seemed the just and natural culmination of a well-spent day. I think that food, though not necessarily chocolate soufflés, assumed a substantial role in all our day-dreams.

At last, almost six weeks after boarding *Otranto*, we reached Durban and the cold misery of the Trade Winds was replaced by the damp heat of a Natal summer. When at last, after hours of unnecessary parades in webbing and full packs, we were allowed ashore, the thermometer stood at 104° in the shade. Whether Luke found the steward for whom he was looking, I don't know; but I, in impetuous mood, sat in a café and wrote a long letter to the Prime Minister, saying that if the Government wanted to encourage mutinous despondency, and to damp the ardour of those who had set out from home keen to fight for their country, they should continue to allow troopships to sail in the conditions which, with many lurid details, I described.

I was hoist with my own petard. The Prime Minister was impressed by my invective. Carefully erasing my name, he caused my letter to be laid before the Chiefs of Staff. And when, a year later, I sailed home from South Africa, resplendent with my pilot's wings and expecting every luxury and privilege on the ship, I found that an egalitarian régime had been established. All ranks were subjected to an equally dreary austerity; nevertheless, by comparison with the *Otranto*, it was paradise.

24. Pillars of Empire

Throughout the war it was the function of the Secretary of State for the Dominions to keep the Dominion High Commissioners informed about military and diplomatic affairs. Churchill supplemented this regular briefing by telegrams to their Prime Ministers with whom he established a personal association ranging from intimate friendship to dutiful attention. When one of them came to London he was invited to attend the meetings of the War Cabinet and his counsel was sought on a wide range of political and strategic matters. They were, after all, part of a family with which Churchill felt keen emotional ties and each of their countries had soldiers, sailors and airmen fighting, from the very outbreak of hostilities, side by side with the British forces.

Foremost in Churchill's esteem was General Smuts, whom he easily persuaded the King to create a Field Marshal. No active statesman, apart from Churchill, had longer practical experience. He had sat in the Imperial War Cabinet during the First War; he had resolved a strike in the Welsh coalfields when Lloyd George himself failed; he was a philosopher as well as an astute politician; but what raised him to the pinnacle of Churchill's temple was the fact that he, who had once been our enemy, was now, as the result of a generous peace settlement after the Boer War (in drafting the terms of which Churchill himself played a prominent part) a loyal subject of the Crown and supporter of the Empire. When Smuts came to England, Churchill would drop all else and listen attentively to the accented words of wisdom, spoken in high staccato tones, which poured from the South African patriarch on all the issues of present and future policy. In Pretoria they called him 'Slim Jan'; at Downing Street he was the Prince Charming. South African troops were fighting in North Africa and Smuts was often in Cairo, whence his advice and his warnings sped by telegram to

London. This advice was usually shrewd, and it was always imaginative. There were few of Churchill's colleagues in the British Government whose opinions carried the same weight.

One April day towards the end of the war Smuts arrived to stay at Chequers bringing his son Jappy. He invited me to accompany him up Beacon Hill in the Chilterns. We set off at a brisk pace, climbing several slopes, and when we reached the foot of the highest hill, the 75-year-old Field Marshal, who had been discoursing volubly about wild flowers, sprinted ahead, leaving Jappy and me panting and breathless as we struggled along further and further behind the nimble Obaas. Finally Jappy sat down. His father was, he said, a wonderful man, but he was totally out of touch with the modern technological age. He still had old-fashioned interests such as philosophy and wild flowers and, he added bitterly, hill-climbing.

That same day at luncheon the opinionated American financier Bernard Baruch, six foot five in height, his bespectacled face crowned with a mop of thick white hair, joined the party. There was a heated debate on the future of gold, which Baruch asserted would always remain paramount because it alone gave people confidence. Churchill argued in favour of a Commodity Dollar, tied in value to an agreed number of commodities of which gold would be only one. Smuts made the final contribution. Gold, he said, must be like the British monarchy: it must cease to rule but remain a constitutional stabilising influence.

Later on gold gave way to diamonds as a topic of conversation. Churchill told a story which Smuts, who said he had entirely forgotten it, confirmed as being absolutely true. It seems that shortly after the Treaty of Vereenigen which ended the Boer War, the great Cullinan diamond, far the biggest in the world, was discovered. Grateful for the restoration of self-government, the Government of the Transvaal presented the jewel to King Edward VII on his 66th birthday. The British Liberal Government, too mean to pay the account of the Amsterdam diamond cutters, who had divided it with consummate skill into several large stones, told them to keep the chips of the diamond in payment of the work. The honest Dutch cutters declared that the value of the chips was far greater than the cost of the work. His Majesty's Government cared

nothing for this, provided the Treasury was not required to foot
any bill; but when the news of the transaction reached South
Africa, Generals Botha and Smuts organised a public subscription to
buy the chips in Amsterdam and to re-present them to the British
Crown. Churchill said it was the most humiliating episode in the
history of any British Administration with which he had been
associated. The two biggest Cullinan stones were mounted in the
Sceptre and the Imperial Crown; the re-presented 'chips' were set
in a brooch which is today the property of the Queen.

A close second to Smuts was Robert Menzies. He came over
from Australia early in 1941 and spent many months in London. He
was a guest at Chequers week-end after week-end, invited not only
because his views, and the way in which he expressed them, were
refreshingly original, but because he fell into a category to which
Churchill attached importance when he was off duty, that of men
'with whom it is agreeable to dine'. His contributions at the Cabinet
table were generally agreed to be constructive, and it was thus not
merely as a courtesy to Australia that he was welcome. Churchill
was glad to have him at the dinner table where he could hold his
own with all comers, from de Gaulle and Sikorski to the Chiefs of
Staff and Lord Beaverbrook. When the Australian Government
changed, so that he ceased for a spell to be Prime Minister, his
advice and his presence both at the Cabinet and in less formal
surroundings were sincerely missed. During Churchill's 1951
administration Menzies, by then an elder statesman in his own right,
was an eagerly awaited visitor to London and it was appropriate
that he should in due course be given the honourable, if honorary,
distinction of succeeding Churchill as Lord Warden of the Cinq
Ports.

Peter Fraser, Prime Minister of New Zealand, came on the scene
late in the war. New Zealand, smallest of the Dominions, held a
special place in the hearts of the British, partly from memory of her
soldiers' gallantry in the First War and perhaps partly because in
1938, when a new war had loomed so close, New Zealand alone
of the Dominions had declared unequivocally that Britain's war
would be hers too. Churchill had never ventured as far as the Anti-
podes, for the journey took three months there and back, and that
was a long time in the life of an active politician. Nevertheless, he

shared the British public's gratification at the thought of New Zealand's loyalty. Bernard Freyberg, whose courage in battle was famous, seemed to him to reflect all that was noble in the character of the New Zealanders. So Peter Fraser was welcomed for what he represented. The first impression, by contrast with the dashing Smuts and the eloquent Menzies, was disappointing. An emigrant from Glasgow, who had settled in New Zealand shortly before the First War, Fraser was the embodiment of Scottish caution. His apparent lack of fire gave a false impression of dullness, but as with so many of the best things in life his value was savoured more fully because it became apparent by degrees.

The last time I remember him at Chequers was just before the war ended. Churchill listened attentively to his measured views on the coming peace and the aftermath. Then after luncheon, while Churchill took his young cousin, Sunny Blandford, away for a shooting match in a revolver-pit he had had constructed in the woods (so as to keep himself in training against the eventuality of an enemy parachute descent), Peter Fraser suggested a walk up Beacon Hill. I was happy to find his pace substantially slower than that of Field Marshal Smuts. His wife had just died and he was a sad man who spoke thoughtfully of the dangers ahead. The statesmen were assembling at San Francisco to create a World Organisation which would settle the disputes of the future peacefully. Euphoria was rampant elsewhere, but Fraser spoke in a sombre tone. The new World Organisation was wrongly conceived. The veto of the great powers would remove any chance of its being effective and once 'The Big Three' fell out, as they assuredly would, the United Nations would be just a meeting place for airing the grievances of the small nations. He would give much to be wrong, and he could have no part to play in promoting a saner conception; for New Zealand carried little weight in the counsels of the world powers. As I listened to this wise but melancholy old man, I was reminded of Sir Robert Walpole's words: 'They are ringing the bells now. Soon they will be wringing their hands'. Would it not have been wiser, I asked, for the victorious powers to approach the whole matter on a less ambitious plane, starting with regional associations which would each elect one representative to send to a small Council of the World? He replied that indeed he thought it would; but he stood gazing at the cherry blossom, outlined against the blue sky, and pursued the unsettling topic no further. Mr Fraser was one of the few realists at large in those heady days of approaching Victory in Europe.

Churchill liked to refer to Canada as 'The Great Dominion', and he made a point of going there, if he possibly could, whenever affairs of state took him to North America. The valiant fight of the Canadians at Vimy Ridge in the First War was firmly imprinted on his memory, and he recognised that in the Second War the Canadian divisions and the RCAF had lived well up to their fathers' challenging record. Be all that as it might, he could never quite bring himself to enjoy the company of Mr Mackenzie King, though he sometimes tried quite hard to do so and he did value the unflinching support provided by the Canadian Prime Minister during the worst months of the war. When Mr King came to London, he was accepted as an honorary member of the War Cabinet, and every opportunity was provided for him to visit No. 10 and discuss whatever he wished. But when it came to meals, Churchill's sole wartime hours of relaxation, then it seemed better to leave Mr King's nourishment to the understanding care of the Canadian High Commissioner or the Secretary of State for the Dominions.

Thus, apart from greeting Mr King at No. 10, and once taking notes at a meeting when he was present, the only time I had an opportunity of conversing with him was at the Second Quebec Conference. To my surprise I found him agreeable and entertaining, possibly because Roosevelt and Churchill were deeply engaged in conversation at the other end of the dining room table and on this particular occasion there was nobody else for him to talk to. He waxed eloquent on the vital importance to Canada of the English-speaking provinces learning to give more consideration to the poor, populous French Canadian province of Quebec and, speaking as a devout son of the Nonconformist Manse, he displayed commendable breadth of mind in his sympathy for the Roman Catholic community. He had, he said, always believed that when a battle was over, the contestants should be the better friends simply because they had once fought an honourable fight. As a young Liberal MP he had been glad to participate years before in a commemoration of the storming of Quebec by Wolfe and the Battle of the Heights of

Abraham. The families of Wolfe and Montcalm had been invited. Unfortunately the organisers of the event had failed to introduce them and the first meeting of the heads of the two families had been in an acrimonious dispute over the use of a bathroom at the Château Frontenac Hotel. All the same, said Mackenzie King, he intended to pursue his endeavours for a better understanding between the factions.

After the war, when Churchill was again Prime Minister, he paid several visits to Canada. One of them had an inauspicious start. He had read in the newspapers that the Canadian Government of Monsieur St Laurent had decreed that the Royal Canadian Navy should no longer play *Rule Britannia*. Churchill knew *Rule Britannia* by heart. He loved it passionately: it represented all that he treasured in the history of the British Empire. So St Laurent's nationalist measure was a crime akin to blasphemy. A stern, reproving telegram was sent from Downing Street, recalling to me a surviving remnant of my classical education, Juvenal's description of the terrifying missives sent by the Emperor Tiberius from his villa at Capri: *Verbosa et grandis epistola venit a Capreis*. Monsieur St Laurent was unmoved. He explained in reply that Canada, though deeply conscious of her links with the British Crown, was a free and independent country with her own navy ruling her own section of the waves. Churchill was furious. He tried once more, against the strong advice of Lord Ismay, the new Secretary of State for Commonwealth Relations, and received a second polite but uncompromising refusal. Very well; after his forthcoming journey to the United States in a few weeks' time, he would cancel the plans for a visit to Ottawa. He would show these infamous, republican upstarts what he thought of them.

Wiser counsels prevailed. Lady Churchill said that if he insisted on behaving like a spoilt child, she would not go to America with him. In fact she had a good mind to shut up Chartwell and move off by herself to Brighton. Others took a firm if somewhat less dramatic stance. Nevertheless it was an ill-humoured, unco-operative Churchill who eventually boarded a special night sleeper at Washington bound for Ottawa. In the morning St Laurent and his whole Cabinet were assembled at the railway station to greet him.

Behind them were the massed bands of the Canadian army, navy and air-force. As the old man stepped down on to the platform, the massed bands struck up *Rule Britannia*. He stood there, hat in hand, with tears pouring down his cheeks; and thenceforward nobody ever dared to utter even the mildest criticism of Monsieur St Laurent or of Canada.

25. Flight to Gibraltar

In December, 1943, I was recalled from my Squadron in the RAF, stationed at North Weald and engaged in photographic reconnaissance of the V1 sites and of enemy shipping, to resume my duties as a Private Secretary to the Prime Minister. Churchill, who felt that war was only enjoyable when one was in action, implied that I had had enough fun and must return to the serious war-work of helping to look after him.

After a few days' leave, I arrived at Euston and was met by an official car containing John Peck, another of the Secretaries at No. 10. I was impressed by his civility in coming to meet me until I discovered that his sole object in so doing was to tell me to put on my uniform and be prepared to go forthwith to Lyneham in Wiltshire whence I should be flying to North Africa with Mrs Churchill and her secretary, Miss Hamblin. It was, he explained, a deadly secret: the Prime Minister was desperately ill, probably dying of pneumonia, and the doctors had recommended that Mrs Churchill go to his bedside without delay. It was, however, obvious that if it were known Churchill was ill, German morale would receive the boost it so badly needed, coupled with alarm and despondency at home. It was unthinkable to send Mrs Churchill without an escort and as she would be going into the war zone, that escort must be an officer in uniform. Even a humble Flying Officer would do.

We drove on a murky winter's night, in bitter cold and through dense fog patches, until at about 11.00 p.m. we reached the inhospitable Lyneham tarmac. A Liberator bomber with an RAF crew awaited us, but such was the secrecy that even the Station Commander had no idea why we had come or where we were going. The bomb-racks had been removed from the aircraft; there were no seats; and the furnishings consisted of some rugs and RAF blankets on the floor and several thermoses of coffee.

We took off into the blackness and Mrs Churchill, who in spite

of a gay and apparently unconcerned exterior was deeply worried
about her husband, announced that she could not possibly sleep
and that she had brought a backgammon board with her. So
crouched on one rug and swathed in two others we played backgammon and drank black coffee while the Liberator plodded out
into the Atlantic before turning southwards, well away from the
enemy-occupied Biscay coast. As the first grey light of dawn
appeared we touched down on the Gibraltar runway, the first and
most dangerous leg of our journey safely completed. We must have
played at least thirty games of backgammon and I was £2 10s od
to the good.

The four engines were switched off and the crew prepared to
open the door of the aircraft. 'Be a good boy', said Mrs Churchill,
'and go and see what is happening outside'. Steps had been pushed
up to the plane and as I emerged I saw three figures standing in line
some ten yards from their base. Behind them I could also see, in the
dim light, rank upon rank of soldiers who, as I stood at the door of
the aircraft, presented arms. The hands of the three figures directly
in front of me went to the salute, and so I naturally saluted back. I
walked down the steps and was soon close enough to see through the
gloom that the three figures were very high-ranking officers indeed.
In the centre was the Governor of Gibraltar and he was flanked by
Sir John Cunningham, Commander in Chief of the Mediterranean
Fleet, and an enormously important looking Air Marshal. They
for their part gazed with bewilderment at the single ring round the
sleeve of my uniform.

'Who are you?' asked the Governor. 'I am not allowed to say,
Sir', I replied, for I had been given strict orders to that effect before
leaving. 'Well, who is in that plane?' said the Governor with
obvious exasperation. Abashed by the importance of the company,
and the vast ceremonial parade behind them, I decided to disobey
orders. 'Mrs Churchill', I said, feeling that I was committing an
unpardonable breach of the Official Secrets Act. 'Why on earth?',
said the Governor; but to that enquiry I gave no reply.

The parade was dismissed and the Governor took us to the
Convent, his official residence, for breakfast. What had happened
was that when we were airborne, a signal had been sent in cipher
to Gibraltar announcing the ETA of a Liberator containing 'One

VIP and one Secretary'. The Governor had been asked to receive them and provide every facility. The message was deciphered in Gibraltar to read: 'One VIP and one Secretary of State'. The Governor showed great acumen. If, he concluded, a Secretary of State was not a VIP, then it could only mean that the VIP was the King. The feelings of the Gibraltar Garrison, turned out on parade before dawn to present a royal salute to a Flying Officer in the RAF, are fortunately not recorded.

26. Mrs Brown

After our surprising reception at Gibraltar, Mrs Churchill and I flew on to Tunis and were received with the news that the Prime Minister's life was no longer in danger. He was making a remarkable recovery at the White House, a villa on the sea-front at Carthage so named because Roosevelt had used it as his headquarters on the way back from the Tehran Conference.

There was no room for me to stay at the White House, where two of Churchill's Secretaries were already lodged, and so I was quartered in the exquisite d'Erlanger Villa at Sidi-bou-Said, which was also occupied by several Commanders in Chief and a staff of American GIs who walked about the courtyard offering the Admirals and Generals orange juice but declining on principle to clean their shoes or polish their buttons. I deposited my scanty luggage in this Arabian Nights billet and walked down to the White House. I had scarcely seen Churchill for two years and as soon as Mrs Churchill had left his bedside, John Martin, the Principal Private Secretary, suggested I should go in and present myself. He was sitting up in bed, wearing a scarlet dressing-gown embroidered with golden dragons and working on his papers as if there were nothing wrong with him at all. He did not look up as I entered the room, but said in a querulous voice: 'I will not be disobeyed. Mrs Brown *shall* have a CBE'. This was an unexpected greeting, but I felt I must say something.

'Who is Mrs Brown?' I asked.

He raised his eyes, dropped his papers and greeted me with an affectionate warmth that almost reduced me to tears. But after five minutes, when I rose to leave the room, he said: 'Tell them Mrs Brown *is* to have a CBE'.

I passed on the message. It was received by my colleagues with wry smiles. I asked who Mrs Brown might be and this is the story that General Ismay told me.

Operation TORCH had been the simultaneous landing of a British and American Army on the north-west coast of Africa under the supreme command of General Eisenhower. The task of the newly landed armies was to fight their way eastwards to join hands with General Montgomery's 8th Army advancing westwards from Tripoli.

The detailed plans for this first joint operation were of such secrecy that in Whitehall only the three Chiefs of Staff had a full copy. Those who needed to work on a particular section received the minimum extracts relevant to their task. The landing had been made early in November 1942.

One of the officers working in the office of Sir Charles Portal, Chief of the Air Staff, was an Oxford don of high intelligence and integrity. He did, however, suffer from an irrepressible curiosity to know what was afoot, and he was led into temptation. It was his duty one night to lock up the Chief of the Air Staff's safe when all but he had gone home, and in the safe was Portal's full copy of the plans for operation TORCH. It would, he reasoned, be easy for him to take the document home, so as to satisfy his thirst for fuller knowledge, and to replace it first thing in the morning. Nobody would know, nobody would suffer and he, of course, would not tell a soul what he had learned.

He put the plan in his overcoat pocket and walked out of the Air Ministry into the blackout. There was an impatient queue waiting for a bus and he was jostled by the crowd as he fought to get a footing on the bus platform. When he arrived home the pocket of his overcoat was empty.

At first light Mrs Brown, a lady who helped clean the Home Office every morning, was walking along Whitehall when she espied a bundle of papers in the gutter. On picking them up she saw that the top sheet was headed by three important looking green lines and on further inspection she read the words 'Operation TORCH. Most secret. Personal copy of the Chief of the Air Staff'. Mrs Brown was not quite sure what to do, but she had a nephew who was a Sergeant-Pilot and she knew that he was home on a few days' leave, staying with her sister in Tooting. Instead of going into the Home Office she took a tram to Tooting.

Her nephew was incensed at being disturbed so early in the

morning on one of his few days off duty. However, when Mrs Brown
showed him what she had brought, he wasted no time. 'This is not
for the likes of me,' he announced; and as soon as he could put on
his uniform he set off for the Air Ministry.

On arrival he demanded to see the CAS and in spite of repeated,
increasingly irritable refusals, he declined to leave the building or
to hand over the papers to anyone but Sir Charles Portal himself.
Finally an angry Squadron Leader, Personal Assistant to the CAS,
came downstairs and ordered the Sergeant-Pilot in sharp tones to
leave the Air Ministry at once. This was, he assumed, some pilot
suffering from operational strain who wanted to air a grievance. He
advised him to go back to his Squadron and talk to his Commanding
Officer.

Mrs Brown's nephew stood his ground. 'Can you prove, Sir,
that you really are the CAS's Personal Assistant?' The Squadron
Leader, baffled by this obstinate insolence, ordered the Service
Police on duty at the entrance to confirm his identity and to remove
the intruder. Only then, and with extreme reluctance, did Mrs
Brown's nephew disclose his errand.

An American Convoy, bound for Casablanca, was already at sea.
The British 1st Army would shortly be sailing from the Clyde. And
lying in the Whitehall gutter, for all and sundry to see, had been the
key to their objectives and the time-table of their movements.

The delinquent officer confessed his misdeed without any attempt
to justify himself. The three Chiefs of Staff assembled in a hurry.
They went straight to 10 Downing Street and unfolded the full
horror of the situation to the Prime Minister, who was also Minister
of Defence. They asked for guidance on the action to be taken. They
added that the perpetrator of the crime would be court-martialled
and perhaps charged with treason.

According to General Ismay, Churchill was remarkably unperturbed. It was, he pointed out, inconceivable that any ill-
intentioned person should have found this document in the blackout, copied it and replaced it in the gutter. Operation TORCH
should proceed as if nothing had happened. Nor should they be too
harsh on the officer who had lost the plans. His motive, though
totally reprehensible, had nothing to do with treason. He was, they
had said, a highly educated and honourable man. He must now be

suffering excruciating pains of guilt and would certainly never do anything so foolish again. 'Let us', said Churchill, 'waste no more time on discussing his future; but Mrs Brown must be made a Dame Commander of the Order of the British Empire'.

By the time I came back on the scene, a whole year later, Churchill had grudgingly accepted that a DBE was too high an honour; but he declared that a CBE she should have.

By the end of 1944, he was fighting against the entire Whitehall establishment for a MBE. Even that was opposed and so in July, 1945, he wrote a BEM for Mrs Brown into his Resignation Honours List. It was the only award that had been deleted when, a few weeks after he ceased to be Prime Minister, the List was published.

27. The American Connexion

To dispute accepted beliefs and interpretations has always been a sure way of attracting attention. In some cases it is a wholesome exercise: in others the motive may be suspect and the product unconvincing. There have been many followers of this technique among 20th century historians, but so far none have denied the importance of the relationship between Roosevelt and Churchill in the conduct of the Second World War.

I think this relationship was at its firmest and most fruitful between the spring of 1940 and the end of 1943, notably before the United States entered the war and above all during the year between the collapse of France in June, 1940, and Hitler's assault on Russia in June, 1941. The British Isles were at that time constantly subjected to air attack and almost as constantly threatened with invasion. Throughout the months of anxiety, Roosevelt, despite the fact that 1940 was an Election year in America, moved fast to Britain's aid. He often did so, especially in the case of the generous Lend Lease Bill, faster than his own Government thought public opinion would accept. I believe that to the extent it was in his nature and emotional capacity, he opened his heart in the letters and telegrams that poured eastwards across the Atlantic. Churchill's heart, in which cynicism had no lodging place, was always open to the President, as indeed it was to Stalin. There is, in retrospect, pathos in the gleam of pleasure which could be seen on Churchill's face if there was so much as an ember of warmth in Stalin's replies to his messages.

In the last eighteen months of Roosevelt's life, I thought the openheartedness diminished. By the beginning of 1944, the United States had become the senior partner, even though the British Commonwealth and Empire still had twice as many men in combat with the enemy. Britain had given all she had in five years of war. Her resources were exhausted and it was clear that after the final

British effort of sending one million men across the Normandy beaches, almost the entire future supply of material and manpower would have to come from America. The brotherly tone of the President's messages seemed to change: there were times when I thought others might have drafted them, and this became a certainty after the Second Quebec Conference as Roosevelt grew increasingly frail. There can be no doubt that of the Big Three, Churchill must be awarded first prize for consistent sincerity and, indeed, fraternity.

What has been less carefully examined by historians than the Churchill–Roosevelt correspondence, and the many meetings of the two leaders, is the part played by other men in cementing the Grand Alliance and interpreting the thoughts of their governments. Those concerned, on both sides of the Atlantic, were numerous and distinguished. All I seek to do is to depict the personalities of a few whose impact on life in Downing Street brought them directly into my view.

In 1939 the United States was still subject to the Neutrality Act, an isolationist measure intended to bar assistance to any belligerent country and thus ensure that America should never again be drawn into a European war. The American Ambassador in London was Joseph P. Kennedy. On his arrival in England early in 1938, accompanied by an attractive wife and a long retinue of smiling children, he was greeted with warmth and hospitality. His pleasant manner, his friendliness to all and sundry and the immediate appeal of his sons and daughters to their British contemporaries, quickly established the popularity of the Kennedy family. They gave dinner parties and small dances at Princes Gate, to some of which I went with great enjoyment, and it was not long before they became notable figures of the British 'Establishment'.

In those days social acceptability was still a matter of political significance, since most of the people who counted for something in the conduct of affairs were to be seen regularly in the dining rooms and ball-rooms of London and to be met at week-end parties in the larger country houses. However, in the world of international politics the United States was withdrawn from intervention, and to some extent from influence, by its refusal to join the League of Nations. The Americans were only now recovering from the shattering effects of the Wall Street crash and the great depression, were still affected by isolationist propaganda and were feeling so secure within the ramparts of 'Fortress America' that the strength of their army and air-force was derisory. The US navy, though large in tonnage, was far from being ready for battle. Lest any American who reads this book should take offence at the word 'derisory' applied to the United States army before the war, let me explain that it was the adjective used by General Marshall when reminiscing about those days during a visit to 10 Downing Street in the 1950s.

Thus Mr Chamberlain's Government was more concerned with the attitude and intentions of quite small European nations, whose choice between the German–Italian 'Axis' and the Anglo–French alliance of Democracies might affect the balance of power in Europe, than with either the friendly, but politically and militarily impotent, United States or the inscrutable Soviet Union, weakened by Stalin's liquidation of its military leaders and suspected of planning to sow the Dragon's Teeth of Communism in the furrows ploughed by a European war.

In consequence, Joseph Kennedy, though well-known socially to every member of the Government and doubtless received regularly at the Foreign Office, was seldom found anywhere near the centre of power at 10 Downing Street. In the detailed diary I kept between the outbreak of war and the fall of the Chamberlain Government on 10 May, 1940, these are almost the only references of any kind to the United States:—

'*November 29th, 1939.* I learn [from outside sources] that Mr Kennedy is talking about our inability to win the war. To the PM and the Foreign Office he poses as the greatest champion of our cause in the United States.'

'*December 31st, 1939.* The United States is aloof, and critical of what everybody in Europe is doing and thinking, without shewing the least inclination to step in to redress the balance of the Old World.'

'*February 6th, 1940.* President Roosevelt is proposing to send Sumner Welles over to Europe to visit the various capitals concerned and to examine the prospects of peace. This has been expected, because Hitler well knows how to play on neutral fears of an extension of the war and on the world-wide terror of bolshevism. The PM thinks this move comes, very indirectly of course, from Germany, where Goering and others have long been posing as moderates and putting out peace-feelers. The danger is that Welles' visit will give an opportunity to the 'peace-at-any-price' minority here to raise their voices, while the controlled public opinion of Germany will present a united front. Moreover, such an initiative, which could never really achieve anything, since the destruction of the Nazi régime is from our point of view an essential pre-requisite of peace, may open up endless possibilities of which the German propaganda machine will know only too well how to make use.'

On 10 May, Churchill became Prime Minister and Anglo–American relations at once entered a new phase. Although Kennedy was now a less infrequent visitor, the main channel of business was direct from No. 10 to the White House. Kennedy's pessimism increased. On 27 May, Lord Lothian, the British Ambassador in Washington, reported a conversation with the President from which he deduced that if Britain really was *in extremis* the United States would enter the war. Kennedy for his part, assuming the role of Cassandra, sent home nothing but prophecies of woe; but fortunately his second-in-command at the Embassy, the steadfast, loveable and unpretentious Herschel Johnson, was unrattled by the crescendo of disaster to the allied cause and maintained an attitude of commendable firmness.

While the Battle of Britain raged and the Blitz on London began, Roosevelt was fighting to be re-elected President of the United States for a third term. It was remarkable that even at the height of the electoral struggle he contrived to maintain his concentration on the desperately critical war situation and, behind the scenes, to pursue his plans to support us in our hour of need. He was helped in this by the public declaration for Britain made by the Republican candidate, Wendell Wilkie, so that in spite of the isolationists a bi-partisan foreign policy was established. All the same Roosevelt thought it necessary to tread delicately and go slow in his acts of overt assistance. Churchill well understood the position. When I drove with him to Chequers on 1 November, 1940, he told me he was sure Roosevelt would win the election by a far greater majority than was supposed, and he believed that America would come into the war. He praised the instinctive intelligence of the British press in showing no signs of the eagerness with which we desired a Roosevelt victory. He quite understood the exasperation so many English people felt with the American attitude of criticism combined with ineffective activity; but we must be patient and we must conceal our irritation. All this, as I recorded, was punctuated with intermittent bursts of the song 'Under the Spreading Chestnut Tree'!

After Christmas, when the Presidential Election was over and Roosevelt had been triumphantly elected for a third term, the defeated Wendell Wilkie arrived in England bearing Longfellow's poem, *Sail on, O Ship of State*, which Roosevelt had written out in manuscript for Churchill. Its concluding lines are:

> 'Humanity with all its fears,
> With all the hopes of future years
> Is hanging breathless on thy fate.'

Churchill's easily tangible emotions were deeply affected and he rightly took this as an earnest of the President's intention to place at the very least the whole weight of American economic power behind Britain and, if opportunity allowed, to join us in the fighting itself. Wendell Wilkie, speaking as the leading Republican, once again made it clear that he stood behind the President in all matters relating to support for Britain.

A man of immense power behind the Washington scenes, Harry Hopkins, also came to England for the first time in January, 1941. Shortly after his arrival I found myself alone with him. 'Do you know why I have come here?', he asked me. He answered his own question by explaining that the President required an endorsement of his belief that British public opinion was solid behind Churchill in his determination to pursue the war vigorously, against whatever odds and in the face of whatever discouragements, until the régimes of Hitler and Mussolini were utterly destroyed. Kennedy, he said, had reported to the contrary. Throughout the summer and autumn of 1940 he had assured the President that it was a question of weeks, if not days, before Britain followed France into capitulation, that the morale of the people was disintegrating and that a compromise peace, which the Germans might be generous enough to offer, was the sole alternative to invasion and conquest. Roosevelt, said Hopkins, wanted him to check Kennedy's assessment, and he also wanted to know why, when the heavy air-raids began early the previous September, the American Embassy had been the first to leave London. The President would have wished it to be the last. It was clear to me that Hopkins had already reached certain conclusions, even in advance of the closer investigations he proposed to make.

That same week-end Hopkins told me that he had once been anti-British. Perhaps he could be accused of being absurdly sentimental, and the quality of his judgment might be questioned; for his attitude to Britain had been changed by a single incident. After the death of his wife, he had been invited by the Roosevelts to move into the White House with his small daughter. They were there in the spring of 1939 when, for the first time in history, a reigning British Sovereign visited the United States. As the Monarchy seemed to represent many of the things that Hopkins thought he disliked about Britain, the arrival of King George VI and Queen Elizabeth meant nothing to him personally; but it meant a lot to his small daughter who had read all the Fairy Tales and was excited by the prospect of seeing a real Queen. As ill-luck would have it, on the night of the State Banquet at the White House the child had a high temperature and the doctor would not allow her out of bed even to look over the staircase at the King and Queen. She was bitterly disappointed and somebody (though not her aloof father, who would have died rather than ask a favour of British royalty) told of the tears she was shedding. So when the Queen was dressed for the banquet, wearing a beautiful crinoline dress, the Order of the Garter, a blazing array of jewels and a splendid tiara, she went upstairs to the sick-room and the child did see a real Queen, adorned as she imagined Queens always were. As this particular Queen had the gift of charming into a state of ecstasy people of all ages and as, alone with little Miss Hopkins, she doubtless exercised that gift, the account which the child subsequently gave her father must have been enthusiastic indeed. 'And that', said Hopkins,'is how I first came to think you people must have some good in you after all'. And that also illustrated how a small act of kindness, undertaken without any calculation of policy, can have an indirect effect on the affairs of nations; for in those days Harry Hopkins had a great, if unpublicised, influence.

Few people in England knew much about this man of power in the White House. I do not think Churchill had even heard of him. I certainly had not; but of course Brendan Bracken was familiar with his whole history and background. Bracken was characteristically mysterious, assuring Churchill that this was the most important visitor to Britain since the outbreak of war, disregarding any interest the American Embassy or the Foreign Office might have in the arrival or movements of Hopkins and setting off in his own car to meet him at Portsmouth. He delivered him straight to 10 Downing Street and persuaded Churchill to lunch with him alone. The lunch went precisely as Bracken had hoped. Churchill and Hopkins were so impressed with each other that their tête-à-tête over the dining-room table lasted till 4.00 p.m. Then, because the moon was full and Chequers was an easy target for enemy bombers, we set off to spend the week-end at Ditchley.

I travelled with Bracken who discoursed about Hopkins and his influence with the President during the entire journey. He was in the process of telling me that Hopkins had said Lord Halifax, who had entered the Potomac on the battleship, *King George V*, just before Hopkins left for England, was the best possible choice as British Ambassador in Washington because Roosevelt was impressed by his deep religious faith combined with a Fellowship of All Souls and a passionate interest in fox-hunting, when we collided with a fish and chips wagon and everything went up in flames. We finally arrived at Ditchley singed, shaken, but unhurt.

The mutual respect and interest which Churchill and Hopkins felt for each other blossomed during the week-end. They talked at length about the existing situation and the future of the world after the war. Hopkins stayed on in the United Kingdom, visiting the industrial areas and the bombed towns so as to acquire a first-hand impression of the seriousness of the British war effort and the morale of the people. On 24 January he went with the Prime Minister to see the batteries at Dover. Churchill took special pride in an 18″ naval gun called 'HMG Bosche-Buster' which dated from the First World War and which he had had erected on an eminence above the town so that when the Germans shelled and bombed Dover, a suitable reply could be despatched to the Pas de Calais. Hopkins was moved when, as Churchill walked past, he heard one workman on the site say to another in tones of enthusiastic affection: 'There goes the bloody British Empire'. 'I think', Hopkins commented, 'there must be something to be said for that Empire of yours after all'. In fact he admitted to being increasingly puzzled. He had dined a night or two previously with Ernest Bevin, Herbert Morrison and Sir Andrew Duncan. He was astonished to see on what friendly and familiar terms a great industrialist could be with Labour leaders. He insisted that such a thing could not happen in America. 'Yes', he said, 'there are a lot of things about your country I got wrong'.

That week-end at Chequers the blossoming friendship which had been evident at Ditchley a fortnight previously ripened into a close and lasting intimacy. Hopkins had brought with him the blue-print of the American rearmament programme. Its conception was vast and Hopkins was sure it would impress; but Churchill warned him that it must be at least eighteen months before the results were seen. As events proved, this estimate was correct.

After dinner on 26 January, Churchill and Hopkins, with the Chief of the Air Staff Sir Charles Portal, Professor Lindemann and myself as the audience, discussed the past, the present and the future with entire frankness. They agreed that what Churchill called 'The Unnecessary War' could have been avoided and that both Britain and America should be ashamed of their blindness and apathy. They spoke of Reparations and how the victorious allies, having extracted a huge sum from Germany, had given back double what they had taken and thus financed her rearmament. They discoursed on monetary reform, a topic which gave Churchill an opportunity to dilate on his cherished conception of a Commodity Dollar with a floating value based on the price of a list of selected commodities. Hopkins said, to my surprise, that Roosevelt had had ideas which were not dissimilar, but had met intense opposition in Wall Street. He then launched into an attack on financiers but Churchill argued on their behalf that while everybody desired credit, nobody had any patience with creditors. The following

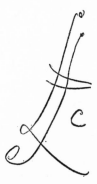

Drawing of a Commodity Dollar sign by W.S.C.

extract from my diary contains an account of how the conversation continued.

'The PM said that when the war was over there would be a short lull during which we had the opportunity to establish a few basic principles, of justice, of respect for the rights and property of other nations, and indeed of respect for private property so long as its owner was honest and its scope moderate. We could find nothing better than Christian Ethics on which to build and the more closely we followed the Sermon on the Mount, the more likely we were to succeed in our endeavours. But all this talk about "war aims" was absurd at the present time: the Cabinet Committee to examine the question had produced a vague paper four-fifths of which was from the Sermon on the Mount and the remainder an Election Address!

'Japan and the US was the next topic, and Hopkins expressed the belief that if America came into the war the incident would be with Japan. The PM said that the advantage of America as an ally to the disadvantage of Japan as an enemy was as 10 to 1. Why, look at their respective power of steel production – and "modern war is waged with steel". Besides Japan must have been greatly affected by the fate of the Italian navy, which on paper had been so strong. "Fate holds terrible forfeits for those who gamble on certainties".

'The PM sat down heavily on the sofa, said he had talked too much, and asked Hopkins for his views. Speaking slowly but very emphatically, Hopkins stated that the President was not much concerned with the future. His preoccupation was with the next few months. As far as war aims were concerned, there were only very few people in America, liberal intellectuals, who cared about the matter; and they were nearly all on our side. He believed the same to be true of people in this country. All he would say of the future was that he believed the Anglo–Saxon peoples would have to do the rearrangement: the other nations would not be ripe for co-operation for a long time. He thought the problems of reconstruction would be very great, greater than the PM had implied, and we should have to send men to the conference table who were tough and not sentimental.

'As far as the present was concerned, there were four divisions of public opinion in America: a small group of Nazis and Communists, sheltering behind Lindbergh, who declared for a negotiated peace and wanted a German victory; a group represented by Joe Kennedy, which said "Help Britain, but make damn sure you don't get into any danger of war"; a majority group which supported the President's determination to send the maximum assistance at whatever risk; and about 10% or 15% of the country, including Knox, Stimson and most of the armed forces, who were in favour of immediate war.

'The important element in the situation was the boldness of the President, who would lead opinion and not follow it, who was convinced that if England lost, America, too, would be encircled and beaten. He would use his powers if necessary; he would not scruple to interpret existing laws for the furtherance of his aim; he would make people gape with surprise, as the British Foreign Office must have gaped when it saw the terms of the Lend Lease Bill. The boldness of the President was a striking factor in the situation. He did not want war; indeed he looked upon America as an Arsenal which should provide the weapons for the conflict and not count the cost; but he would not shrink from war.'

Hopkins came to England again in July, 1941, with plans for the despatch of American tanks to the British army in North Africa, the suggestion that a maintenance unit in civilian clothes might accompany them (despite the obvious breach of neutrality this entailed) and a description of the increased supplies of food and materials which would be shipped to the British Isles. America might not be at war with the Axis, but the world now knew where her almost unchallenged sympathies lay and those sympathies were to be underpinned by everything she could spare.

The years passed and Halifax, as well as Churchill, looked on Hopkins as their principal friend at Court. But it is in the nature of Courts that favourites change, and the Court of President Roosevelt was no exception. Why Hopkins ceased to be close to Roosevelt, I do not know. He was in London again in 1942, privately supporting Churchill and Alan Brooke in their determination that the first joint Anglo–American enterprise should be in North Africa and not, as Roosevelt and General Marshall proposed, take the form of a premature, ill-prepared invasion of Europe with the object of relieving the pressure of the German onslaught on Russia. 'Second Front Now' was daubed on the walls of London by the Communists and their friends who cared nothing for the casualties which such a policy must entail. They were encouraged, incongruously enough, not only by Aneurin Bevan and his small band of dissidents in the House of Commons, but also by the White House and the American Chiefs of Staff (except for Admiral King who wished to solve the problem by transferring all military effort to the Pacific theatre of operations). This American support for an ill-conceived and dangerous strategy arose from chivalry towards a hard-pressed ally and neither from ideological nor military considerations. Hopkins must have seen the Writing on the Walls of London, but I am sure that in his own clear mind he accepted the logic of the stand which Churchill and Alan Brooke successfully made, even if he felt obliged to pay some lip-service to his instructions from the White House. A salubrious blast of the trumpet came from A.P. Herbert, MP.

> 'Let's have less nonsense from the friends of Joe,
> We laud, we love him; but the nonsense, No!
> In 1940, when we bore the brunt,
> We could have done, boys, with a Second Front.'

This 1942 visit to London took place during my excursion into the RAF. By the time I returned to Downing Street, Hopkins was no longer the man of power at the White House. I remember

Churchill saying on the way home from the Second Quebec Conference, after a brief detour to stay with the Roosevelts at Hyde Park, that he feared Roosevelt had only invited Hopkins to luncheon to please him. However, neither the Prime Minister nor Halifax were fair-weather friends. Hopkins was discarded and he had not long to live, but right to the end both Churchill and Halifax kept in contact with him and left him in no doubt of their unaltered esteem. The last time I saw him was in January, 1945, when, temporarily restored to Presidential favour, he passed through London on his way to the Yalta Conference. Churchill cancelled his existing arrangements so that they might dine alone and sat talking to him until the early hours of the morning. At Yalta Hopkins must have been distressed by the line which the American delegation followed, for the President, like Hopkins himself, was a man facing death and he was surrounded by new advisers deeply committed to the appeasement of Russia and (with a few exceptions such as Mr Lewis Douglas) believing that an era was dawning in which there would be only two great powers, the United States and the Soviet Union, working side by side to guarantee peace and justice. Whether Hopkins concurred, or his opinion was even asked, I do not know. I expect he remained silent.

I have dwelt at length on the part played by this thoughtful, gay and yet sad man, because his influence, once so formidable both in London and in Washington, is easily forgotten; but there were other American actors prominent for still longer on the Whitehall stage. In addition to the Generals and the great communicators, like Raymond Gram Swing, Quentin Reynolds and Ed Murrow, there were two men who not only represented their country with exemplary skill but contrived to become close personal friends of Churchill, his family and his entourage without for one moment losing their independence of thought and action. This was an achievement for anybody continually exposed to the persuasive charm of Winston Churchill.

The two men were Gil Winant, successor to Joseph Kennedy as American Ambassador, and Averell Harriman, who was given Ambassadorial status, designated Personal Representative of the President and entrusted with a wide responsibility for shipping, for the provision of supplies and equipment and for special missions to

Russia, Egypt and India. During 1941 it was rare for one of them not to be found at Chequers at the week-end. Often both would be invited, as much for the pleasure of their company as for the business to be done.

Winant was proud of the fact that everybody said he looked like Abraham Lincoln. This may not have been his only pride, but the others were hidden beneath a gentle, unassuming exterior. He arrived early in 1941, just after Hopkins had left, went straight to Windsor and received the honour, unique for an Ambassador, of being met at the station by the King in person. So important was the American connexion now deemed to be. He was allowed no time to acclimatise himself in his new surroundings, but was immediately plunged into the discussions arising from Churchill's proposal to lease bases in the West Indies to the United States for 99 years in return for fifty obsolete destroyers. In Churchill's calculations the destroyers were of secondary importance; and in the event most of them were never used. What did matter was that America's neutrality should be stretched to breaking-point by her adoption of what clearly amounted to a quasi-belligerent measure.

It was by no means plain sailing. The West Indian Colonies were resentful. There were murmurs both in the Caribbean and at Westminster that the conditions for which the Americans were asking amounted to 'Capitulations' such as we had been accustomed to demand from China and Turkey in the 19th century. Sir Edward Bridges thought that if the Government accepted all the American requests, they would be defeated in the House of Commons. The Colonial Office was concerned that we might impetuously cede much that we should subsequently regret. Lord Cranborne detected a dangerous American emphasis on hemisphere defence and feared this might lead to Western Hemisphere isolationism. Bitterness was aroused and it fell to the newly arrived Winant, wisely advised by his second in command, Herschel Johnson (whose contribution to the smoothing of rough edges and surfaces during the war has never been adequately recognised) to present the American case with a mixture of delicacy and firmness. He had the *puissànt* support of the Prime Minister. I wrote in my diary: 'The PM is ill satisfied with the point of view expressed by his colleagues. He believes the safety of the State is at stake, that America, in providing us with credits, will enable us to win the war which we could not otherwise do, and that we cannot afford to risk the major issue in order to maintain our pride and preserve the dignity of a few small islands.'

Having ridden this initial squall without losing an iota of good-will, Winant secured himself in the Prime Minister's confidence. From now onwards the American Embassy became little short of an extension to 10 Downing Street, and like others of my colleagues I made frequent journeys to the offices at No. 1 Grosvenor Square, on the side of the Square opposite the present Embassy. Thus on 8 April, 1941: 'The PM spent all the afternoon composing his speech for tomorrow. After dinner I took it round to the American Embassy to show Winant. He made four pertinent observations in respect of the effect on US opinion and I was deeply impressed by his unassertive shrewdness and wisdom. I afterwards explained these points to the PM who accepted them. While I was with the Ambassador a "blitz" started. He did not even raise his head.' The American Embassy was back morally as well as physically from Virginia Water whither Mr Kennedy had so precipitously removed it, to Roosevelt's scorn and indignation, when the first bombs fell on London.

A few days later Churchill took Winant, Harriman and Robert Menzies with him to Bristol, which was savagely bombed during the night. On the following morning the ruins were still smoking, but members of the University Senate put on scarlet gowns over their Home Guard battle-dress and ARP Warden uniforms. Churchill, in his capacity as Chancellor of Bristol University, donned the black and gold robe which had belonged to his father, Lord Randolph Churchill, when he was Chancellor of the Exchequer, and con-ferred Honorary Degrees on Winant and Menzies. For several months the Greeks had been fighting victoriously against a large but not conspicuously martial Italian army; so it was appropriate that Churchill should compare the fortitude of the people of Bristol to 'that which we are accustomed to associate with Ancient Rome and Modern Greece.'

That evening when we reached Chequers from Bristol, Winant received a message from Roosevelt announcing America's intention to extend her naval patrol area as far west as the 25th meridian. I asked Winant and Harriman if that might not mean war between the United States and Germany. 'That's what I hope', said Harriman. Winant smiled his assent.

Thenceforward Winant was seldom far away. His popularity with Churchill did nothing to prevent his fighting for the American point of view when it conflicted with British intentions. Thus on 25 May, while the *Bismarck* was at sea, and there was deep anxiety reigning at Chequers, Winant arrived to put forcibly to the Prime Minister Roosevelt's objections to conscription in Northern Ireland. The President wanted to be helpful in all possible ways, but the terror of losing Irish support in New York and Massachusetts was sufficiently endemic to excuse his interfering in the internal affairs of the United Kingdom. So, at least, Winant argued against Churchill's decreasingly adamant objections, while the telephone rang every few minutes with the latest news about the hunt for the *Bismarck*. He was at Chequers, too, on 22 June, when Hitler invaded Russia. For once his analysis of the situation was profoundly wrong: he expressed a conviction that there was no genuine invasion, but that the whole affair was a subtle plot engineered by Hitler and Stalin in collusion. The subtlety of it evaded me. Luckily Churchill was too busy writing his speech upstairs to hear Winant's view. Otherwise his faith in the Ambassador's judgment might have been shaken; but this was a rare and uncharacteristic folly.

Winant stayed in London throughout the war, never losing Churchill's affection and confidence. In the autumn of 1944 he joined Gousev, the Soviet Ambassador in London, and the British representative, Sir William Strang, to form a European Advisory Council which was established to make proposals for the future of Germany. He thus played a part of some importance in shaping the post-war settlement. After Truman became President, he stayed on at the Embassy long enough to see the change of Government in Britain, the explosion of the Atom Bomb and the victory over Japan. Then he made way for a well-loved successor, Lewis Douglas.

In the bleak winter of 1946–7, Gil Winant had rented a small house off Park Lane. He asked me to dine one night, saying that he wanted my advice about a book he was writing. I found him alone, the same courteous, soft-speaking replica of Abraham Lincoln whom I had known so well in the war. We dined long and well, for he had imported food and wines which were unobtainable by ordinary mortals in those stringent times. The difference from former days was that on this occasion Winant, who had been wont to listen and to supply the occasional thoughtful comment, wanted to talk. He talked unceasingly throughout a six-course dinner. We moved next door. He produced brandy and long cigars, and continued to talk. He told me sagas of the elections he once fought for the Governorship of New Hampshire. It was past midnight. He switched to reminiscences of the International Labour Office at Geneva. I was deluged with work at the Foreign Office and wished to avoid a late night; but he had not even started to show me the galley-proofs of the book which he had spread out on the table for that purpose. It was nearly 2.00 a.m. He began, at first shyly and then with almost feverish vigour, to tell me what had gone wrong with his marriage. Three o'clock came and passed. I said it was high time I went home. He seized the galley-proofs and started to read parts of them. It was after 4.00 when I finally rose. I said firmly that I really must go.

I had a pouch full of papers on which I had intended to work before going to bed. 'Don't leave me', he said; '*please* don't leave me'. Perhaps I should not have done so. I realised he was lonely and that something strange was happening under the surface; but I was very tired and I imagined we were both a little drunk. A day or two later he went back to the United States and shortly afterwards he killed himself.

The tragic Genius which pursued, and finally overcame, both Harry Hopkins and Gil Winant was happily a stranger to Averell Harriman, last but not least of the eminent Americans who were so much to the fore in British public life during the war years.

I first saw him in March, 1941. Churchill invited him to dine at No. 10, together with Drexel Biddle, American Ambassador to the whole host of our fugitive allies who had established their governments-in-exile in London. After dinner there was a heavy raid and so Churchill, by way of entertaining his guests and his staff, ordered us all to put on tin helmets and led us up to the roof of the Air Ministry to watch the display. For Harriman it was a good introduction to life with Churchill, and he did not turn a hair.

He was often invited to accompany Churchill on his travels and I well remember his presence at Plymouth, just after a devastating raid, at Bristol and at Liverpool. I don't think he was asked for any reason other than the pleasure of his company and the fact that he had unofficially, and almost inadvertently, become an adopted member of Churchill's entourage. As he did not, like Harry Hopkins, lose Roosevelt's personal favour and confidence, his energies were soon required for so many other ploys, such as haggling with Stalin, that later in the war he had less time for constant attendance on the Prime Minister; but, like Winant, he was never far away.

Without knowing it, Harriman saved my life. When he devoted his energies to something, he was only content to excel. In the world of sport he would not rest until he was expert. Thus he had been one of America's best polo players and was a champion at croquet. On the lawn at Chequers he totally defeated Mrs Churchill at croquet, a feat never before witnessed by anybody present. He even played six-pack bézique well. Now it happened that on board the *Queen Mary*, returning from the Second Quebec Conference, I re-taught the Prime Minister bézique, a game he had played many years before but had entirely forgotten. This was a serious error of judgment on my part because for the next twenty years I frequently found myself playing bézique at hours of the morning when I should have preferred to be in bed and asleep.

In January, 1945, Churchill proposed to take two of his Private Secretaries, John Martin and Leslie Rowan, to the Yalta Conference. A few nights before the party was due to leave, Churchill had finished all the work he intended to do, had read the next day's morning papers and was, I hoped, about to say Good Night, when he suddenly felt an urge to play bézique. At about 3.00 a.m. he announced that as the Yalta Conference was bound to have its *longueurs*, I had better come too. A few games of bézique would be an agreeable contrast to Plenary Meetings and neither Martin nor Rowan, remarkable though all their other qualities were, knew how to play the game. It was not mine to reason why; but next morning my colleagues were far from gratified by the news. It meant that the office in London would be understaffed and anyhow there was no room in the Prime Minister's plane. I should have to travel separately in a York transport aircraft which would be conveying some other members of the so-called 'Argonaut' party to the Crimea.

The night before our departure, Averell Harriman came to dine with Churchill. He could, it seemed, play bézique. He was, no doubt, as great a master of the game as he was of polo and croquet. There was therefore no need for me to go to Yalta after all and, said Churchill, it had been forcefully represented to him that my absence would leave the office short-handed in London. I unpacked; I was disappointed; I was privately indignant with Martin and Rowan, devoted though I was to both of them, and felt they had behaved in a curmudgeonly way. As for Harriman, it seemed the worst luck in the world that in addition to his other skills, he should know how to play bézique. I was wrong on all counts, for the York, on which I should have flown, crashed off Pantellaria and its passengers were killed.

28. D-Day

When, in December, 1943, I was recalled to Downing Street from my Squadron in the RAF, I immediately learned that we and the Americans were planning a full-scale invasion of northern France the following spring. Although the details and the date were a deadly secret, my duties were such that I could not fail to be informed. It was unthinkable not to take part in what was certain to be the largest military operation ever planned. Happily the Prime Minister, part of whose charm was that he had never quite grown up and remained incurably romantic, was eventually persuaded to share this view, although he did ask me to bear in mind that 'this war is not being waged for your amusement'.

Thus, on 20 May, 1944, I put on my uniform and set out for the RAF Station at Odiham from which No. 168 Squadron was flying its P.51 Mustangs, taking low level photographs of target areas, firing cannon shells at trains in occupied France and sweeping the enemy coast in search of shipping. Much time and effort had been wasted in trying to prevent a totally unimportant and admittedly rather spoilt Flying Officer from getting his way. The Secretary of State for Air had come in person to tell Churchill that it was unsafe and unwise to allow a man who knew the invasion plans to fly over enemy territory. Professor Lindemann, by now Lord Cherwell, made similar representations. My colleagues at No. 10 pointed out that a replacement for me would be necessary and they well knew how much the Prime Minister disliked unfamiliar faces. However, Churchill replied that he had given his word and would not go back on it. The security point could be met by my being forbidden to cross the coast until 'D' Day, by when my knowledge of the time and place of the landing would be useless to the Gestapo, should I fall into their hands. Moreover, he added, the German Intelligence were far too sophisticated to suppose that a junior RAF officer taking an active part in operations could be the Prime

159

Minister's Private Secretary. I might, he decided, have three months' fighting holiday, but if still alive must report back for duty at No. 10 at the end of August.

On reaching Odiham I was taken aback to be greeted by Flying Officer Tubby Hussey, a dashing, rotund, most likeable but not, as I had hitherto thought, deep-thinking New Zealander, with the comment that my return to the Squadron obviously meant the fun was going to start shortly.

'Don't be alarmed', he said, 'I am not going to ask you any awkward questions. Anyhow, I know where it will be and when'.

'Do you?', I asked with a painfully superior smile.

'Yes. Caen or thereabouts, on the 5th or 6th June'.

I was aghast. Here was the most closely guarded piece of information in the world, and a junior officer in an RAF Squadron knew all about it.

'You are, in fact, absolutely wrong', said I, lying as convincingly as I could. 'But what gave you that silly idea?'

'Well, anybody who has been flying over the north coast of France for two years can see that the only beaches, within range of air support, on which an army could possibly land are between the Cherbourg Peninsula and the River Orne. And obviously it has got to be the full moon. With all the preparations in all the ports which you can see from the air, it can't be as far ahead as July. So it must be June 5th or 6th'.

I assumed that if my New Zealand friend could make these deductions, the German High Command must assuredly have done so too. The odd thing was that they had not. They were convinced we were going to land in the Pas de Calais and it seems that they expected us in July.

June 5th, the chosen day, was unseasonably vile; but if the Operation was to proceed as planned – and there had been months and months of detailed planning by some of the ablest men in Britain and the United States – then it must be 'go' on the 6th at the latest. Otherwise the whole invasion must be postponed till July. A postponement would bring inestimable damage to London from the German V weapons, which were all but ready to be launched, and would mean the loss of one vital summer month's campaigning. On the evening of the 5th, General Eisenhower made the decision to risk the weather and to go. It is his claim to imperishable fame.

That evening we were all confined to camp. The Group Captain summoned the pilots to the Operations Room where a map show- ing the objectives for D-Day was displayed. At dawn, he told us, Operation Overlord would go forward whatever the weather and with or without air support. 'That is', he commented, 'a decision calculated to deflate the ego of the Royal Air Force'.

At 3.00 a.m. I was awoken for briefing. The skies had cleared and in the early light I set off with one accompanying aircraft to perform a tactical reconnaissance of an area in Normandy near Falaise. As we set course for Selsey Bill, flying over the somnolent Hampshire villages and fields flecked by the rising sun, it was impossible not to feel exultantly melodramatic and I doubt if I was the only pilot that morning who told himself with commonplace self-satisfaction that 'Gentlemen in England, now a-bed, shall think themselves accursed they were not here, and hold their manhood cheap. . . .' I even wished it were St Crispin's Day.

The Channel was teaming with ships: convoys of landing craft, large and small; big troop-ships; destroyers and cruisers: thousands of ships with their white bow-waves and thousands of barrage balloons. In the sky we mingled with an equally vast array of Spitfires and Typhoons of the RAF and Lightnings and Thunderbolts of the US Army Air Force. We were in the van of the greatest Crusade of all times, elated to the extent of spiritual intoxication, and so instilled with a sense of unity with those thousands of others who were setting forth on the same venture that the hazards ahead were of no consequence, and fear was a forgotten emotion. War in these conditions is, for a short span, magnificent.

A long line of men-of-war lay off the Normandy coast, their big naval guns blazing and the burst of their shells inland distinctly visible. The trajectory of their missiles was high and that very morning one of my brother officers in 168 Squadron was struck by a 15″ shell from the *Warspite*, he and his plane entirely disintegrating. The chances of being hit by a 15″ shell when flying at 5000 feet must be small indeed.

There were landing craft on the beaches, a series of smoke screens, the constant fountains of sand and earth as the shells exploded and the flashes of the German batteries. Once across the coast, we dived to roof-top level, for though England and the Channel were bathed in sunshine, northern France was still under cloud. The contrast was immediately striking. Not a man nor a machine was visible. The countryside was as green as Hampshire and as peaceful. The cows stood placidly in the fields and the white farmhouses showed no sign of human life. Nobody fired at us; no enemy aircraft came to meet us. The Germans had been taken unawares and the French, too far inland from the coastal battles to be disturbed, were still asleep.

It was not always like that. I crossed the Channel again that evening and many times in the next few days until our Squadron moved to a landing strip near Bayeux and we pitched our tents in a Normandy orchard. The Germans brought up their divisions, their flak guns and their fighter aircraft. The war grew fierce and in my Squadron alone we lost a quarter of our strength in the first week after D-Day. Thanks to that defensive, artificial skin which nature provides in war, a skin not thick but temporarily anaesthetised, I forgot the horrors and the sorrows that came later. I shall never forget that glorious June morning when even in the enclosed cockpit of a Mustang, I knew that all the birds were singing and believed that I had no unfulfilled ambition in life.

29. Second Quebec

Enjoyment of war may indicate a debased nature; but I found it difficult not to enjoy the summer months of 1944, living in a tent in a Normandy orchard, soaring once or twice a day over the lines of battle and flying low down the streets of small French towns, far from the Front, where the inhabitants waved ecstatically if there were no Germans or collaborators about and showed a marked lack of enthusiasm if there were. I escaped injury although my aircraft was hit on three separate occasions by anti-aircraft fire, twice by the Germans and once by the Americans who thought I was a Messer-schmidt. I should have been on firmer ground in complaining about the poverty of their aircraft recognition skills, had I not, that very morning, missed my only opportunity of shooting down a Focker-Wulf 190 because I believed it to be an American Tomahawk.

By September my campaigning days and my three months leave were over. I was translated once again to Downing Street and chosen to go with the Prime Minister's Principal Private Secretary, John Martin, to an Anglo–American Conference in Quebec. Since the end of 1941, when I first left No. 10 for the RAF, there had been many such conferences, so that the participants, civil and military, knew each other well at all levels of seniority. It is difficult to exaggerate the contribution these close personal relationships made to the efficient conduct of the war, to the avoidance of those misunderstandings which so often arose with the Russians and, at least until the Yalta Conference, to the settlement of differences of opinion on an entirely frank basis. It is, on the other hand, now easy to forget that in the summer of 1944, the British Empire and the United States were still partners of comparable strength. American industrial capacity, undamaged by bombardment, was far the more powerful; but in size and fire-power of armies, fleets and air-forces there was little to choose between the two Anglo–Saxon allies. At the end of the war the

RAF and the US Army Air Force had each dropped approximately 680,000 tons of bombs on Germany and over Europe as a whole the RAF had lost 10,800 aircraft against America's 8,300. The British and the Americans both had approximately one million men on French soil during that summer of 1944 and, in the Far East, the British Imperial Forces guarding India and fighting Japan in Burma were as numerous as the Americans deployed in the whole Pacific theatre of war.

This was the Second Quebec Conference, for there had been one in the same city a year earlier; and by the time it began the outcome of the war was no longer in doubt. Most of Italy was in Allied hands; our armies, having freed Brussels, were racing eastwards towards the Rhine; and the Joint Planning Staff thought that Germany might collapse and surrender within weeks. Thus the object of the Conference was to consider such matters as the Allied Zones of Occupation in Germany, finance in the post-war period and the prosecution of the war against Japan. The peace terms would, of course, have to be discussed with our absent friends, the Russians, of whose good faith and intentions none of the Americans and only a few of the British had serious doubts.

The long hours and hard work inseparable from these conferences were compensated by the provision of luxuries unfamiliar in wartime Britain with its rigid blackouts, adequate but unpalatable rations and drab landscape of dirty, unpainted buildings interspersed with bomb-sites. Release from austerity began on the *Queen Mary* where, the first night on board, my eyes opened wide with delighted amazement at the sight of oysters, champagne and other sybaritic pleasures long forgotten. Later, as I lay in my spacious cabin on 'A' deck, I remembered the Mess Decks in the *Otranto* and found myself thinking guiltily of the nineteen thousand American troops travelling in other parts of the great ship. At least their travail would only last five days; and they were going home.

The Prime Minister's own entourage, which fed in his private dining room, was small; but the main Conference party was large enough to fill the huge First Class dining room of the ship. The three Chiefs of Staff, the Chief of Combined Operations and the Office of the Minister of Defence had brought all their principal acolytes. The Foreign Office and the Treasury were well represented.

Lord Leathers, Minister of War Transport, was not travelling unaccompanied. There were clerks, secretaries, cipherers and orderlies by the score. A substantial part of Whitehall was bound for the Western Hemisphere and all day long meetings, drafting of papers and staff discussions went on exactly as if the participants were still in their London offices. A judiciously aimed torpedo would have earned the almost bankrupt Hitler a refreshingly large dividend, and for that reason strict wireless silence was enjoined. Since Churchill was constitutionally incapable of not sending telegrams, his messages had to be enciphered and flashed by Aldis Lamp to one of the escorting destroyers which would then dart away out of sight before daring to wireless the signal home.

On 10 September we moored at Halifax where the Governor General's train awaited us and the Mounties were present in full regalia. While the luggage was being loaded on the train, Churchill stood on the balcony of his drawing room coach and a crowd of enthusiastic citizens sang patriotic songs to him. He responded with a hilarious impromptu speech which all but caused a riot. There is no doubt that wars do make people feel friendly.

The next morning the train steamed into Wolfe's Cove at Quebec where President Roosevelt, seated in his car, was waiting to greet the Prime Minister. They drove together to the Citadel, the Governor General's residence placed at Roosevelt's and Churchill's disposal; and there for six days of Plenary Conferences and subsidiary staff meetings, the fortunes of war and the plans for peace were discussed without a trace of disagreement. Seldom can a meeting between two great nations have been conducted without a jarring note of discord. Perhaps it was so on this occasion because the war machine was, to all appearances, working faultlessly; because neither the disaster to the British Airborne Division at Arnhem, nor the German break through the American lines in the Ardennes, had yet occurred; and because Roosevelt, whom Churchill thought very frail, found it less tiring to say 'yes' than to say 'no'. Certainly the British left Quebec with a favourable answer to every one of the questions on which they had expected the Americans to prove difficult. It was to be a different story five months later at Yalta.

There was, of course, the occasional crisis. One, which affected me, arose when it was discovered that Churchill had failed to read the papers about the vexed 'Zones of Occupation' problem. The British having, to their entire satisfaction, been allocated the south of Germany had now changed their minds and wanted to occupy the north so as to control Hamburg and the other German ports. It was believed that the Americans would quite reasonably object to this capricious change of plan. However that might be, Churchill had not read his brief and the discussion with the President on this issue was to take place after dinner. The Prime Minister said he did not need to read his brief: he knew all about the matter. The Foreign Secretary and the Chiefs of Staff, disbelieving him, enjoined me with severe mien to make absolutely sure that he read it. Like Uriah the Hittite I was flung into the forefront of the battle by men who themselves seldom succeeded in persuading Churchill to do anything against his will.

I waited till he went up to dress for dinner and volunteered to read the brief aloud. He vanished into the bathroom. I followed, sat on a chair and started to read. Every now and then he submerged completely under the bath-water and it was necessary to pause in mid-sentence until he reappeared. I finished the document just before he went downstairs and was subsequently reprimanded for being late for dinner myself. The time-factor was something which Churchill never understood.

Roosevelt agreed to a zone-swap immediately the subject was raised. The arguments carefully martialled in the brief were not required; and had they been, Churchill would probably have used totally different ones with equal or greater effect.

There were two side-shows, neither of them in any way related to the agenda for the Conference. The first was introduced by Mr Morgenthau, Secretary to the United States Treasury, who strayed far from his budgetary responsibilities and tried his hand at the exercise of racial retribution. He proposed that all German industry should be dismantled and the country 'pastoralised'. He enlisted the support of Lord Cherwell whose hatred of all things German knew no bounds. Together they persuaded the President to initial the plan. Having succeeded to that extent, they invited Roosevelt to secure Churchill's initials too; and he agreed. Cherwell, to whom Churchill was devoted, but whose opinion on matters of this kind he would never have thought worth considering, would have secured no initials; but to refuse Roosevelt, especially when he was being so generally amenable, was quite a different matter. The following day Anthony Eden and Cordell Hull, the American Secretary of State, both horrified by the document, of which they had known nothing, succeeded in turning it into a dead letter. It remains a mystery why Churchill, whose attitude to the Germans, as opposed to the Nazis, was consistently generous, and who well knew what a contribution Reparations after the First War had made to the conditions which led to the Second, did not immediately reject the Morgenthau Plan. It was unlike him to agree, or even pretend to agree, with something of which he disapproved, for his independence of spirit and of judgment was unquenchable. What I do know is that he never referred to the plan on the long journey home nor, at any rate in my presence, did he ever express views which could be construed as sympathetic to it.

The second side-show was at Roosevelt's home, Hyde Park, where Churchill stayed two nights on his way to rejoin the *Queen Mary* at New York. There he persuaded the President to initial a paper agreeing that since the British, originally far more advanced than the Americans in nuclear physics, had voluntarily handed over their entire knowledge and experience in 1940 so as to create a joint Anglo–American team for the development of an atomic bomb, all atomic bombs produced in the United States should be shared between the two countries. At that time there were no atomic bombs, but in less than a year there would be, and I have no doubt that if Churchill had returned to power in 1945 he would have held the American Government to their pledge.

I had never realised how lax great men can be when asked to initial documents.

30. A Tale of Two Berlins

Once a week during the latter part of the war the distribution of Foreign Office telegrams included a long savings telegram (which meant that for the sake of economy it had come by bag and not through the ether) giving a summary of all the notable leading articles, feature articles and comments on the news that had been published in the American press. The summary was not only vividly and compactly presented, but was so informative as to be one of the few in the thick pile of Foreign Office telegrams that the Prime Minister always read with meticulous care.

One morning a heap of papers from Churchill's black box was returned to his Private Office for action, and was distributed among the Private Secretaries. My quota contained the latest Washington press summary on which Churchill had written in red ink: 'Who is the author of these brilliant if somewhat perfervid reports?'

I enquired of the Foreign Office and returned the telegram to the Prime Minister's box, in the folder entitled 'Answers to Questions', with a note saying: 'The author is Isaiah Berlin'. I assumed that the name of this well-known Fellow of All Souls and of New College was familiar to Churchill.

Weeks passed. In February, 1944, the Churchills gave a luncheon party in the Garden Rooms at 10 Downing Street. These rooms on the lower ground floor, level with the garden and directly beneath the Cabinet Room, had been vacated by the typists when the bombing started; but now, shored up by massive wooden pillars against the possibility of a hit in the sporadic air-raids which were again afflicting London, they were furnished as a dining room and a sitting room. The guests invited to lunch were the CIGS, Sir Alan Brooke, and his wife; the Chief Whip, Mr James Stuart; the Duchess of Buccleuch; my mother, Miss Juliet Henley and myself. Mrs Churchill told me just before lunch that at short notice the Prime Minister had insisted on her inviting Mr Irving Berlin whose

High Summer

arrival in London to entertain the American troops had been widely reported in the newspapers. She was, she said, delighted to ask him, but could not quite think why the Prime Minister was so anxious to meet him.

Irving Berlin arrived and was introduced; but since he can only have had the haziest idea who his fellow-guests were, he kept a discreet silence throughout most of the meal. My mother, who was sitting next to him, thought he was a distinguished civil servant and discoursed about social problems. The Duchess of Buccleuch, on his other side, camouflaged her ignorance by exerting all her well-known charm. The Prime Minister talked to the table at large about the war situation. The food, as always when Mrs Churchill was involved, was superb; the drink, as always when the Prime Minister was entertaining, was admirable. There was total serenity.

At the end of luncheon, the trouble began. Churchill, turning towards Irving Berlin, said: 'Now, Mr Berlin, tell us what in your opinion is the likelihood of my dear friend, the President, being re-elected for a fourth term.'

'Mr Prime Minister, I am honoured and flattered that you, the great Winston Churchill, should turn to me for an opinion on a matter of that kind. I shall tell my children and my grand-children of this outstanding honour in my life. Gee, to think that Winston Churchill should ask me, Irving Berlin, a question of that importance on which I am so little qualified to speak.'

'Come, Mr Berlin. As the author of those brilliant if somewhat perfervid reports, your impressions will be of great interest.'

So Irving Berlin began a rambling assessment of the forthcoming Presidential Campaign explaining that Roosevelt would win because the American people were so dynastically minded. I soon saw that Churchill was wilting and was on the verge of interrupting. The penny had dropped, as far as I was concerned, for I remembered the Washington telegram. Fearing that the Prime Minister might give himself away still further, and embarrassed by the thought that Irving Berlin would realise he had been invited in error, I kicked Churchill under the table.

'What are you kicking me for?', he asked loudly. I muttered some idiotic remark about keeping an eye on the clock for Questions (although there were indeed none for the Prime Minister to answer

169

that day), and James Stuart, realising that something was awry, gallantly introduced a new topic of conversation.

Afterwards, Churchill maintained that he had never heard of Irving Berlin, although it transpired that he knew and liked many of his songs. He would certainly have preferred talking about them to hearing a long, ill-informed discourse on American politics.

I could not resist telling the story. It got back to Isaiah Berlin who received it with ecstasy. I hope it did not get back to Irving Berlin.

31. Greek Fire

It was partly my fault; not, of course, the situation in which we found ourselves, but at least some of the initial heat and anger which were engendered. A British Force under General Scobie had landed in Athens in October, 1944, as the Germans began their withdrawal. It was greeted with enthusiastic cheers; but it soon became evident that this contingent was too small to control the well-disciplined bands of ELAS, a Communist guerrilla body supplied with British arms for use against the Germans and now determined to use those arms to seize control of the country. Having occupied Corinth and most of Attica, and murdered all prominent men likely to oppose a Communist takeover, ELAS held General Scobie's men and the British Embassy besieged in the centre of Athens.

President Roosevelt had recently pronounced that 'the two great Republics, American and Soviet, standing shoulder to shoulder, each the sentinel in its own hemisphere, will together guarantee the peace and order of the world.' Thus the American Government, smitten with acute short-sightedness in Foreign Affairs, was wearing thick rose-coloured spectacles through which it looked on left-wing Liberation Movements with benign approval. Its myopia was matched in Great Britain by *The Times*, the *Manchester Guardian* and Mr Aneurin Bevan, but not by General Scobie's soldiers who, war-hardened though they were, saw and abhorred the atrocities committed by ELAS against an anti-Communist Greek population. Churchill, for his part, had no intention of allowing Greece to be seized by a Communist minority and the eastern Mediterranean to fall under Soviet domination. He persuaded the British Cabinet to agree to intervene and caring nothing for the views of the American Government on this matter, nor of *The Times*, the *Manchester Guardian* and Mr Aneurin Bevan, he resolved to take action.

That was not my fault, but the immediate consequences were. On the night of 4 December, 1944, Churchill sat up till after

4.00 a.m. wrestling with the text of the orders he proposed, as Minister of Defence, to issue to General Scobie. Reinforcements would be sent, but meanwhile the General should not hesitate to use all the means at his disposal against the ELAS bands. Finally he handed me the telegram. It included the words: 'Treat Athens as a Conquered City'. I made a feeble effort to have its despatch delayed till the following morning, so that the Foreign Secretary might see it; but Churchill was in a mood which brooked no argument. 'Have it sent off immediately,' he said. I did.

It was nearly 5.00 a.m. and I was tired. There was a rule that those telegrams which were for British eyes only, but which were routed through Allied Forces Headquarters at Caserta in Italy, should be marked: 'Guard'. I forgot to write this important word on the top of the typed telegram. I put it in a red box, with a red label, and gave it to a Marine orderly to take over to the Foreign Office for immediate despatch. I went to bed.

The following morning, the American Minister at Caserta, Mr Kirk, found on his desk at AFHQ a copy of the Prime Minister's telegram. He at once had it repeated to the State Department. The President, though deploring Churchill's attitude to Greece, doubtless recognised that it was a British sphere of influence and that no American troops were involved. However, Mr Drew Pearson, a journalist working for the *Washington Post*, had unauthorised means of access to the White House and to the State Department of such efficiency that almost any paper, however secret, was at his disposal. A week after it had been sent, the text of Churchill's telegram appeared in Drew Pearson's column in the *Washington Post*. The headlines blazed. The entire American press were joined by *The Times*, the *Manchester Guardian* and Mr Aneurin Bevan in pious denunciation of Churchill's monarcho-fascist initiative

I felt obliged to confess my delinquency. Churchill, who was nothing if not magnanimous, said that it was his fault for keeping me up so late. He rather enjoyed the firework display; and it made no difference to his resolution to save Greece, if necessary single-handed.

For the next fortnight the Cabinet were exasperated by Churchill's concentration on this sole issue. Sir Edward Bridges and Sir Alexander Cadogan said that no business could be done at the

Cabinet table, and item after item had to be postponed because the Prime Minister was only prepared to discuss the Greek theme. Shortly before Christmas he said he would go to Greece and take the matter in hand himself, and when we arrived at Chequers for Christmas he told me to order his aircraft, a recent present from the Chief of the American Air Staff, General Arnold, to stand by for a flight to Athens. I did not take him seriously, because Mrs Churchill, Anthony Eden, Brendan Bracken and Lord Moran were all conspiring to prevent him and I thought their combined efforts would succeed; but luckily I obeyed orders, though I was loth to spoil the RAF crew's family Christmas to no purpose.

On Christmas Eve it seemed that the project was abandoned, or at least postponed. At luncheon, however, the Prime Minister said he would go. He told me to warn the crew of the aircraft to be ready to leave at 11.00 p.m. and to invite a reluctant Anthony Eden to accompany him. At a few minutes before midnight we took off into the still Christmas night, bound for Naples en route to Athens.

Field Marshal Alexander, Harold Macmillan and General Scobie awaited us at Athens airport. It became bitterly cold in the aircraft where a Council of War was held lasting a full two hours, and then the entire party embarked in a fleet of armoured cars; for in order to reach the Piraeus we had to pass through a part of Athens held by ELAS. 'Where is your pistol?' Churchill asked me, and since the last thing normally required by the Prime Minister's Secretary is a revolver, I had to admit I had none. Churchill, who apparently visualised our having to fight our way through ELAS territory, said that he was astonished I should come so unprepared and I was ordered to borrow a Tommy-gun.

Fortunately the journey was uneventful and in the dusk we reached the Piraeus, where pinnaces were waiting to take us to our quarters on HMS *Ajax*, a six-inch cruiser moored in Phaleron Bay. As we came alongside, the ship's company, ignorant that the Prime Minister, Foreign Secretary, Commander in Chief and Resident Minister in the Mediterranean were about to become their guests, were holding a carol service on the quarter deck. We climbed the gangway to the sound of some 400 naval voices bellowing *The First Noel*.

Churchill was in no mood for carols. He demanded immediate action and it was not long before the Greek Prime Minister, Mr Papandreou, came on board. While he and Churchill were closeted together, His Beatitude Damaskinos, Archbishop of Athens, a man of splendid appearance who had once been champion wrestler of Greece and whose surname, by strange coincidence, was also Papandreou, arrived on board and was left with me. The British Ambassador, Reginald Leeper, thought the Archbishop should be appointed Regent until conditions were such that the Greeks could decide whether they wanted their king back. Churchill was not so sure: he wanted to see Damaskinos and form his own opinion, and the interview was to take place as soon as Papandreou had left. So the Archbishop, his interpreter and I sat waiting in a cabin, encouraged in our conversational efforts by a bottle of the Greek liqueur Ouzo which the Admiral thoughtfully provided.

A messenger came to say that Papandreou had left. I rose to escort the Archbishop and his British military interpreter to Churchill's cabin, but we had only gone a few yards when we came face to face with a man wearing a bowler hat, a false nose and a hunting stock. Behind him were others attired in equally strange disguises and all were carrying a glass of gin in their hands. It was, it seems, a naval tradition to organise 'Funny Parties' at Christmas and much relaxation of naval discipline was permitted. Totally unaware that their ship was now occupied by the highest imaginable dignitaries, and seeing before them a man dressed as a Greek Archbishop and two others in military and RAF uniforms, they naturally assumed they had chanced on a rival 'Funny Party'. The conversation became awkward as they tried to penetrate our disguise and I feared that the Leading Seaman in the bowler hat was going to pull the Archbishop's long beard in the expectation of finding the face of a well-known shipmate underneath. In the nick of time the Admiral appeared, appraised the situation, explained that we really were what we pretended to be and ushered us into Churchill's presence.

The Archbishop made an immediate impact on Churchill and he emerged from the meeting Regent in intention, if not yet in name. It was agreed that a message should be sent to the ELAS rebels inviting them to a conference on the following afternoon.

Boxing Day was cold, bright and sunny. Standing on the bridge of

"Souvenir d'Athènes
Christmas. 1944.
— Osbert."

His Beatitude Damaskinos, Archbishop of Athens.
A drawing by Osbert Lancaster.

Ajax we could see the smoke of battle from the street fighting west of the Piraeus, hear the noise of shell-fire and machine guns and watch a squadron of Beaufighters diving to attack an ELAS stronghold on one of the surrounding hills. Evidently we could be seen too, for as we were about to go ashore a salvo of shells straddled the cruiser and five minutes later a second salvo struck the shore quite close to us as we landed. After another drive by armoured car through enemy-held territory, and a preliminary conference in the besieged Embassy, the British party left for the Ministry of Foreign

175

Affairs. There, to the sound of bursting mortar shells, we arrived to find the Archbishop and the Greek Government awaiting us. That night I wrote the following account of what happened.

'The Conference was due to start at 4 p.m., but there was doubt whether the ELAS representatives, who had been offered a safe conduct through the British lines, would come and several post-ponements had to be made. The security officials had had a field day: tanks patrolled the streets, an armed cordon surrounded the building, and the passes of everybody approaching the Ministry were closely scrutinised.

'The Ministry of Foreign Affairs must at best be a gloomy building, and with the electricity cut off its dinginess was accentuated. Followed by the rest of the party, the Prime Minister was ushered through a seething mob of Greek politicians, of all ages and Parties, of security officials and of heavily-armed soldiers, into a large rectangular room devoid of all furniture except an immense table about which some 30 chairs had been placed. The room was lit by hurricane lamps, of varying degrees of brightness, placed on the table, and was heated by evil-smelling oil stoves. Apart from a yellow glow thrown by the lamps on the faces of those seated round the table, darkness prevailed. It was a scene such as would normally be associated with the meeting of some hunted band of conspirators and this no doubt helped the ELAS delegates, when they finally arrived, to feel at ease and at home.

'No seating arrangements had been made, but the Archbishop, who was Chairman of the Conference, sat down in the centre of the table on the right hand side of the door. Mr Churchill sat on his right with Mr Eden next to him, and on the left of the Archbishop sat Field Marshal Alexander. The other British representatives spread themselves on either side, facing members of the Greek Government. Monsieur Papandreou sat opposite Mr Churchill and next to him was General Plastiras, whose fierce mien and waxed moustaches were the cynosure of all eyes. At the end of the table facing the door were the American Ambassador, Mr MacVeagh, the French Minister, Monsieur Beynet, and the Soviet Military representative, Colonel Popoff.

'Room was left at the other end of the table, near the door, for the representatives of ELAS should they decide to come. But as time passed and they made no appearance, it was decided to begin the Conference. The Archbishop rose to his feet, a tall and impressive figure in his black robes and high black hat. He made a speech welcoming the Prime Minister and Mr Eden and when he sat down Mr Churchill began his address.

'He had not been speaking for more than four or five minutes when noises without heralded the belated arrival of the ELAS delegates. They were first well searched, and General Mandakas, who had brought with him a Mauser rifle and large quantities of ammunition, was required to lay them aside. He refused on principle to hand his weapons over to British troops, but eventually a compromise was reached whereby the arms were placed in an empty room, the door locked and a guard placed outside. The Conference waited patiently while all this took place, and then the three ELAS leaders, dressed shabbily in khaki battledress and glancing furtively around as if they expected a trap, shuffled into the room. Following the Prime Minister's example, the British representatives and the Allied observers rose to their feet with one accord and bowed to the new arrivals. The Archbishop followed suit, but the members of the Greek Government remained firmly seated and did not so much as turn their heads to the door. The ELAS delegates sat down, Monsieur Partsalides on the right, Monsieur Siantos, the Secretary and brains of the rebel committee, in the middle and General Mandakas on the left.

'It was decided to begin the proceedings again. The Archbishop repeated his speech and Mr Churchill then spoke for half an hour addressing his remarks largely in the direction of the ELAS delegates. Gradually, as Mr Churchill proceeded, the three rebel leaders lost their look of intimidation and seemed to abandon their suspicion of an intended "coup de main". Perhaps it was wholesome that whenever they raised their eyes from the table they looked straight into the glittering spectacles, spotless uniform and impeccable bearing of Colonel Popoff, whose appearance was every inch that of an officer and a gentleman.

'While the Prime Minister was speaking, the sound of gunfire went on ceaselessly without, and at one moment the roar of descending rockets, launched by Beaufighters at some nearby enemy position, almost drowned his words. Field Marshal Alexander followed with a short but powerfully-reasoned speech which clearly left its effect on his audience. When he had finished, the Archbishop enquired whether any of the Greek representatives had questions to ask. There was an awkward pause and it was evident that a difference of opinion existed in the ELAS ranks. However, just as the Prime Minister was suggesting that the British representatives should depart and leave the Greeks to their own deliberations, an aged Royalist, Monsieur Maximos, rose to his feet and, instead of asking a question, made a short and highly coloured speech of welcome. He was followed by Monsieur Papandreou, whose speech was equally ponderous but a great deal longer, and who spoke with evident shyness and embarrassment. Then Monsieur Partsalides of ELAS arose and, beginning with the utmost diffidence, his eyes bent downwards, paid a glowing tribute to Mr Churchill. However, as he warmed to his subject, his excitement got the better of him, he raised his eyes which flashed in the lamplight and spoke with such speed and vehemence that the interpreter was unable to get a word in edgeways and was obliged to give up the unequal task. As it was clear that his speech was largely based on a misunderstanding of the intention of the Conference, Mr Eden said a few words of explanation.

'The time had now come to leave the Greeks to their own devices and so, headed by the Prime Minister, the British representatives walked out of the room, shaking hands as they left with members of the Greek Government and lastly with the delegates of ELAS, whose bows could not have been lower, handshakes warmer nor protestations more friendly had they been ambassadors of a party under the deepest obligation to Great Britain.

'On the steps of the Ministry of Foreign Affairs, while Mr Churchill was entering his armoured car, there was a further alarm, and indeed excursion, as various Greeks, headed by the 84 year old Liberal leader, Monsieur Sophoulis, made a desperate effort to flee from the Conference chamber. They were, however, firmly held and persuaded to return to their places at the council table.

'So ended the opening session of what must surely be the strangest conference which a British Prime Minister and Foreign Secretary have ever attended.'

The ensuing negotiations between the Greek antagonists were much affected by the fact which Mr Churchill had mentioned in his speech, and Field Marshal Alexander had emphasised, that large British reinforcements were on their way to Athens from Italy. Thus, for the next twenty years or so, Greece was assured of freedom and democracy.

32. Fire Extinguisher

Leaving the Greek protagonists to a Homeric battle of words, the British leaders and their acolytes returned to the Embassy. There was much clearing up to be done. The speeches to which we had been listening had to be typed and prepared for issue to the world. The task was lightened by the Press Attaché, Mr Osbert Lancaster, whose notes on the proceedings were adorned by drawings of the Archbishop and other participating dignitaries. But a full two hours were needed before I could leave the Embassy. Meanwhile the Prime Minister and most of his party had returned to the ship. As they left they were good enough to say that once safely on board they would send a ship's launch back to the Piraeus to wait for me. On this occasion the kindness of their intention was not matched by the retentiveness of their memories.

By the time my work was done, darkness had fallen and it was icy cold. I set off on the long drive to the Piraeus with Miss Marian Holmes, one of the secretaries from 10 Downing Street who had accompanied us on this venture and had stayed behind with me at the Embassy. It had been thrilling to gaze at the Acropolis and the Lycabettus by the light of the full moon. It was no less thrilling to share that romantic pleasure with Marian Holmes who was not only shyly charming and highly efficient, but closely resembled one of the prettier species of gazelle. What rapture it was going to be to glide with her across the smooth moon-lit waters of Phaleron Bay in the snug warmth of a spacious and spotless naval pinnace!

We reached the Piraeus. The driver, announcing that he was urgently required at the Embassy, dropped us near the quay, turned the car round and vanished. Miss Holmes, I noted, was shivering. I hoped it was with emotion, but feared it was with cold. So with a gesture of gallantry, and spurning her protestations, I took off my RAF overcoat and draped it around her shoulders. I may just possibly have comforted myself with the thought that we had scarcely more than a hundred yards to walk.

The quay was deserted. No boat was to be seen and on anxious investigation we found nothing but a solitary watchman sheltering in a hut. The boat must even now be on its way from *Ajax*, we said. Ten minutes passed, and then twenty: we felt like lost explorers of Antarctica. By means of gestures and the constant repetition of *Ajax* and Royal Navy, I made our plight known to the watchman. He pointed to a distant illuminated building and indicated by signs and a few broken words of English that it was a Greek nautical establishment containing a wireless transmitter. We could doubtless arrange for a message to be sent to *Ajax* and, while we waited, take temporary refuge in the hospitable warmth within.

We set off through an olive grove. In the moonlight Marian Holmes' long golden hair transformed her into the Lorelei; but romance had frozen within me. In the circumstances Casanova himself would have been a blameless escort. We were half way to our objective when a dozen swarthy men, carrying every kind of firearm, emerged from behind the olive trees. They pointed their weapons at us and uttered harsh cries. At first I assumed they were an ELAS band and that a quick, merciful death was the best for which we might hope. But I had been told categorically that this particular area was entirely ELAS-free, and, after the initial panic, I correctly deduced that this must be the Greek Home Guard. I addressed them in English; I addressed them in French. It had no effect. So I tried a few still-remembered lines of Ancient Greek, such as 'My son, mayest thou be more fortunate than thy father', and 'There is no way in which I may call false things beautiful'. This had no effect either, for my accent bore no resemblance at all to modern Greek. Finally, in rash, thoughtless despair, I switched to German. This they immediately recognised and, coupled with my blue uniform, it confirmed their worst suspicions. We were clearly a remnant of the Wehrmacht. There was an ominous clicking sound. It took a long time to convince them and I feel sure that in the end it was Marian Holmes' beauty rather than my unlikely explanations that saved the day; but they refused to let us go further and pointed with stern gestures back towards the quay. We had no choice but to retrace our steps.

In our absence a boat had come alongside the quay. It was not a

smart pinnace from *Ajax*, but a ramshackle launch, with an open
cockpit in the stern from which two steps led down to a small
covered engine-room. A Lieutenant of the Royal Hellenic Navy was
in command and he had a crew of two bearded seamen. He spoke
a quaint but fluent English. On hearing our distressful story, he at
once offered to ferry us to *Ajax*, lying though she was a good mile
out in the bay. It would, he said, be an honour to bring his boat
alongside a ship of the Royal Navy with which it had not hitherto
been his good fortune to co-operate.

We chugged off into the darkness of Phaleron Bay. There was
now a fresh breeze and we pitched heavily. By the light of a hurricane lamp I could see Marian Holmes growing paler and tightening
her lips; but I sensed that she was determined not to disgrace her
country in the presence of the Royal Hellenic Navy even though she
scarcely felt well enough to reply graciously to the flowery compli-
ments which the Lieutenant, upright in the stern and grasping the
tiller, never ceased to heap on her.

After ten uncomfortable minutes we were approaching *Ajax* and
the Lieutenant made a wide sweep to bring us alongside. He was not,
I suppose, an experienced helmsman nor, since the Greek Navy
had long been safely moored in Alexandria harbour, can he have
had many opportunities of going alongside a large cruiser in a rough
sea. We made three unsuccessful attempts and it was just possible,
above the wind and the waves, to hear the laughter of the unfeeling
starboard watch in *Ajax*.

The Lieutenant was desperate. His country's honour no less than
his self-esteem was at stake. At the fourth attempt we seemed to
be doing better when in the capricious way that the Greek Gods
have, the wrong one – perhaps it was Apollo getting his own back
on Aphrodite – intervened. As we swung round towards the gangway, the Lieutenant shouted an order, presumably the Greek for
'Hard Astern'. The engineer pulled the lever the wrong way and we
went 'Full Ahead', straight into the side of *Ajax*. We made quite a
large dent.

At this point the other crewman, who had been standing silent
in the bow, could no longer control his feelings. He flew at the
engineer and punched him. Within seconds they had tripped up on
the step leading down to the engine room and were rolling on its

greasy floor in furious combat. Slowly we bumped down the side of *Ajax*, ramming her afresh as each wave propelled us forward. The Lieutenant burst into tears. He had, he sobbed, been made to look ridiculous in the eyes of the Royal Navy which it had been his lifelong ambition to impress. I was less moved by this indisputable fact than by the prospect of slipping under *Ajax*'s heaving stern.

We were saved from disaster by two British sailors with exceptionally long boat-hooks. We clambered up the gangway. 'Good night, Miss Holmes', I said, for I had not even succeeded in getting on to Christian name terms. 'Good night, Mr Colville', she replied as, brave to the last, but deathly pale, she rushed off towards her cabin without any thought of food.

As for me, I made my way, cold and hungry, to the Ward Room, where a large party was dining. The Prime Minister interrupted the flow of conversation as I sat down. 'You are disgracefully late for dinner', he said and picked up the thread of what he had been saying. I was chilled to the marrow, but I was indeed late and the soup was tepid.

33. Plunder

Travelling with Churchill was never dull. Travelling with him to one of the war zones was sure to be especially exciting because nothing would induce him to keep far from the conflict, though he expected to be constantly supplied with papers, telegrams and everything relating to affairs of State as well as with the physical comforts to which he was accustomed. To forego a hot bath, even within a few miles of the enemy, was unthinkable.

So it was with high expectations that I set off with him on 23 March, 1945, to watch Operation Plunder, the crossing of the Rhine. He thought it fitting to be accompanied by his Flag Commander, Tommy Thompson, in naval uniform and by me, temporarily reconverted into a Flying Officer, RAFVR. No doubt to emphasise that it was a combined operation, he himself was dressed as Colonel of the 4th Hussars. We stayed in Field Marshal Montgomery's collection of caravans at 21st Army Group Headquarters, who were encamped in a rectangular clearing in the middle of a pine forest. All the caravans were decorated with photographs, mostly of Monty himself (some even signed by himself) but also of the German Commanders he admired. There were three of Rommel, one of Rundstedt and about thirty of Monty.

As Churchill sat in his caravan after dinner, poring over the maps of the operation with Monty and Alan Brooke, I brought him a venomous telegram from Molotov complaining that the Russians were bearing the sole brunt of the war. The hundreds of thousands of British and American troops waiting tensely for dawn were in themselves the reply, but Churchill pushed aside the telegram and concentrated on the maps.

The day of the assault broke clear and cloudless. Churchill set off with Montgomery and Brooke to join Eisenhower on the top of a convenient hillock. Leaving a competent rearguard to deal with incoming messages, I went with one of Monty's Liaison Officers,

Captain Gill, to a hill near Xanten. Fighters flew ceaselessly over-
head and 2000 guns thundered away in a deafening barrage, alter-
nating with minutes of total silence. In one of these interludes we
saw, far away to the north east, a trail of white condensation climbing skywards. It seemed to travel slowly and we could trace its
vertical path up to 30,000 feet or more. We knew that it was a V.2
rocket on its way to Antwerp or perhaps London.

The guns had been silent for twenty minutes and the dust on the
far side of the Rhine was settling, when a host of Dakotas appeared
flying low and in close formation, the doors in each fuselage wide
open and a parachutist standing ready in the aperture. A solitary
Flying Fortress accompanied them. To our left came another great
fleet and behind yet a third. They vanished in the haze across
the Rhine, but not before we had seen hundreds of parachutes open.
Fleet after fleet of Dakotas followed while the first contingent
streamed back empty over our heads. The Fortress reappeared, on
fire, and the occupants baled out one by one as the aircraft flew
steadily on, the flames spreading towards its tail. Soon there were
fleets of gliders too. As each was released over the river, its tug-
aircraft turned steeply away for home. Several of the returning
Dakotas were in trouble and three or four crashed before our eyes,
bursting into flames as they struck the ground. One, struggling low
over Xanten, lost height irrecoverably and there was a great
explosive flash as it crashed at the bottom of our hill, right on top
of one of our heavy gun positions. For two and a half hours this
apparently endless Armada flew over the Rhine, the last and
inexorable destroying angel launching itself at Hitler's crumbling
Reich. Even Molotov might have been impressed.

Captain Gill and I did not wait for the end of the air display. We
made our way to the river. It flowed peacefully before us and there
was a small boat. Long before the Airborne Operation was completed we stood on the eastern bank of the Rhine. There seemed
to be mines everywhere and we watched the sappers exploding
them. Prisoners, newly taken, came marching towards us, their
hands clasped behind their heads, some of their faces registering
relief, others despair. We walked up a short, steep road towards the
little village of Marwick where, on a bluff above the river, stood the
'Gasthaus Die Drei Könige', filled with wounded and with more

German prisoners keeping a strained and depressed watch on the Rhine.

I stood talking to Gill in front of the inn. An Airborne Colonel arrived, in claret-coloured beret, complete with jeep and driver. I stared through the windows at the prisoners and one of them, with his cap aslant, stared back defiantly. Suddenly a shell exploded in the river, and others began to fall nearer. Gill, quite unmoved, suggested it would be fun to talk to the prisoners and find out their impressions. We walked towards the front door of the inn to ask the officer in charge if he had any objection. Just as we reached the door, an 88 mm shell landed precisely where we had been standing. We were less than ten yards from the burst and the Airborne Colonel's driver, who was next to me, had an artery severed. My tunic was drenched in blood. The next shell brought a tree down across the courtyard and as we made our way to the cellar, carrying the wounded driver, a third missile landed by the front door. A medical orderly took charge of the unhappy driver and as soon as the shelling stopped, we picked our way over the German prisoners, lying flat on the floor, and crawled out from among the debris.

We met two tank officers, who gave us some eggs they had collected from a nearby farm and told us that the enemy were less than a mile away. We had crossed the Rhine in the belief that we were at least ten miles behind the lines. It seemed wise to retreat and so we recrossed the Rhine in an amphibious machine called a Buffalo which proceeded to charge the opposite bank at the wrong angle, toppled back into the river and flung us all, including the man with the severed artery, into a writhing heap on the floor.

Finally, we succeeded in jumping ashore, recovering our jeep and driving back through devastated Xanten, where the German children seemed well-fed and the populace curious rather than resentful. The sun beat down as it should in July and the dust was as thick as I remembered it in Normandy. We had a picnic lunch in a quiet lane followed by a leisurely return to 21st Army Group Headquarters. As we reached the entrance we all but collided with the Prime Minister and the Field Marshal, the former, as I later discovered, glum and rather angry because he had not been allowed to cross the Rhine.

They looked at my blood-stained tunic. What, they asked, had happened to me? I poured out what was, I thought, my exciting story. Monty was livid with rage. How dare I, a Civil Servant, get in the way of the battle! My job was back at Headquarters. I had deserted my post and, without permission, made free of the zone of operations under his command.

His eyes blazing with anger, he said: 'This is an intolerable act of insubordination and I shall . . .'.

Churchill, who had been listening to the tirade, interrupted him:

'Before you say what you will do, Field Marshal, pray remember Mr Colville is my Secretary, not yours. It is for me and not for you to issue a reprimand'.

Much later, when he was going to bed, he said with a kind smile: 'I am jealous. You succeeded where I failed. Tomorrow nothing shall stop me. Sleep soundly; you might have slept more soundly still'.

34. Captains of the Host

The British Chiefs of Staff, collectively and individually, played a part in the conduct of affairs which was not solely professional; for they were men of fine intellect and strong character whose almost daily contact with the Prime Minister, usually in harmony but sometimes in conflict, influenced thought and policy in a sense wider than the purely military. At times Churchill exasperated them all, but they admired him and, perhaps with the exception of Admiral Cunningham, who seemed to me the only one impervious to Churchill's spell, their admiration was combined with affection. They stood in awe of him, but they seldom failed to stand up for their convictions, nor would he have respected them if they had been a tamer body. He complained of their obstinacy and would grumble to their combined faces that he was expected to wage modern war with antiquated weapons; but I never remember his denigrating them as men.

The one in whose judgment he had the greatest confidence was the quiet, unemotional and unassuming Wykhamist, Sir Charles Portal, Chief of the Air Staff, who only spoke when he had something significant to say, listened intently and neither made promises unless he knew he could fulfil them nor allowed himself to be the victim of undue optimism or pessimism. Churchill rated high the military flair of Sir Alan Brooke, Chief of the Imperial General Staff, and found him a stimulating companion; but in after years he was hurt and distressed by the publication of the General's diaries, although to many readers their praise of Churchill's leadership seemed more pronounced than their criticism of his methods. At the beginning of the war, and for more than three years after Churchill became Prime Minister, the First Sea Lord was the dour old sea-dog, Sir Dudley Pound, sure, cautious and so conscientious that he literally worked himself to death in the belief that if the captain of a ship must be on the bridge in times of danger, still more must the First Sea Lord be available and on duty night and day in times of war. Alan Brooke, according to his diary, thought Pound insufferably slow and complained that he dozed at long meetings (although that was doubtless when supplies for the Army or RAF were under interminable discussion). Churchill, on the other hand, had an affectionate esteem for him, though he bullied him on the telephone when he thought the Admiralty was being unimaginative. The affection was returned and the Admiral's serious wrinkled face would flicker with pleasure and amusement when Churchill teased him. One summer night at Chequers we were walking in the rose-garden after dinner. The poor old Admiral, who was lame but unquestionably sober, fell down the steps and lay flat on his back. 'Try to remember', said Churchill, 'that you are an Admiral of the Fleet and not a midshipman'. A slow smile spread across Pound's face as we helped him to his feet.

Naturally Churchill knew the American Chiefs of Staff less intimately than his own, but by the end of the war, after many Anglo–American conferences and frequent visits, they had become his friends. For General George Marshall, doggedly though Churchill fought him over the policy for the landing in Normandy and strongly as he regretted and opposed 'Operation Anvil' (the American landing in the south of France) he always felt confidence and regard. Marshall was, after all, a diplomat and a statesman of towering stature. It was those qualities, even more than his professional abilities as a soldier, which counted in the highest counsels of the Allied war effort; and he combined a prepossessing appearance with irresistible charm. There were few people who could mes-merise Churchill: Marshall was one of those few who came close to doing so, and it is to Churchill's credit that when he opposed Marshall's strategy, as he quite rightly did in the case of 'Operation Anvil', he managed to resist the General's charm and to fight him vigorously without diminishing the respect in which they held each other. General Arnold, Chief of the American Air Staff, may have been less striking than Marshall, but he was no less efficient and his esteem for Churchill was marked by the gift of a splendidly equipped C.54 aircraft for the Prime Minister's personal use on his foreign journeys. Then there was Admiral King, known for his belief that the main weight of the American war effort should be placed in the Pacific rather than in Europe. He was suspicious and resentful of Churchill's undoubted influence in the reverse direction with President Roosevelt and the other American Chiefs of Staff. Lastly, on the American side, there was Admiral Leahy, close to Roosevelt, an admirer of Marshal Pétain and implacably hostile to General de Gaulle. Except on French matters, he was generally believed to be helpful and to lean more to the Marshall side than to that of his fundamentally anti-British fellow-Admiral, King.

Although the British Chiefs of Staff were physically in London, there was in Washington a Combined Chiefs of Staff organisation and there, from the beginning of 1942, the views of the British were mainly represented by Sir Alan Brooke's predecessor as CIGS, Field Marshal Sir John Dill. In London he had often seemed weary and lacking in spirit. He had wilted before the blast of Churchill's sleepless energy. When he went to Washington all was changed. He was greeted with frankness and goodwill; he became a close personal friend of the American war leaders and of General Marshall in particular; his radiant and smiling good looks, as well as his transparent honesty, won all hearts and his position became such, both in London and Washington, that most differences of opinion between the British and American military leaders were resolved with graceful ease and those which persisted were debated without leaving any personal ill-will behind. His tenure of office as CIGS had been widely regarded as a failure. He had, as it were, set sail for the New World to repair his fortunes. He did so brilliantly, serving his own country and the Allied cause with such acclaim among Americans that when he died in Washington, at the pinnacle of his well-earned popularity, they buried him among their own heroes in Arlington Cemetery.

The fighting soldiers came and went. There was seldom a week-end at Chequers without a General, and there were often two or three. Churchill would, of course, have liked to be a General himself and I have always suspected that in the fantasies of his day-dreams, in which like the rest of us he must sometimes have indulged, he saw himself commanding the Allied armies on the road to Berlin. With the solitary exception of Wavell, whose merits were a closed book to him, he respected all military commanders, even those who failed. Two were especially prominent in his catalogue of honour: Alexander and Montgomery. When they were at home, it was all but impossible for them to escape from Chequers or 10 Downing Street; when they were campaigning abroad, Churchill sought every excuse to visit them.

Widely respected for his gallant First War record as an officer in the Irish Guards, Alexander had commanded, with cool efficiency, first the rearguard on the Dunkirk beaches, and then the fighting retreat of the British Army in Burma. Like General Marshall in America, like Eisenhower and like Sir Jóhn Dill, he had a personal charm which enabled him to allay discord. He explained his plans with a quiet confidence that won immediate attention without seeming to demand it; and he stuck to his guns with as much courage in the Council Chamber as on the field of battle. To be a successful Supreme Allied Commander required patience, tact, impartiality and the capacity to win and retain the confidence of political chiefs. Alexander had precisely those gifts and he was therefore cherished by the Americans and the Canadians, the French, the Poles, the Brazilians and all the others under his Command, as much as by his own compatriots. Churchill led the field of those who admired him as a soldier. His artistic endeavours – for he was a painter of quality – still further cemented the friendship and though Churchill did not consider modesty a virtue essential for his friends and boon-companions, he could not fail to recognise and value it in Alex. He thought and said that Alex scarcely received the full popular acclaim which was his due; but he did his hero no good in seeking to redress the balance after the war by dragging a reluctant, though always obedient, Field Marshal away from a successful Governor-Generalship of Canada to become Minister of Defence, an office to which the politically analphabetic Alexander was entirely unsuited in peace time.

From 1943 onwards, General Dwight Eisenhower was as constant a visitor as the British Generals. He had many of Alexander's qualities, though he had not in either war had Alexander's experience on the field of battle. It may even be that Monty was right in considering Eisenhower to be lacking in tactical knowledge and strategic skill. However, he had under his command Generals, American and British, who supplied all that he lacked. He had Patton and Bradley; he had Montgomery and Dempsey. What he did do, supremely well, was to co-ordinate a group of allied armies with absolute fairness to all, to establish an integrated Anglo–American staff in which friction between officers of different nationality was recognised as an unforgivable sin, and to preside over one of the greatest military operations in history to the universal satisfaction of politicians, soldiers and the entire general public of the United States and the British Empire. This was no mean achievement nor can there often have been post-war tributes to a Commander comparable to the generally accepted phrase: 'I like Ike'. It would perhaps have been better for him, as in the last century for Welling-ton and Grant, if he had rested on his military laurels. From the time of Oliver Cromwell to the present day, the English-speaking peoples have generally regretted their occasional experiments in selecting a General to lead them in the changed circumstances of peace.

After the war, comparisons, often invidious, were made of the merits of the Generals. In 1969, a few days before Alexander's sudden death, I went to have luncheon with him to ask his advice on a book I was proposing to write about Lord Gort, the Commander in Chief of the British Expeditionary Force in 1940. Alexander said Gort was not, in his view, the man to be a Commander in Chief; but he was the ideal Commander of an independent fighting force. Gort should, he said, have been the British Rommel and he believed that because he had a thorough Staff training, whereas Rommel had none, he would have been the better of the two. He paused for a minute and then he added: 'In fact if Gort had been in command of the 8th Army, I think he would have beaten Rommel quicker than Monty and I did'. Whether this would have been so, we shall never know; but it was certainly not said for effect and it is rare to find such humility in a successful man, particularly when the statement was likely to be published.

Montgomery would never have said such a thing, even if he had believed it. His very inability to be modest or self-deprecating was one of the hall-marks of his success, for he would not admit inferiority of any kind for himself, his troops or his country. This had an endearing as well as an infuriating aspect. It involved jealousy: he was jealous of Alexander, whose part in the North African victories he minimised; he was jealous of Bradley whose

military skills he denied; and he was above all jealous of Eisenhower, to whom he would allow scarcely any credit at all for the
conduct of the 1944 Campaign against Germany in Northern
Europe. Yet, in the circumstances of the time, these defects were
virtues, for they enabled Monty, a brilliant if self-taught, leader of
men, to instil into his armies the self-confidence he personally
exuded. Churchill recognised the fact and when there was a
serious dispute between Montgomery and Eisenhower about the
strategy for the later stages of the attack on Germany, he exercised
his power of conciliation to satisfy Eisenhower without abandoning
Monty.

Off the battle-field and away from the centre of affairs, Monty
could be cosy and engaging. He lived not far away from us after the
war, and used to come over to luncheon, bringing chocolates for
the children and for me a bottle of port given to him by Salazar, or
a bottle of Slivovicz from Tito. He enchanted the children to such
an extent that after one visit my four-year-old daughter confided to
her mother that 'I think I would like to have Gomery as my daddy,
and Daddy can be the gardener' (on hearing of which Monty at once
sent her an inscribed book). Yet he could be shabbily ungenerous.
One week-end we had staying with us Tony Pepys, who had
commanded 'The Royals' in North Africa and had lost a leg in
action. Monty came to luncheon and asked Pepys, with the mono-
tone bark of a machine gun:

'Did you serve under me?'

'Yes, Field Marshal; I commanded The Royals.'

'Ah, under Lumsden. I had to sack him: he was yellow.'

'I can't agree, Field Marshal. He personally saved my life when I
had my leg blown off. He was one of the bravest men I ever knew.'

'Can't help it. I sacked him. He was yellow.'

The unconquerable spirit which drove Rommel from Africa,
saved the day in the Ardennes Offensive and drove the Germans
relentlessly over the Rhine, was less easy to recognise in a peace-
time Hampshire dining room; but it is always easy to snipe at great
men posthumously, and for all his lack of good manners, modesty
and tolerance, Monty was a great general and a great man.

Churchill admired Monty's qualities of leadership, thoroughness
and efficiency to such an extent that he gladly overlooked his

failings, submitted to his whims (such as drinking no alcohol or going early to bed), listened with patient amusement to his strictures on all politicians and most of our allies, and even allowed Monty to remove, practically by *force majeure,* no less than four of his own paintings from Chartwell. Towards the end of Churchill's life, when he was old and often sad, and Monty was lonely in his retirement, there was scarcely a week-end on which his name did not appear in the Visitor's Book at Chartwell. He was usually self-invited, but I believe that he was always welcome.

Part 3

THE COLOURS CHANGE

35. The Canadian Stimulant

By the time Churchill became Prime Minister in 1940, the close friends of his early political life had mostly left the scene. F.E. Smith, Freddy Guest and the Duke of Marlborough were dead, and Lloyd George had retired to a twilight world of his own. Lord Beaverbrook was the only survivor. Churchill, enchanted by Beaverbrook's inexhaustible and effervescent energy, also had a solid faith in his qualification for high political office, a faith which was not shared by his Sovereign, his wife or the Conservative, Liberal and Labour Parties. He had to override some formidable opposition in appointing him Minister of Aircraft Production; but the rapid and irrefutable success of Beaverbrook's activities, piratical though they were in conception as well as in performance, both disarmed the critics and left Churchill loyally and lastingly indebted to him. He never failed, in private or in public, to give him all the many ounces of credit that were his due.

Once the Battle of Britain was over, Beaverbrook became a mixed blessing. He could be counted on to stimulate; but he was for ever resigning or threatening to resign; he could not be trusted to refrain from attacking his colleagues (apart from Churchill) publicly; he praised Stalin loudly and criticised the Americans incessantly; and his irrepressible addiction to political intrigue, at a time when politics were officially dormant, was a source of embarrassment.

There was no doubt of his admiration and affection for Churchill, even though he laughed at him behind his back; but at the same time he was, in his self-contradictory way, jealous of him. One way in which this jealousy showed itself was his consistent effort to win for himself the first loyalty of Churchill's friend and protégé, Brendan Bracken. He did not wholly succeed, for Bracken's veneration for Churchill was unshakeable; but in the latter part of the war, and particularly when Churchill formed his Caretaker Government in May, 1945, he encouraged Bracken to believe that

197

Churchill had shown himself ungrateful in a number of ways and particularly by not offering him the Chancellorship of the Exchequer, an office for which Bracken would in fact have been wholly unsuitable. Soon after the war, Bracken renounced politics and while he saw much of Beaverbrook, he saw less and less of Churchill. Yet when Churchill had his stroke in June, 1953, no friends could have been more assiduous in their attentions or more genuinely anxious for his recovery, than Beaverbrook and Bracken, both of whom had been conspicuously aloof during the two preceding years.

In the War Coalition there was no love lost between Ernest Bevin and Herbert Morrison. When somebody said that Herbert Morrison was his own worst enemy, Bevin was reported as replying: 'Not while I'm alive, he ain't.' Churchill, like Attlee, was an admirer of Bevin who could seldom do wrong in his eyes. Beaverbrook, doubtless for the impish pleasure of it, gave all his support to Morrison and set himself the task of persuading Bracken to follow the same course. As the war in Europe drew to its close, it was clear that the Coalition was likely to dissolve and that party politics would be resumed. Churchill at first regretted it; Beaverbrook and Bracken were delighted.

On 7 April, 1945, Bevin fired an early shot by making a political speech attacking the Conservative Party while Churchill, and Attlee too, were still hoping that the Coalition could be held together until Japan, as well as Germany, had been defeated. Most of the constituency agents of the Conservative Party were away fighting; but whereas the principal Labour leaders, loyally working in a Coalition team, had given little or no attention to party organisation during the war years, Dr Hugh Dalton was the exception. On 27 July, 1945, the day after the Election results were announced, he walked into the room where I was working and I made the not profoundly original comment that he must be pleased with the result. 'Yes', he said, rubbing his hands and smiling broadly, 'I think I can take a good deal of personal credit. In the last year or two, while everybody else pretended to be so busy, I have taken pains to ensure that our electoral machine was put in good order'. This explained to me why he was so widely known as 'The Dirty Doctor'.

If Beaverbrook and Bracken had been less methodical than Dalton, and if their party political instincts had only recently reawakened, they none the less threw themselves into the forthcoming contest with frenzied vigour; and playing on the Bevin–Morrison antipathy seemed to them one fruitful method of creating dismay in the opposing ranks. The Prime Minister was only spasmodically interested.

In the middle of April, Churchill was heavily concerned with manifold problems created by the imminence of victory, and Anthony Eden was away in San Francisco where efforts were being made to shape a new post-war world. Beaverbrook thought that he had the field largely to himself. On 1 May, Churchill decided that he must apply himself more assiduously to party politics, since everybody seemed to think an early election was certain. First, declaring that Beaverbrook was being too high-handed about the Tory Party and its election strategy, he sent for him in order to remonstrate. The same evening he gave a political dinner party to which he invited Beaverbrook, James Stuart (the Chief Whip), Oliver Lyttelton and the Chairman of the Conservative Party, Ralph Assheton. He did not invite Brendan Bracken because he was well aware that the official Tory Party, represented at the dinner by Stuart and Assheton, were looking askance at the Beaverbrook–Bracken Axis. I interrupted their deliberations by walking into the dining room towards the end of dinner with the announcement, broadcast by the Nazi wireless, that Hitler had committed suicide. 'Well,' said Churchill, 'I must say I think he was perfectly right to die like that'. Being offered a glass of brandy, I sat down and listened to the conversation which was thenceforward concentrated more on the late Hitler than on the future election.

Victory in Europe, marked as forcibly by foreign complications as by home celebrations, put a temporary stop to electioneering thoughts, at least within 10 Downing Street, and on 18 May Churchill wrote to the Opposition leaders expressing the hope that they would agree to preserve the Coalition until the end of the war with Japan. Attlee called in person to say that he was favourably disposed to the idea, that Bevin supported him and that he would do his best to secure the agreement of the Labour Party at their Whitsun Blackpool Conference; but on 21 May he telephoned from Blackpool and said that he had been unable to do so. Churchill thereupon wrote him a letter, formally accepting the end of the

Coalition. After a struggle Beaverbrook persuaded him to leave out the last paragraph which contained generous references to the help of his late Labour colleagues. Churchill was far from being elated, but other Tories broke into a wild stampede and right in the fore-front was Beaverbrook. Bracken was not among the early starters. I wrote in my diary: 'Brendan, who is offended with the PM over a number of minor slights, is sulking in his tent'.

On 24 May, Churchill formed a Conservative Caretaker Government. Beaverbrook, more interested in manipulation than in office, made it clear he did not wish to be included. Bracken, offered neither the Exchequer nor his alternative choice, a combination of the Board of Trade and the Ministry of Production, finally settled for the Admiralty. Churchill for his part took the advice which Polonius gave Laertes. He had been chary of entrance to a quarrel, but being in he decided that the opposed should beware of him and he flung himself into the fight with all his natural, not always well-judged pugnacity. I was never sure that his heart was in it, but as the weeks passed he was buoyed up by the vociferous applause with which millions greeted him as he stumped the country. I remember his saying to me, when he rejoined the train after addressing vast crowds in Glasgow and Edinburgh, that nobody who had witnessed their enthusiasm could doubt the result of the Election. I replied that I would agree if it were a Presidential Election.

At the end of May Beaverbrook asked me to his house at Cherkeley for the night and the account which I wrote of my visit is an attempt to draw a sketch of this unpredictable, mischievous, but always attractive and, in many ways, loveable man.

'He was alone when I arrived and he took me for a long walk to see his chickens, to look at the little house he gave Mrs Norton (whose death last winter was a grievous blow to him) and back through the woods and valleys. He told me at length the story of Bonar Law's resignation and Lord Curzon's disappointment, and then he switched off to sing the praises of Brendan (whom he is backing against Eden for the Leadership of the Tory Party) and to complain that the PM had maltreated him in a number of ways over appointments.

'When we got back to the house Harold Balfour, just returned from West Africa, arrived, followed by Lord Queensberry and Brendan. Before dinner there was an incident indicative of the social chip on Beaverbrook's shoulder. In the course of attacking Eden, he claimed that he owed his success solely to his birth and education. He then turned on us all and said that true men of quality, like Brendan and himself, had worked their way up from nothing by sheer hard work and ability. Having made this attack with flashing eyes, he proceeded to send for the Scottish Psalter and read aloud several of the Metric Psalms, presumably in order to make amends to the Almighty.

'We had an excellent dinner with a magnum of Champagne and lots of brandy, followed by a rotten film. When Balfour and Queensberry had gone, there followed a long political conversation, with attacks on Bevin, praise of Morrison (the Beaverbrook–Bracken theme) and abuse of Eden and Anderson and of the recent appointment of Dunglass (who is pro-Pole while they are violently pro-Russian) as Under Secretary at the Foreign Office. The evening was fun, with a real buccaneering, racketeering atmosphere. Of course, they are both utterly mischievous and will do the Conservative Party countless harm, at this election and afterwards.

'*Monday, 28 May.* Awoke to a glorious view through the Dorking Gap and to a single poached egg accompanied by the *Daily Express*. Brendan had said that he would be ready to leave for London at 9.30 but was not in fact ready until 11.30. Meanwhile I sat in the sun or poked about in Lord B.'s library in the belief that books often tell one much of their owner. His were mostly dull: the lesser novelists and the standard biographies. But on a reading desk, by the side of two dictaphones, stood the Bible open at the Psalms and, nearby, Wilkes' notorious *Essay on Woman*.

'Lord B. came down, sat beside me in the sun, carried on some politico-journalistic intrigue by telephone, told some unidentified caller that he would surely try and get him the Financial Secretaryship of the War Office (which he subsequently made no attempt to do), blackguarded James Stuart to somebody else as a Highlander, at once treacherous and loyal (James stands up against the Beaver–Brendan schemes and wields too much influence over appointments for their liking), discoursed cheerfully on a variety of unrelated subjects and, finally, after a debunking description of Charles

Dickens' private life, presented me with one of the maligned author's First Editions.

'Brendan came down and talked politics for an hour, saying that the Socialist plot was to nationalise only the mines, the Bank of England and electricity, but that if they nationalised the last they controlled industry as a whole and the second would tie finance to their apron. Eventually I left in Brendan's car and by way of contrast he talked the whole way up to London in an absolutely sane and sensible way.

'Later in the day Lord B., who had argued with me that the Prof. [Lord Cherwell] had been utterly wrong about the V. Weapons (the Prof. is unpopular for opposing him about the Bretton Woods financial project) sent me part of his dossier on the matter, each page taking one instance in which the Prof. could be shown to have been utterly wrong. He must be an uncomfortable colleague.'

The truth was that Lord Beaverbrook enjoyed the thrill of the chase, but was not much interested in the kill. He was an engaging companion, a generous friend and sometimes sincerely dedicated to a worthwhile cause. His failing, and his danger, was that if some political stunt or personal vendetta amused him, he would pursue it with all his energy and give little or no thought to the aftermath. Here is an illustration.

I long wondered why Churchill had put his political survival at risk and antagonised the entire House of Commons by supporting Edward VIII at the time of the Abdication. It was a delicate subject, but one day there was an opportunity to ask him. Had he, I enquired, really visualised Mrs Simpson as Queen of England? He replied that he certainly had not. He was, however, always loyal to his Sovereign and Edward VIII, whom he had known, liked and admired as a young Prince of Wales, was the King. His duty was to save him if he possibly could. He had believed, wrongly as it turned out, that the King's love for Mrs Simpson was a temporary passion. His plan, therefore, was that the King be pronounced ill, too ill to undertake his royal duties. He would be persuaded to retire to Windsor Castle for a few months during which, as Churchill put it, 'we should raise the draw-bridge and place the doctors on guard, Lord Dawson of Penn at the front door and Lord Horder at the back door'. He sought the advice and support of Beaverbrook who immediately gave both. They agreed that the first thing to do was to persuade 'Cutie', as they irreverently called Mrs Simpson, to leave the country so that the King might have a chance to recover from his emotional prostration.

'Then', said Churchill, 'terrible things began to happen. Bricks were thrown through her dining room window, letters arrived threatening her with vitriol, angry slogans were written on the walls of neighbouring houses.'

'*You* didn't do things like that?' I asked incredulously.

'No,' he replied. 'But Max did.'

A few weeks later I sat next to Beaverbrook at dinner. I told him what Churchill had said. He roared with laughter. 'Did you really throw bricks through the dining room window?'

'Perhaps some young man from the *Daily Express* did.'

'Do you think Winston was prepared to destroy his career entirely from personal loyalty to the King?'

'Yes, I think that was Churchill's motive. Would you like to know what mine was? I just thought it was all a lot of fun.'

He was capable of irresponsible, indeed discreditable, acts. Yet in 1940 the war might have been lost without Beaverbrook, and, despite all his acts of mischief, British politics gained something from the mixture of salt and vinegar in which he soused them. And he revolutionised British journalism.

36. The Gestapo Speech

Having with some reluctance agreed to fight a General Election before the war against Japan was over, Churchill would have been untrue to himself if he had charged into battle at anything less than a full gallop. He had not forgotten the excitement of an election campaign, nor was he a man whose youthful enthusiasms were dulled by advancing years. At seventy he was as invigorated by a political jousting-match as he had been when he was twenty. All the same, for five years he had been the leader of the nation, his authority seldom disputed and never successfully. He had grown accustomed to explain and defend his actions in the knowledge that there was none but a small, self-appointed and unrepresentative Opposition; and he had all but forgotten he was the Leader of the Conservative Party with which, indeed, he had few emotional bonds of sympathy, however hard he tried to convince himself that he had. In 1940, when Neville Chamberlain died, he had even hesitated before accepting the Leadership and Mrs Churchill had urged him to decline. He liked and respected most of his Labour colleagues in the Coalition Government and his relationship with them, free from Party spite, had been one of joint dedication to the broad national interest. The effort he now made was thus to some extent an artificial one and the deep-throated growl seemed to me to lack conviction. There can be no doubt that the electorate, for their part, regarded Churchill as a lofty mountain peak towering into the skies, the supreme hero above and apart from party politics.

But if Churchill had to brace himself to be a Tory, he did have a profound antipathy to the doctrine of Socialism. He had often spoken, in private as in public, of a fairer Society based on the increase of material prosperity to which the world could look forward. Those who had borne the brunt of the fighting and the bombing of the cities deserved a fuller share of the riches the future would bring. This was quite different from advocating an egalitarian society since men are neither born equal nor do they have equal deserts. Although a strong supporter of *la carrière ouverte aux talents*, he had no hesitation in giving Liberty precedence over Equality. The Liberal Party, to which he was proud to have belonged at the time of its apotheosis, had withered because it had achieved its programme. Like a beautiful flower it had bloomed to perfection and faded when its purpose was fulfilled. It had left an edifice of wholesome social benefits which must now be expanded and mended by the Conservatives or the Labour Party, but in such a way as to improve the lot of the needy without shackling the endeavours of the enterprising. The Coalition Government had accepted the Beveridge Report and the other basic proposals for a Welfare State. To translate these into law would be the task of the first post-war Government. Once this was achieved, the less the State interfered with the individual, and the smaller the programme of legislation submitted to Parliament, the better. This was Churchill's thesis.

The antithesis was Socialism in the guise he believed it must eventually assume. Not, indeed, the Fabian Socialism of Attlee and Bevin or even of Morrison and Cripps; for there was little to distinguish that from Liberalism or progressive Conservatism except for the regrettable addition of an element of nationalisation and a tendency to be too lavish with the taxpayers' money. The Socialism he feared was that foreshadowed by the words written in the Labour Party Creed. Some members of the Party might, like many Christians, dutifully repeat the words of the Creed without accepting the literal meaning of every single sentence; but that was not a safe assumption for the future. State ownership of the means of production, distribution and exchange would one day be sought by a Socialist Government and Churchill was not alone in believing that to be the prescription for totalitarianism. Socialism carried to its logical conclusion would destroy the character of the British people.

Part of Churchill's strength stemmed from his simplicity. He had always had a gift for eliminating the complex and concentrating on the essential. If a particular theme seemed to him to contain an essential truth he would seize on it, play with it like a cat with a mouse, expatiate on it at the dinner table and, provided it stood up satisfactorily to all his own tests, finally offer it to the public. One such theme had settled firmly in his mind as the result of reading two books by Maeterlinck, *The Life of the Bee* and *The Life of the Ant*. The latter in particular, with its description of the orderly, un-thinking regimentation of life in an ant hill, seemed to Churchill a realistic picture of what Society would eventually become under Socialist control.

This was the background of the so-called Gestapo speech, the first of four election broadcasts which Churchill delivered on the BBC. It was all his own composition. Contrary to the general belief, neither Lord Beaverbrook nor Brendan Bracken had a hand in preparing it. He wrote it during a week-end at Chequers and broad-cast it from there on the evening of 4 June, 1945. I sat with him in a little sitting room, hung with Constable landscapes, while he delivered it. I noted with amusement that his gestures to the micro-phone were as emphatic as those he normally used in a public speech to a large audience. For the first time he was speaking to the Country within a given time limit, for the BBC could not allow the Prime Minister one second longer for a Party Political Broadcast than had been approved for all Election Broadcasts. This new and unwelcome restriction on his oratory put Churchill off balance, so that he spoke hurriedly, without the pauses and unscripted inter-polations which had always been a feature of his oratory.

He said what he really believed. 'A Socialist policy is abhorrent to the British ideas of freedom. Although it is now put forward in the main by people who have had a good grounding in the Libera-lism and radicalism of the early part of this century, there can be no doubt that Socialism is inseparately interwoven with totalitarianism and the abject worship of the State. . . . Look how even today they hunger for controls of every kind, as if these were delectable foods instead of war-time necessities. . . . The State is to be the arch-employer, the arch-planner, the arch-administrator and ruler and the arch-caucus boss. . . . But let me tell you that once a Socialist Government begins monkeying with the credit of Britain and trying, without regard to facts, figures or confidence, to manipulate it to Socialist requirements, there is no man or woman in this country who has, by thrift or toil, accumulated a nest-egg, however small, who will not run the risk of seeing it shrivel before their eyes.' He had preceded these remarks by asserting that a Socialist State could only be kept in power by a political police, 'Some form of Gestapo', and that all the power would be gathered 'to the supreme party and the party leaders, rising like stately pinnacles above their vast bureaucracies of Civil Servants, no longer servants and no longer civil.' Churchill was, of course, drawing his conclusions from Soviet Russia, the only country in which the experiment of Marxist Socialism had then been made; for the no less tyrannical Marxist régimes in all the countries of Eastern Europe were still for the most part nightmares of the future. What he did believe was that a Socialist experiment in Britain, however humane and respectful of individual liberty in its early stages, must inexorably evolve into the soul-less régime of the ant hill which Maeterlinck had described.

Hostile criticism of the speech was immediate, even from his own supporters. The Chief Whip, James Stuart, said to me on the telephone after the broadcast: 'If that is the way he wants to conduct the campaign he must decide. He is the Leader of the Party. But it is not my idea of how to win an election.' Yet it must be doubtful whether Churchill's speeches that summer, whatever their content and however delivered, would have made any difference at all to the result. The country wanted a change of Government. The voters had been taught to believe that the nation's unreadiness for war in 1939 had been exclusively the fault of the pre-war National Government. They had been taught this (and had swallowed the story uncritically) by pamphleteers and propagandists like Michael Foot whose own party had done its utmost to retard rearmament, had opposed the doubling of the Territorial Army and, only four months before the outbreak of war, had voted against even a limited measure of conscription. The great majority of the Electorate loved and respected Churchill. They would have voted for him under a Presidential system of Government; but after fourteen years of National Government, with an overwhelming Conservative majority, their instinct for change was understandable and doubtless whole-some, even if their conscious decision to vote Labour may have been taken, at least in part, on false propagandist premises.

I copied the quotations I have made from the first draft of the Gestapo Speech, part of which I kept and still possess. Churchill always consigned the first, corrected drafts of his speeches to the waste-paper basket, retaining only the text from which he spoke.

Socialist Government conducting the entire life and

industry of the country could afford to have *allow* free, sharp

or even violent *violently worded* expression of public discontent.　They

would have to fall back on some form of Gestapo, no doubt

very humanely directed in the first instance.　This woul

nip opinion in the bud;　it would stop criticism as it

reared its head and it would gather/to the supreme Party *all the power*

and the Party leaders, rising like stately pinnacles abov

their vast bureaucracies of *civil* servants no longer, civil. *servants & no longer*

And where would the ordinary simple folk - the common

people, as they like to call them in America , be, once

this mighty organism had got them in their grip? I am

not against this nation or against that.　I am against

tyranny, in whatever liveries it marches or slogans it

mouths.　I stand for the sovereign freedom of the

individual; against any Government, however powerful

which is against the rights of the ordinary man to say

what he thinks of the government of the day, and to turn

them out, neck and crop, if he thinks he can better his

temper or his home thereby But, you will say, look at what has been done in

*A sheet of the amended typescript of the Gestapo speech retrieved from the
waste-paper basket.*

Keeping relics and mementoes is, I suppose, almost as reprehensible a habit as keeping a diary; but it is one to which I used to have a guilty addiction. Having extracted from the waste-paper basket part of this text, and having previously appropriated a draft of one of the famous war speeches, my conscience was uneasy. It was the more so because although I should have to be on the bread-line before selling either, I realised after the war that these two documents would have a high market value. So I decided to confess and to offer restitution.

The opportunity came one day at 28 Hyde Park Gate, where Churchill lived after the war. We were lunching alone together and I confessed my delinquency. He was silent a full minute, looking at me intently with those penetrating eyes. Then he said: 'I think you are one of the Wise Virgins.'

37. Balkan Blues

At the end of 1945 I went back to the Foreign Office where I was placed in the Southern Department with responsibility for our relations with Yugoslavia. Marshal Tito had consolidated his mastery of the Serbs, Croats and Slovenes, had nonchalantly discarded his obligations to the Allies, to King Peter and to the lawful Government in London, had captured and was about to hang his former rival Mihailovic and was only prevented from annexing Trieste by the forceful obstruction of Field Marshal Alexander's army. It was a cheerless parish to administer.

London, too, was cheerless. Rationing was even more severe than during the war, the people were grey and disgruntled, wine and spirits were unobtainable, and the squares and streets were disfigured by jagged gaps which the bombs had left. The elation of victory was already forgotten. Travel was restricted by a pitiful foreign exchange allowance, but reports were received of gaiety and rapidly returning plenty in Paris and even in the cities of our lately defeated enemies, the Italians. Germany alone presented a scene of starker misery, and the Government's brave talk of a fairer society and the equal division of the national cake did nothing to make the people happier. The new Chancellor of the Exchequer, Sir Stafford Cripps, was known to be a man of honesty, sincerity and deep religious faith. He was also suspected of believing that the hair shirts which he chose for his own wardrobe should be manufactured and distributed to the whole community. There was a Limerick which expressed the feelings of many:

> It was gay in the days of Maid Marian
> E'er we'd heard of the word proletarian,
> But our land's in eclipse
> In the grips of old Cripps,
> That teetotal totalitarian.

The Colours Change

The Foreign Office was still much as I had known it before the war, except that it no longer waited till 11.00 a.m. to open its doors. There was friendliness, high intelligence, a touch of cynicism, a deep reverence for the Secretary of State (by this time Ernest Bevin), a readiness of wit and a capacity for laughter. There was also an almost unbearable load of work. Because of some administrative error, the affairs of Yugoslavia had been left untended for a full three weeks before my arrival at my new desk and the backlog was vast. As quickly as I emptied trays and boxes they filled up again. I felt less harassed if I disposed first of the fattest files, but these often contained the least important papers, while the thinner ones were sometimes urgent. People started to ring up angrily about letters or telegrams to which I had not even penetrated. For six months I took cases full of papers home every night and worked till 2.00 or 3.00 a.m. I could well believe that life had been gayer in the days of Maid Marian.

Some of the members of the new Administration suffered from illusions. One of the junior Ministers asked me to go and see him. He had before him a blistering minute I had written about the Yugoslav Government's oppressive measures.

'Mr Colville,' he said, 'I do want to impress on you that times have changed. The People's Democratic Republics in Eastern Europe represent the hopes and aspirations of a new world. I know that it is difficult for people like you and others in the Service, with the background and upbringing you have had, to realise that Europe, this country and the whole world have changed. We in the Labour Movement make full allowance for the time it will take you to adjust your outlook; but do, please, try to see what magnificent possibilities lie ahead for the Yugoslav people and for us all.'

The illusions did not last long. A year later, after drafting endless notes to the Yugoslavs, which were good practice for rhetoric but achieved no practical result whatever, I wrote a paper suggesting a change of tactics. We might see whether limited co-operation and a more friendly attitude would reduce the hostility. One day it could well prove that Tito was not quite so firmly tied to Stalin's apron strings as we all supposed. We should prepare for a crack, however improbable, in the granite of the block which the Russians had

hewn. The next day the same Junior Minister asked me to go and
see him.

'Jock', he said (for we were now on Christian name terms), 'I
wonder if you realise how unreasonable these people are, how
totally impervious to argument, how immune from the finer and
kinder feelings? They are obsessed by the inevitability of political
developments, by the doctrine of economic determination which
Marxism lays down. I can assure you it is a waste of time to make
gestures of friendship and goodwill. They respect nothing but
strength.'

In addition to drafting long and fruitless diplomatic notes, which
gave full scope to my vocabulary (and were doubtless untranslate-
able into Serbo–Croat), I did have one serious and worrying ploy.
When the British troops in Italy captured Yugoslavs whose names
appeared on the Allied list of War Criminals, Tito's Government
demanded that they be returned for punishment, which usually
meant execution, not necessarily by the quickest available method.
It was the policy of the Allies to hand back the captured nationals of
any allied country who could be proved to have fought with the
Germans; but in the case of Yugoslavs it had been decided that
Allied Forces Headquarters at Caserta should first seek instructions
from the Foreign Office in each individual case, for Tito's men were
known to have massacred in cold blood a large body of Croat
soldiers whom the Allies had refused to accept as political refugees
when the fighting ended. It usually fell to me, in effect, to make the
decision and I much disliked the task. The Yugoslav Government
complained bitterly that we were sheltering pro-Nazi traitors, their
hands red with the blood of innocent peasants and gallant freedom-
fighters. Left-wing MPs, Mr Kingsley Martin of the *New Statesman*
and other well-meaning but ignorant observers maintained that if
we returned the guilty men, they would be submitted to a gentle
course of re-education and then take their place, as free but
reformed citizens, in the new Utopian state.

We were, of course, hardened by six years of war. Death was
no stranger and condign punishment for war crimes was the policy
accepted by almost everybody. Yet it is difficult to sleep well after
signing a letter which may condemn a man to die. I made a decision.
I refused to allow the repatriation of any Chetniks, the guerrillas

who had fought under General Mihailovic, even when it was clear
they had collaborated with the Italians and even when the Yugoslav
Ambassador came round in person to protest that we were breaking
our pledge to return traitors. I did agree to hand back some, though
by no means all, of the fanatic Croat Ustasi, but only if there was
well-attested evidence that they had been guilty of massacre and
brutal terrorist crime.

I was released in some degree from these unrewarding and, on
occasions, ghoulish duties by being selected as Assistant Head of the
Southern Department. This meant that Roumania, Bulgaria,
Hungary and Albania, where even viler oppression and much nastier
tortures were practised than in Yugoslavia, were added to my
responsibility. I was like a curate in charge of a group of parishes in
every one of which he knows the Black Mass is celebrated daily.
There was, however, one – Greece – where, largely thanks to
Churchill's timely intervention, there was no Black Mass and, at
least temporarily, a constitutional Monarchy with Parliamentary
Government was established. This had its disadvantages, because in
consequence we had to pay attention to what the Greek Government said, and they were already beginning to say embarrassing
things about Cyprus.

One day I wrote a memorandum suggesting that as in the long run
we should probably have to abandon Cyprus, it would save a lot
of trouble if we did so right away, on condition that the British
were allowed to retain their military bases in full sovereignty and
local autonomy was provided for the small Turkish minority. The
Head of my Department, William Hayter, thought well of the
memorandum, but I did not expect it to go further than Christopher
Warner, the Under-Secretary overseeing the Southern Department.
I thought he would be interested by the argument but would strongly
deprecate the conclusion. If by any chance he sent it further along
the hierarchic corridor, there was a sure long-stop in the person of
Sir Orme Sargent, Permanent Under-Secretary of State, who could
be counted on to return it with a good-humoured but cynical
comment.

None of these things happened. I don't know what came over Mr
Warner and Sir Orme, but when my memorandum returned to me
they had merely written their names in full under William Hayter's

and mine and sent it up to the Secretary of State.

The telephone rang. Mr Bevin wished to see me. I had known him well, and respected him greatly, at No. 10 during the war. In my new, lowly position in the Foreign Office, I had been nowhere near the great man.

'Look 'ere, Colville, what is all this nonsense you've written about Cyprus? Churchill said Cyprus was British and on things like that Churchill is always right. While I'm Secretary of State, Cyprus stays British. And, I say, you're looking rather peaky. You ought to 'ave a 'oliday. 'ose the 'ead of your Department?'

'William Hayter, Sir'.

'Well, go and tell 'ayter from me that you're to 'ave a 'oliday. Take my advice: go to 'ove. The air at 'ove is wonderful. Mrs Bevin and I went there last year and it did us all the good in the world. Now, be a good boy, go off to 'ove and when you come back you won't look 'alf so peaky and you'll stop writing all that bloody nonsense about Cyprus'.

It is not surprising that the members of the Foreign Service, who once upon a time used almost always to worship their Secretary of State, did so with particular fervour in the case of Ernest Bevin.

38. Burgess and Maclean

When I knew Guy Burgess at Cambridge, he never pretended to be anything but a Communist. He wore a high polo-necked jersey and looked unwashed, which were notable Party badges in those days; and though he made no pretence to like proletarian company, and indeed revelled in the flesh-pots, he professed dedication to the destruction of the political system and the social order. He hoped for a Fellowship at Trinity but was not quite up to the intellectual standard required.

I made Donald Maclean's acquaintance when I joined the Foreign Office. He, too, walking across St James's Park on the way to lunch, would profess that he was a Communist. He was good looking and I remember seeing him, dressed in a tail coat and a white tie, leaning against a pillar during a great ball at Dudley House. He was surrounded by a throng of entranced débutantes to whom he was explaining his political philosophy. One of them said: 'But why, Donald, if you feel like that, do you come to this sort of party?'

'Because', he replied, 'the more people do so, the quicker the system will be discredited'.

And yet when Maclean and Burgess fled to Russia, all their acquaintances and most of their friends were astonished. Indeed, the senior ranks of the Foreign Office declared they did not even know they were Communists. Burgess, though much liked by the Minister of State, Hector McNeil, and by Harold Nicolson, was not generally admired; but Maclean was the blue-eyed boy of the Diplomatic Service, regarded by everybody, including successive Secretaries of State, as the brightest and best of his age-group. Their contemporaries, knowing well that in the 1930s Communism was the fashionable creed at the Universities, assumed that like most other intelligent people of the same generation they had grown out of it.

I shared the general astonishment, at least in the case of Burgess, because of one incident.

In 1946, while I was still working in the Southern Department of the Foreign Office and dealing with the much-vexed Balkans, terrible things were happening there, by no means for the first time in their chequered history. In the House of Commons there were some thirty pro-Communist Labour MPs who believed, or affected to believe, that the spotlessly pure governments of Bulgaria, Roumania and the rest were being constantly maligned through the machinations of the reactionaries in the Foreign Office. These MPs were known as Fellow-Travellers and they were cordially disliked by the Foreign Secretary, Ernest Bevin, and by the Minister of State, Hector McNeil. The dislike was returned and they devoted a lot of effort to putting down Parliamentary Questions which might cause embarrassment. Both Bevin and McNeil were realistic and resolute men on whom the Fellow-Travellers' shock tactics had no effect whatever, but this did nothing to diminish their persistence.

The Bulgarians had recently condemned to death and executed a middle-of-the-road, strongly anti-fascist (but also anti-communist) politician called Petkov. His crime was that he did not admire Stalin and was in favour of honest and fair elections in Bulgaria. His party also enjoyed much more popular support than did the Communist Party, and this in itself was sufficient to warrant a death sentence.

Petkov's execution gave rise to an impotent outcry in the West. One of the dedicated Fellow-Travellers at once felt bound to put down a Question, no doubt intending to declare in supplementary questions that Petkov deserved no sympathy and that the Bulgarian Government should receive praise rather than obloquy. It fell to me to draft the reply which Hector McNeil would give.

In order to procure evidence against Petkov, who had displayed a totally incorrect and unacceptable unwillingness to confess, his secretary was seized by the Bulgarian police. She was a young girl, but she must have been intolerably obstinate because she died rather than incriminate Petkov. Her body was exhumed by her friends and relations and a detailed account of what the political Inquisitors had done to her was smuggled out of the country. It reached the Foreign Office.

I need not have feared that Hector McNeil would deal mildly or apologetically with his questioner; but I felt that if even Homer sometimes nodded, so Hector might just conceivably have an off-day or be smitten by some improbable notion about appeasing the Left Wing of his own party. So I attached to my draft reply the account of what had been done to Petkov's secretary, put the documents in a red box and rang for a messenger to take it along to the Minister of State.

An hour later Guy Burgess, who was McNeil's Secretary, stumped into my room. He was shaking with emotion. Hector, he said, must read this nauseating document to the House. He hated to know that such vile men existed; but since they did, their abominations must be revealed to the entire world. I told him it was impossible: otherwise the friends and relations who had exhumed the girl's body would suffer as she had. With tears rolling down his cheeks he begged me to think how justice might be done, how these villainies might be exposed and checked. Sadly, he walked back to his office declaring that his only aim from now onwards would be, with Hector's help, to see justice done.

So I, too, was surprised when he defected to Russia, especially as Stalin was still conducting the music and the Bulgarian Government was still performing the role of a savage dancing bear.

39. A Pearl Necklace

On 20 November, 1947, Princess Elizabeth was married. For the first time since the end of the war a little colour and pageantry were restored to a country, and indeed to a world, in the grey grip of austerity. Food, petrol and clothes were still severely rationed. Although bombs no longer fell, there were large unfilled gaps in the London streets and squares, and it was years since a coat of paint had been applied to public or private buildings. Suddenly romance returned: a beautiful young Princess was marrying a handsome Prince and all the stories in the Fairy Tale books were coming true. Vast crowds assembled; the Blues and the Life Guards put on full dress uniforms for the first time since 1939; and magnificent carriages emerged from the Royal Mews, the horses glistening and the coachmen and postilions resplendent in State Livery. The war, it seemed, really was over.

I had recently been appointed Private Secretary to Princess Elizabeth and was to drive in her procession to Westminster Abbey. So I put on my discarded RAF uniform since, except for the Household Cavalry, Service Dress was the order of the day, and contrived to reach Buckingham Palace through the Electricians' Entrance, far removed from the excited and almost impenetrable throng in front of the Palace. There were to be two processions to Westminster Abbey: first the Queen and representatives of every Royal family in Europe; and then the King, driving with his daughter and followed by carriages containing her Household. All had been arranged with that precision and efficiency which no other country in the world has ever contrived to equal on State Occasions.

Half an hour before the Queen's procession was due to leave, I received an urgent summons to go to Princess Elizabeth's sitting room. She stood there, radiant and entrancing in her wedding dress. One thing and one only had gone wrong. The superb pearl necklace which the King had given her had been left with the other presents at St James's Palace, where they were to be on display to the public, and she particularly wanted to wear her father's present at her wedding. Could I, somehow, make my way to St James's Palace and retrieve the necklace?

I looked at my watch. I rushed along the corridor. I galloped down the Grand Staircase and into the main quadrangle of Buckingham Palace. Take any car, the Princess had called after me. So I ran towards a large Royal Daimler. 'To St James's Palace', I cried to the chauffeur, and I flung open the door of the car. Before I could leap in, a tall elderly man, ablaze with Orders and Decorations, began to emerge. It was King Haakon VII of Norway. 'You seem in a hurry, young man', he said. 'By all means have my car, but do let me get out first'.

The Daimler sped through the forecourt and down the Mall, but the police had allowed the crowds to fill the road across Marlborough Gate and they were at least fifteen deep. There was nothing for it but to bid the car remain in the Mall and to force my way on foot through the close-knit crowd. I ran as fast as I could to Friary Court, St James's Palace. All was still and there was not a living soul to be seen. I rang the doorbell and nothing happened. I rang again and after a minute or two a suspicious face appeared as the door opened a few inches. I was asked what my business might be. My story sounded improbable and the ancient janitor evidently thought it so. He was clearly undecided, so that I began to wonder whether to push him aside and force an entry. Finally he let me in with a warning that upstairs, guarding the wedding presents, I should find representatives of the CID.

There, indeed, they were: several dour but well-built young men who were obviously going to stand no nonsense. I told my story again. They were in a quandary. If I were telling the truth and they declined to let me take the pearls, there would be trouble. If, on the other hand, I were a brazen burglar and they did allow me to steal some of the Crown Jewels, there would be still greater trouble. They looked blank; they glared at me and at each other; two of them held a whispered conference. I suggested they should ring up Buckingham Palace, for the switchboard would know my voice. The line was dead. I insisted that time was running out and that I must be back, with the pearls, before the first procession left for the

Abbey. Finally, in desperation the Senior Officer said: 'What is your name?' I told him and he referred to the Wedding Programme. 'Yes,' he said, 'that coincides with the name in the official programme'; and he allowed me to take the pearls.

Perhaps, as I forced my way back to the car, pushing and apologising, with one hand firmly pressed against the pocket of my tunic where the pearls lay, the Senior Officer may have reflected that any enterprising thief could have put on the uniform of a Flight Lieutenant, RAF and bought, for one shilling, a Souvenir Programme which included the name of Princess Elizabeth's Private Secretary. If so, he must have been relieved when the evening papers appeared with photographs of the Princess, in her bridal gown and wearing the pearls.

40. A Portuguese Interlude

In 1949 I went as Head of Chancery to the British Embassy in Portugal. One October morning my wife and I leaned over the rail of RMS *Andes* as she glided up the estuary of the Tagus. There are few more soothingly beautiful cities than Lisbon approached from the sea, and many that are as monotonously dreary when approached by car from the airport. In 1949 there was no vast bridge to violate the natural majesty of the Tagus: just the seven hills of Lisbon, crowned by castles and cupolas, and the romantic fortresses of St Julian, Belem and St George. San Francisco and its Golden Gates cannot compare with Lisbon, and even Istanbul must yield pride of place.

It was not an easy town in which to find accommodation, and we finally came to rest in a pink villa at Estoril, well-known to the gossip-writers since nearly all the Pretenders to the thrones of Europe had assembled there. They presented a social problem because if invited to dine they expected to act as host and sit at the head of the table, a pretension which His Majesty's Ambassador quite rightly declined to countenance in the British Embassy; and some of them refused to be seen in the same company as the others. Thus King Carol of Roumania and his wife, the former Madame Lupescu, could not be asked to meet the Count of Barcelona, the Comte de Paris or the ex-King of Italy; and Admiral Horthy, formerly Regent of Hungary, was acceptable to none of them, not even to King Carol. In a severely restricted society, which the immoral might penetrate but not the divorced, all this led to social imbroglios. Fortunately such problems, though inescapable by diplomats in a country where protocol loomed large, form was all-important and Society was small, were a source of amusement rather than a preoccupation.

We had an even closer 'special relationship' with the Portuguese than with the Americans. They were, after all, our oldest allies, although we had treated them scurvily from time to time, especially in respect of the colonial carve-up of Africa. That was forgiven and all but forgotten, in spite of Lord Halifax having, as late as 1938, airily suggesting satisfying Hitler's demand for a place in the colonial sun by handing some of the Portuguese colonies over to Germany. The British Embassy was indeed the busiest of all the Embassies: there were endless matters of common concern, and occasionally of dispute, in Africa south of the Sahara; there was a strong trading relationship; there was a large British colony and many old established British firms; there was European Defence and our joint membership of NATO; and there were regular visits by the Royal Navy. Our total staff, from the Ambassador down to the Messengers, was thirty-five. During one of our periodic economic crises, I was instructed by the Treasury to cut the staff by 10% and I received an indignant rebuke when I wrote to ask whether 3.5 meant four as in Auction Bridge, or three as in Contract Bridge.

The American Embassy, which had fewer interests and much less work, numbered 275, whose office hours were longer than we found necessary for our multifarious activities. They included an Agricultural Attaché who was a man of charm and intelligence. He had a staff of five.

'What do they do?', I asked him.

'Well, just now they are analysing the quality of the wheat harvest in the Alentejo province.'

'Where do they get the information?'

'From the newspapers, of course'.

'What will be done with your report when it gets to Washington?'

'It will be filed, no doubt, in the Library of Congress'.

This great American presence and the goodwill which accompanied it was of undoubted value to Portugal, both economically and politically. Some American visitors were less so, for Portuguese susceptibilities were easily disturbed. When Cardinal Spellman paid a visit to the shrine at Fatima, by which he was deeply moved, he gave an account of his experience to a ship-load of Holy Year pilgrims bound for Rome. He ended his remarks by saying: 'And if Our Lady can do all this for a small country like Portugal, what couldn't she do for the great United States?' The local Americans were much amused, for there are no people so healthily prone to criticise and laugh at themselves; but the story was widely reported and the Portuguese were incensed.

Relations with the French were friendly but formal. The elderly French Ambassador, Monsieur du Sault, lived in a magnificent palace which had been seized by the Napoleonic Marshal, the Duc d'Abrantes, and never relinquished after the French defeat. One night we were asked to dine. My wife, who speaks entirely adequate French, panicked at the thought of speaking it to a purist like Monsieur du Sault who might well, by his grave and distinguished mien, have been a member of the Académie Française. So she talked to him all through dinner in Portuguese. For weeks thereafter the French Embassy were up in arms. They were convinced this had been a deliberate attempt by the British, doubtless made on direct instructions from the Foreign Office, to show that French was no longer the diplomatic language. The Portuguese were delighted.

The British Ambassador was Sir Nigel Ronald. A diplomat of the old school, so severely wounded in the First War that his health never fully recovered, he was an erudite bibliophile, knew almost every bar of music in every classical composition and was one of those passionate gardeners who regard the cultivation of rare but dull shrubs as more rewarding than a blaze of colour. He laid playful intellectual traps for his diplomatic staff, who bore this habit with resignation, and extended it to their wives who did not. He assumed that the Service Attachés were illiterate and so let them off lightly. He took the wise view that the more we were all out of the Chancery, learning about the country and its people, the better we were doing our job; and we all regarded him with bemused admiration and affection. So, which was more important, did Dr Salazar, for both were scholars and there was a genuine meeting of minds. Nigel Ronald was the only foreign Ambassador whom Salazar, aloof, unsociable recluse that he was, received with unfailing regularity.

There were indeed few foreigners who ever had the chance of meeting the redoubtable Doctor; but he did make an exception for important Ecclesiastical dignitaries and it was thus that, by pure chance, I once spent two hours with him. The Ambassador was away, and the Counsellor was on a tour, when the Roman Catholic Archbishop of Sydney called at the Embassy. He wished, he said, to

meet Dr Salazar. Could I arrange it? I explained politely that he
might just as well try to go to the moon (which nobody then had)
but that I would enquire. To my astonishment the reply came that
Salazar would be glad to receive the Archbishop and that somebody
from the Embassy should accompany him. That somebody might,
I thought, just as well be me.

We drove to the small fort of St John, on the sea near Estoril,
where the Dictator lived in a modest style verging on austerity.
He greeted the Archbishop with the humble deference he considered due to a high ecclesiastic and invited us to sit with him out
of doors, in upright chairs, looking over a balustrade at the sea. We
conversed for two hours on theology, philosophy and the government of mankind and never once did Salazar give any indication of
spiritual pride or intellectual arrogance. The depth of his learning
was evident, but not more so than his eagerness to discuss things
on an equal footing and to add still more to his learning by listening
to the experience of others. As ruler of Portugal he would brook
no opposition and no indiscipline. He was the schoolmaster who
alone knew what was right and wholesome for his pupils, and he had
no mercy on the wilful or the disobedient. Yet his intentions were
entirely benevolent and his patriotism was fiercely sincere. Seeking
no material gain for himself, he had brought unprecedented prosperity to a country which, when he first came to power in 1928,
had been torn by eighteen years of civil strife, parliamentary chaos
and economic disaster. He loved his people; he strove with all his
might to do the best for them; but he never trusted them and he
denied them the one thing they craved, liberty. All the same, as the
Archbishop and I drove away from the fort, we knew we had been
in the presence of rare greatness and still rarer personal humility.

One thing Salazar had signally failed to achieve was an acceptable
level of social justice. The rich were only moderately so by comparison with other countries. The middle class was a growing body,
flourishing contentedly in what had become a preponderantly
consumer society, sustained not by industry or agriculture, but by
the accummulation of war profits, the remittances of Portuguese
citizens working in other lands and the produce of the African
colonies. The poor, however, were miserable and destitute and
although I am sure Salazar would have wished to improve their lot,

I doubt whether in his ivory academic tower he had any conception what dire poverty means. Nor, indeed, have many of us; but we may have a clearer vision of it than an isolated professor; and perhaps Plato was wrong in maintaining that all would be well with the world when philosophers were kings.

Portugal under Salazar was more akin to the Enlightened Despotisms of the late 18th century than to the dictatorships of the 20th. The fear, the whispering, the anxious look over the shoulder, the nagging anxiety that a man's friends or even his own children might betray him; all the detestable terror of Nazi Germany, Fascist Italy and Soviet Russia which I had sensed in my travels to those countries before the war, and which lay so heavily in the atmosphere that I remember vividly how fresh the air seemed on crossing the frontier into a free country; none of this was to be found in Portugal, nor for that matter in Spain. Certainly those who dabbled in politics, or insisted on expressing publicly views that were unacceptable to the régime, risked penalties for offences that were not, by our standards, offences at all. But the penalties bore no comparison with those inflicted by the Nazi and Communist dictatorships and it was only in exceptional cases that the hand of the political policeman fell anything but lightly on the shoulder.

Poor though so many of them were, the friendliness of the Portuguese artisans and labourers was immediately noticeable. We had been in the country only a few weeks when our car broke down on a lonely stretch of road high in the Serra da Estrela, the Mountain of the Stars. There was not much daylight left and the mountains were still inhabited by wolves. Leaving my wife in the car, I walked a mile or so until I came to a village. As yet I spoke but little Portuguese and I was met with total indifference by the villagers who shrugged their shoulders and made it clear that the garage was closed for the night. Then they discovered I was English. In a moment all was changed. The entire population marched back with me along the mountain road and pushed the car up hill to the village where the garage was miraculously found to be open and entirely competent repairs were made by lamplight. I had difficulty in persuading the garage to accept a few escudos in payment. What nationality they had taken me for in the first place, I never discovered.

Portugal will never lose its romance. There is no land except Greece where the evening light is so ethereal. There are few landscapes which surpass the valley of the Douro. The craftsmanship of the people and its perfectionism are hard to match in the modern world. The country is small and it is poor; but the people were the first of all the navigators, the discoverers, the colonists and the missionaries. They became the prisoners of their own history so that it was their pride in their unequalled pioneering record which long prevented them from facing the facts of twentieth century life. They hung tenaciously and disastrously to their Colonial Empire long after the British, the French, the Belgians and the Dutch had voluntarily renounced theirs. In so doing they believed they were obeying a manifest and historically ordained destiny and I am sure this belief weighed even more with Dr Salazar than did the material benefits of the Portuguese Colonial system. When I was in Portugal the fly was firmly embedded in the amber and it took another twenty-five years, bewildering to the Portuguese and finally most painful, to dislodge it.

41. Portuguese Colonial Rule

The British Consulates in the Portuguese colonies reported to the Embassy, but such was the parsimony of the Treasury that no member of the Embassy staff had ever been allowed to visit them. This was scarcely sensible, for much of our work had a direct or indirect bearing on those colonies. Fortunately the Air Attaché, Cecil Garton, had established a close friendship with the Chief of the Portuguese Air Staff, by whose good offices a journey to Angola was arranged for Cecil and me at no cost at all to His Majesty's particularly stingy Government. It meant travelling in an ancient aircraft by slow hops down the west coast of Africa, often flying at sea level to avoid storm clouds we could not surmount and spending nights at primitive ports of call such as Villa Cisneros where there were tame cheetahs tied up by the city gate for use in pursuit of thieves and nocturnal marauders. Eventually, after a day in the Island of St. Tomé, where contract labourers from Angola were forced to work in the plantations, we arrived at Luanda, the capital of the Province. From there we flew in a small aeroplane the length and breadth of Angola, sometimes staying with missionaries and sometimes accommodated in the small towns of the interior. I made a study of Portuguese colonial methods which, like so much else in Portugal, were based on historical rather than pragmatic considerations.

Brazil did not abolish slavery until after 1889 when the last Emperor, who was also an eminent scientist, lost his throne because he was opposed to slavery. His republican successors were unable to resist international pressures and so in spite of their victory over the Emperor, slavery had to go. This was doubtless a relief to the natives of Angola and Mozambique, who had long been the main source of the illegal Brazilian supply; but by the beginning of the 20th century the two larger Portuguese colonies, and Angola in particular, were sparsely populated by tribes genetically as well as numerically weakened through forcible removal of their more vigorous members to Brazil.

At the time of our visit Angola was little known to foreigners. There was the British-owned Benguela Railway, which the Ambassador had specifically charged us to visit because he believed that, with its terminus on the Atlantic seaboard, it should be the natural outlet for Rhodesian copper; and De Beers had been casting acquisitive eyes on some diamond mines recently discovered in the north. Otherwise it was a country of forests and great rolling plains which, we thought, were well suited to turn Angola into the cattle-raising Argentine of Africa if problems of water supply could be resolved. In all this vast territory, bigger in area than Nigeria and five times the size of the United Kingdom, there were scarcely five million inhabitants. Even though parts of the north were tsetse-fly country, there was fertile space for development and expansion such as few parts of the world could offer.

In remote parts of the country the Portuguese had started to build cities with evocative names such as Nova Lisboa and Silva Goa. They had set about it in an original way. There would be a church, a town-hall, a Court of Justice and several other public buildings, all well built and attractively designed; but no houses. The houses, they explained, would follow when people decided to move there. It was, after all, part of Portugal: the overseas territories were an extension of the home country and an integral part of it. Indigent farmers and unemployed agricultural labourers from Portugal were being brought out to settle. Each was given land, the necessary agricultural tools and a little money. Unhappily, as an old Canadian missionary said to me: 'The soil of Africa corrupts the white man and he soon disdains to use his hands'. The tools were there, but before many months had passed the immigrant peasant, accustomed all his life to toil on the land, was paying primitive, hungry tribesmen a pittance to do the work for him.

In their anxiety to transform Angola into part of Portugal itself, and to endow thousands of their fellow-countrymen with a stake in the country, the Government was obliged to consider what to do about the native inhabitants who were, after all, Portuguese too. The Portuguese minded less than any other European race about miscegenation, and a glance at the passers-by in any Lisbon street reveals that this has been so for centuries. Arabs, Phoenicians, Anglo–Saxons, Africans and Indians have all mixed their blood with that of the native Iberian. Thus inter-marriage would in time help to solve the problem and there were already many half-caste children to be seen in Luanda.

In the meanwhile practical measures must be taken. An African who showed above-average ability could become an Assimilado. This entitled him to wear European clothes and to enjoy the privileges of the Europeans. It had the incidental advantage of neutralising the potential organisers of nationalist discontent, since it was natural for most Assimilados to feel aloof from those of their fellow-tribesmen who had done less well in life. As for the re-mainder, it was thought important to have a cheap work force on the plantations and so Contract Labour was introduced. This meant that, often against their wish, young men were forcibly removed from the villages, and sometimes from their wives and children, to work as indentured labourers for a period of years in the Island of St. Tomé or some distant part of Angola. Recalcitrance was dis-couraged by an implement called the palmatorio, shaped like a table-tennis racket, drilled with a number of holes and applied to the palm of the hand with such vigour that the holes raised the flesh off the palm.

In the towns there were a limited number of school places for African children. Those who obtained them did not suffer racial discrimination, for all colours sat in the same classes. One head-master told me that the black and the white children got on admirably together; they united in bullying the half-castes, who were the least amenable of the three. In the Bush the Government provided neither schools nor hospitals, but their responsibility was assumed with diligence and true Christian charity by a variegated body of missionaries. There were Seventh Day Adventists from Canada, using modern hospital equipment in a remote forest and apparently possessed of a bottomless purse; there were no less worthy and well-heeled Wesleyans from Ohio; there was a Kirk, with school and medical unit attached, in a most improbable setting; there were French and Belgian nuns surrounded by swarms of laughing children; there was a German Pastor who was fighting a ding-dong battle with a Witch Doctor for the souls of his parishioners. They formed an international body of dedicated and selfless men and women, some well supplied from home, others struggling in poverty to teach, to heal and to inspire; and having seen them, I have never felt any sympathy for ill-natured criticism of missionary interference. Those who despair of humanity would profit from a visit to missionary centres in the remoter parts of Africa.

After weeks of travelling we returned to Luanda where we were invited, as an act of great courtesy and generosity, to finish our tour with a Safari in the north. It was tsetse country though it was the time of year when the pernicious creatures hibernate. We should, in consequence, be marching through uninhabited country. It was the old-fashioned type of Safari, and the objective was to capture a baby elephant for the Lisbon Zoo. There was a diminutive white hunter, a sporting zoologist, Cecil Garton, myself and forty bearers. There were no mechanical vehicles and everything was carried on the backs of the forty bearers. It lasted seven days and we saw no other human beings.

Being terrified of snakes, Cecil and I had acquired knee-length boots which were likely to be uncomfortable in the tropical heat. We were therefore surprised that the white hunter was wearing a pair of sand-shoes without stockings. 'Are there no snakes?' I asked. 'The most poisonous in all Africa,' he replied. 'But you won't see them. They will hear you coming and run away'. With some misgivings I removed my boots.

For much of the time we walked through grass so tall that it was impossible to see anything on either side, following a path trampled down for us by a herd of elephants walking in single file. Sometimes we forded fast flowing rivers, carried piggy-back by the porters. Occasionally we penetrated tulgy woods, in one of which I came across a python sleeping on a bough. I was keen not to wake him up. Each morning we started at first light and walked grimly on until, about an hour before sunset, our guide would lead us to one of the small woods with which the countryside was dotted. The porters drew their pangas and in ten minutes cleared the thick undergrowth so that a huge fire could be lit and our camp-beds erected on a patch of bare ground. An antelope or one of the dangerous dwarf buffalo with which the country abounded would be stalked and the steaks cooked for dinner. The water was said to be dangerous, but numerous casks and a generous supply of alcohol were included in the porters' load.

The day came when the white hunter, placing his hand on some elephant droppings, announced that they were warm and that the herd was close at hand. An hour later an advance patrol of two Africans came stealthily back to tell us that our long hunt was over: the herd had halted half a mile ahead. The track made by the beasts divided on each side of a deep wooded gully. I went to the left, with the white hunter and the two African patrol men. Cecil Garton and the sporting zoologist took the right-hand track; while the forty wise porters dropped their burdens and swarmed up trees.

We walked on and on, as quietly as we could, until the white hunter, signalling to me to continue on my way, disappeared into a thicket in search of a tree from the top of which he hoped to see exactly where the herd had gone. The two Africans were well ahead, out of my sight, and so clutching my rifle I went on alone. I had not gone far when the Africans came racing back, their eyes dilated with terror and crying, as they shot past me, 'Arranca, Arranca', which I took to mean: 'He is charging'. I stood hesitantly still and, sure enough, there appeared about thirty yards in front of me a huge cow elephant, with a calf by her side. Her ears were flapping angrily and she stood gazing at me with understandable dislike. I raised my heavy rifle, conscious that in order to kill, a frontal shot must hit a small target area above and between the eyes. Kill it I must, for a wounded elephant would make short work of me, and there was no white hunter to fire a second shot if I missed. My hands were shaking violently and I was totally incapable of holding the rifle steady. The sights swung from one elephantine ear to the other. A 17th-century Muscovite proverb asserts that though flight is contrary to honour, it is good for the health. That afternoon I became a convert to Muscovite philosophy. It was the first time that I had ever been acutely conscious of physical cowardice; but an aggressive Messerschmitt is a mild hazard by comparison with an angry elephant, and for the moment honour stood low in my list of priorities. But where to fly? An elephant, unlike a rhinoceros, charges with its eyes fixed on its objective, turns to right or left with athletic alacrity and roots up any small tree which its opponent contrives to climb. Survival depended on hitting the vital spot and the uncontrollable swing of my rifle made that solution improbable.

Inexplicably the lady stopped flapping her ears and lowered her angry trunk. She turned round and with the calf still beside her ambled slowly away. My hands stopped trembling and now, without much doubt, I could have killed her, for a bullet in an elephant's anus is as mortal as one between the eyes. But she had spared my life and in spite of five days' foot-slogging for the sole purpose of shooting an elephant, I laid down my rifle. As I did so, there was a sound of thunder as the remainder of the herd, having suddenly winded our party, stampeded away. There was no baby elephant for the Lisbon Zoo; and I was in disgrace.

When I returned to Lisbon I wrote a paper about the Portuguese Colonial system. It was sent to London where, I expect, it suffered the same fate as my American friend's report on the wheat harvest in the Alentejo province, except that instead of being filed in the Library of Congress it was probably consigned to oblivion in the Foreign Office Registry.

42. A Gallant Failure

The Conservatives won the 1951 General Election and Winston Churchill invited me to return to 10 Downing Street. He had become Prime Minister for the first time by the declared choice of the electorate, and he set his sights on renewing the intimate relationship with the President of the United States which had made such a contribution to success in the Second World War. Truman was still President and Churchill, having established a basis of friendship with him at the Potsdam Conference, had cemented it firmly in 1946 when the two men travelled together to Fulton, playing poker in the Presidential Train, and Churchill delivered the famous Iron Curtain speech.

On returning to Office he did not seek to establish such a frequent exchange of letters and telegrams as he had had with Roosevelt, but he was determined to maintain close personal contact and he let it be known that the American Ambassador in London, alone of foreign representatives, might have direct access to him at 10 Downing Street. However, there was no longer a World War, but only the tail end of the conflict in Korea. The American Government, though privately convinced that Britain was their closest and most reliable ally, were determined not to parade publicly the display of a special relationship. Furthermore, Winston Churchill, though always received with affection by the Americans, was regarded as a dangerous wizard by some and an old-fashioned Imperialist by others. There was, as John Foster Dulles once admitted to me, terror in Washington that the President might be bewitched by the music of the Churchillian siren. The White House and the State Department clutched their life-belts and prepared to repel boarders.

Early in January, 1952, the boarders arrived at New York in the *Queen Mary*. They were greater in number than the Prime Minister wished, because the Foreign Secretary had insisted on coming and so had the Chiefs of Staff.

On the Atlantic voyage, it was difficult to persuade Churchill to read the array of briefs and memoranda which had been laboriously prepared in Whitehall. When I tried to engage his attention to one or two of the more important, he protested that he was going to America to re-establish relations, not to transact business. A protoplasm, he said, was born sexless. Then it divided into two sexes which, in due course, united again in a different way to their common benefit and gratification. Such, too, should be the story of Great Britain and America and it was not going to be told in a lot of turgid briefs.

The visit was a success. Military matters relating to NATO and the Korean War were fruitfully discussed; and Churchill won a long, loud and standing ovation when he addressed both Houses of Congress. The only fly in the otherwise pure ointment appeared afterwards, in the House of Commons, because Churchill had said in his speech to Congress that if the truce we and the Americans were seeking in Korea were broken, our response would be 'prompt, resolute and effective'.

This caused a stir among the Labour Members who had visions of atomic bombs being dropped; but Churchill told the House that the words were, he thought, better than 'tardy, timid and fatuous'.

The offending words were in fact the only ones in the entire speech to Congress which were not Churchill's own composition. He had, as was so often the case before an important speech, been still in bed toying with the final draft when he should already have been dressed and ready to leave. All demands that he should get up were met with angry frowns and grumbles. Finally into the room came Sir Roger Makins to announce that the car was already at the door. Churchill said he was short of three adjectives: what would our response be if the Chinese and the North Koreans broke the truce? 'Prompt, resolute and effective', said Sir Roger, his eye glued anxiously to his wrist-watch. 'Good,' said the Prime Minister. He then got out of bed, had a bath and miraculously arrived at the Capitol on time.

In the spring of 1952, General Eisenhower decided to resign his post of Supreme Allied Commander of the NATO forces in Europe and to seek nomination as the Republican Candidate in that year's Presidential Election. In May the Churchills gave him a large farewell dinner at which he said that if he were elected, he would pay just one visit outside the United States and that would be to the United Kingdom, in order to demonstrate the special relationship. This was music to the Prime Ministerial ears; and a month later Churchill told me that if Eisenhower were elected, he would have another shot at making peace by means of a meeting of the Big Three. It was the first indication of what later became his theme: he would stay in office with one overriding ambition, namely to bring Stalin (or, as it later became, Malenkov) to the conference table with Eisenhower, and to preside over the ending of the Cold War. The Russians, he said, feared our friendship more than our enmity; and to remedy this state of affairs was his last ambition.

In August Truman agreed to send a message, signed both by Churchill and himself, to the Persian Prime Minister, Mossadeq, who was threatening the British oil installations, ignoring the Shah and invariably fainting or bursting into tears when thwarted or opposed. As this was the first time since 1945 that the Americans had agreed to an overt 'ganging up', Churchill was elated. He had visions of a tripartite Congress in Vienna where the Potsdam Conference might be reopened and the vexatious problem of the eastern German frontier settled by a final Peace Treaty. When, in November, Eisenhower duly won the Election, it seemed appropriate to establish an equally close, or perhaps even closer, association with the incoming Republican administration, though Churchill believed that as a general rule it was easier to work with the Democrats than with the Republicans.

So on New Year's Eve, 1952, we again set forth in the *Queen Mary* with the dual objective of bidding Truman farewell in Washington and greeting the Republicans at their temporary headquarters in the Commodore Hotel, New York. This time Churchill had somehow contrived to shake off both the Foreign Secretary and the Chiefs of Staff.

In his talks with the Republicans there was little reference to Russia, but Churchill quickly decided that he disliked and distrusted the in-coming Secretary of State, John Foster Dulles, whose influence on Eisenhower he thought pernicious and whose views, on the Middle East in particular, he found obnoxious. However, nobody could have been friendlier or more attentive than Eisenhower. He spent many hours visiting Churchill who was staying at Bernard Baruch's appartment in E. 66th Street. He did, indeed, say that we must be careful about collusion; he was in favour of it clandestinely, but not overtly; but in general he seemed to defer to Churchill's greater age and experience to a remarkable degree – especially when John Foster Dulles was absent.

Those who called on Churchill included Harry Luce, founder and proprietor of *Time* and *Life*, and his wife, Claire. Churchill had long been fascinated by Claire's beauty and intelligence, but he was taken aback when Eisenhower asked how he would view her appointment to the London Embassy. A woman, and a former actress at that, as American Ambassador to the Court of St James was, in 1953, something too ludicrous to contemplate. It was an improper suggestion. 'I love her', he said, 'and admire her; but if you were to do any such thing I should feel obliged to advise the Queen to declare her *persona non grata.*'

'I thought you would say something like that', said Eisenhower. 'All right, then, it will have to be Winthrop Aldrich'. Churchill tried to persuade Eisenhower to break with American precedent and instead of continuing the established practice of making party political appointments to important foreign Embassies, to leave in London the intelligent and much respected nominee of Truman, Walter Gifford. Eisenhower said that in principle he agreed, but he was obliged to reward those who had contributed generously to his election campaign. It was not a good system, and he would like to change it; but it was beyond his power to do so.

Here, let me digress. As London was so unchivalrously barred to her, Claire Luce went as American Ambassador to Rome and presided with skill over the distribution of Marshall Aid to Italy. In April, 1955, Churchill decided that on leaving office he would like three weeks' holiday in the sunshine and he invited my wife and me to go with him to the Hotel Politi at Syracuse. It seems that in Sicily the sun is supposed to shine in April; but in 1955 it did nothing of the sort. It rained day after day and Churchill was reduced to setting up his easel and painting in a cave. The Luces announced that they would join us from their Roman Embassy. Churchill was delighted: Lady Churchill, who wanted peace and quiet, was not; but before she could devise an excuse, the Luces arrived.

The Colours Change

The first night, I sat next to Harry Luce at dinner. He was much in favour of the noisome anti-Communist crusade which, with the aid of every conceivable miscarriage of justice, Senator McCarthy was leading in America. I crossed swords with him on the subject. 'Listen', he said, 'I have been reading British history recently. You British had a fine development called the Industrial Revolution. You were the pioneers of machinery, and then a whole lot of Lollards came out at nights and destroyed your fine machines'.

'Not Lollards, Harry. You are getting confused with Henry IV, Part I or Part II. You mean Luddites'.

'Well, I don't give a damn whether they were Lollards or Luddites. The point is they were Communists, and if Senator McCarthy had been in England at that time, it would have saved you a *lot* of trouble.'

The next day was Sunday. Harry was a Wesleyan Methodist, born and bred by missionaries in China and overbrimming with sympathy for Madame Chiang-Kai-Chek, who was also a Wesleyan Communist-fighter. Claire, however, was a Roman Catholic and seeing that she, not he, was the Ambassador, Harry accompanied her to High Mass at the Cathedral. The Italians, conscious how much depended on liberal dollops of Marshall Aid, had left no stone unturned. When the Luces came back to the hotel, there were tears in Harry's eyes. He took me aside.

'It was the most moving ceremony I ever attended. There, right out in front of that vast congregation, were two solitary prie-dieux for Claire and me. And at the end of the Mass, the congregation filed quietly out of the Cathedral, leaving Claire and me kneeling on those prie-dieux while, very gently, the organ played *My country 'tis of thee*'.

I put my tongue firmly in my cheek. 'Harry, I don't like to disappoint you; but you know they were in fact expecting Sir Winston and Lady Churchill; and it was *God Save the Queen* the organ played'.

His face fell. 'Now, Jock, please don't tell Claire that. It will spoil the most beautiful illusion'.

Yet, Harry Luce built from nothing one of the most successful publishing businesses in America; and he was also a good and generous man. Unlike his wife, he was just incurably naive.

I return to Anglo–American relations in the early 1950s. Churchill went home from America in January, 1953, well satisfied with the progress he had made. He was distressed to find that Anthony Eden, for whom he had a deep affection, was seriously ill; but this ill-wind did blow him an opportunity to take charge of the Foreign Office, the only great Department of State he had never held. On 11 May, paying no attention to Foreign Office objections, he ended a speech in the House on Foreign Affairs by unfolding, albeit in guarded terms, his hopes of what he had taken to describing as an 'easement' in relations with Russia and made a plea for a new approach to end the suspicions and misunderstandings dividing East and West. It would be a mistake to assume that nothing could be settled with Soviet Russia unless or until everything was settled, or 'to map things out too much in detail and expect that the grave fundamental issues which divide the Communist and non-Communist parts of the world could be settled at a stroke by a single comprehensive agreement'. This did not, however, mean that a start should not be made. Perhaps the ideal of the Locarno Treaty, signed in 1925 in the hope of preventing war between France and Germany, might be resurrected with the object of ensuring peace between Germany and Russia.

The Minister of State, Selwyn Lloyd, had some sympathy with this aspiration, but the Foreign Office and still more the State Department were alarmed. They feared a weakening in resolve by the NATO powers. Churchill's speech was indeed surprising to all but the few who knew where his thoughts were moving, for nobody had seen more clearly the inexorable purpose of Communism, immune to human sentiment under the malign, determinist spell of Marxist doctrine. As far back as 1944 it had been Churchill who was the first to scent the danger to any post-war settlement foreshadowed by Stalin's intransigent attitudes; and as recently as the previous January he had said to Eisenhower, when speaking of the savage treason trials in Czechoslovakia: 'That they should think it good propaganda is what shows the absolutely unbridgeable gulf between us.'

In March, 1953, Stalin had died and with a degree of wishful thinking it was believed that under Malenkov and Beria a new spirit of compromise would stir in the Soviet Union. Churchill concluded that if there was an opportunity, it must be seized without delay.

The peace of the world might depend on it and at least, as he put it to me, 'there may be a respite in which science can use its marvels for improving the lot of man and the leisured classes of my youth may give way to the leisured masses of tomorrow'. A plan was accordingly made for a journey to Bermuda in HMS *Vanguard* to initiate further talks with Eisenhower. We were to sail on 30 June, and Russia took pride of place on Churchill's personal agenda.

A week before our departure, Churchill presided at a dinner party for the Italian Prime Minister, De Gasperi, and made an entertaining speech about the Roman conquest of Britain. Just before the guests left, he had a stroke. For a few days the doctors doubted if he would survive, but he made a steady recovery. During the summer months of enforced inactivity, he pondered deeply on the means of achieving the appeasement which had now become his supreme aim, although the word itself, for recent historic reasons, was banned. He said that any other course would consign us to years of hatred and hostility, and before long the issue became a contentious one between the Prime Minister and his now convalescent Foreign Secretary. They were also in profound disagreement over British policy in Eygpt and the Suez Canal Zone.

Churchill was distressed to hear from Lord Salisbury, who paid a visit to Washington in July, that Eisenhower had become violent in his hostility to Russia, even more so than Dulles; but having successfully faced the Conservative Conference at Margate and proved to himself, by means of a fifty-minute speech, that his physical ordeal had been surmounted, he put the long-suffering *Vanguard* on notice again. This time it was for a trip to the Azores. Eisenhower flatly refused, much to the relief of the Foreign Secretary, who was at one with his own Department and with Dulles in believing that the slightly more reasonable attitude recently shown by the Russians was due less to Stalin's death than to the constant pressure and increased strength displayed by the Western Powers.

Eisenhower could not go on saying no, and in December 1953, the postponed Bermuda Conference took place. The French, who were in serious trouble in Indo-China, came too. In June they had been in difficulties about joining the party because, as used so often to be the case under the Third and Fourth Republics, they were unable to form a Government. Now, at last, they had a Prime

Minister called Monsieur Laniel, although it was feared, quite correctly, that he might not last long. Much as Churchill loved France, he found her representatives' presence on this occasion regrettable, because it would make heart to heart discussions with Eisenhower more difficult. However, to Bermuda they went and Churchill had taken great trouble to ensure that a Guard of Honour of the Royal Welch Regiment, complete with their regimental goat, should be there to greet the visiting statesmen. Luckily Monsieur Laniel quickly developed a temperature of 104°, and though his foreign minister, Monsieur Bidault, held forth at great length about Indo-China in the plenary sessions of the Conference, Churchill was able to leave him to Eden and Dulles and to monopolise the President. Indeed, immediately on Eisenhower's arrival at the airport, he was dexterously kidnapped by the Prime Minister and driven off to a tête-à-tête luncheon, to the indignation of Anthony Eden and John Foster Dulles neither of whom trusted their Chiefs alone together.

Both at the Plenary Conferences and in private Churchill advocated what it amused him to call his policy of 'Double Dealing'. This he described as a policy of strength towards the Soviet Union combined with holding out the hand of friendship. He said that only by proving to our peoples that we should neglect no chance of easement, could we persuade them to accept the sacrifices necessary to maintain strong armed forces. Alas, speaking for France, Bidault was intransigently anti-Russian; and Eisenhower, for his part, said that however much Churchill might talk about a 'New Look' in Soviet policy, he considered that Russia was a woman of the streets. Whether her dress was new, or just the old one patched, there was always the same whore underneath. America intended to drive her off her present beat into the back streets.

The fact that the French delegation leaked these earthy remarks to the press did not help matters and Churchill wisely decided to keep his powder dry for a more propitious occasion. The delegates conferred about Indo-China, Egypt, the Korean Truce and the proposed European Defence Community: the one topic about which Churchill really cared was swept under the carpet.

Then the President produced a speech which he intended to deliver to the United Nations the following week. It contained one matter of substance, relating to the potential use of the atomic bomb, which was discussed and, after urgent representations, amended. When that had been settled, Eisenhower sent Churchill the full text of the speech for his approval. It was a hot day and the Prime Minister read the text languidly. Then he told me to take it downstairs to the President and point out that it contained two split infinitives, a double past-participle and a totally unacceptable reference to 'the obsolete Colonial mould'.

With some difficulty I made my way past a posse of suspicious 'G-men' and found Eisenhower in his sitting room, cross-legged in an arm chair, going through his speech. Before I could deliver my message, he said that whereas Winston considered the atom bomb to be something new and utterly terrible, he looked upon it as just the latest improvement in military weapons. There was no distinction between 'conventional' weapons and atomic weapons: all weapons in due course became 'conventional'. Much as I disagreed, it was hardly for me to argue with the President of the United States on this delicate subject, and so I turned the conversation to the split infinitives and the double past-participle. 'Gee,' said the President, 'what greater privilege can there be than to have the acknowledged master of the English language correct my grammar for me? Please thank Winston very, very much'.

I turned to the 'obsolete Colonial mould'. The Prime Minister considered that this phrase would cause grave offence both in England and in France. Eisenhower replied that he had known Winston would not like it, but it was part of the American philosophy. However, at this time Eisenhower was indignant with the Indians who were, he thought, prevaricating at the long drawn out Korean Armistice negotiations. I therefore said that whatever the American public might think about Colonialism, a lot of people in England believed that India had been better governed by the Viceroy and the British Government of India than it had been since Independence. 'As a matter of fact,' said Eisenhower, 'I think so myself; but to us Americans liberty is more precious than good government. All the same, if Winston wants it out, I'll take it out'.

Months passed and the Prime Minister continued to brood on his objective. The last phase began in June, 1954, when we again went to Washington and Churchill stayed as Eisenhower's guest in the

Footprints in Time

White House. Since the Bermuda Conference the Americans had detonated the first hydrogen bomb. This had induced Churchill to change his strategic views and had resolved disagreement with the Foreign Secretary, and most of his Cabinet colleagues, who had been pressing him to agree to the withdrawal of the British Military Forces in the Suez Canal Zone; but his almost solitary determination to aim for an understanding with the Soviet Union remained a bone of contention at home as well as in Washington. It was not the only difference of opinion with the Americans. There were disagreements about South East Asia, Egypt, the future role of Germany in Europe (Churchill having long been in favour of inviting Germany into NATO), and atomic policy. So the Foreign Secretary came to Washington too.

On the very first day of the visit Eisenhower, to Churchill's joyful astonishment, agreed to talks with the Russians. Later on in the visit, under pressure from Dulles, he retracted his willingness to take part himself. He said, however, that if Churchill wished to see Malenkov and Molotov (Beria having vanished in a cloud of Kremlinesque intrigue), the United States would raise no objection nor do anything to damage the chances of success. There was also entire agreement on the Indo-Chinese, Egyptian and German problems and the Prime Ministerial party left well content with the wholly satisfactory state of Anglo–American relations.

The storm broke on the way home in the *Queen Elizabeth*, steaming at 30 knots through otherwise calm seas. Churchill, impatient to take advantage of Eisenhower's amenable mood, insisted on telegraphing to Molotov to propose an early meeting with Malenkov in Moscow. After a hard struggle Anthony Eden persuaded Churchill to submit his telegram to the Cabinet in London The Cabinet were deeply disturbed. Lord Salisbury and Mr Harry Crookshank threatened to resign. All was set for a bitter show-down, with Churchill offering the Cabinet the choice of acquiescing or else facing his own resignation on an issue which would split the Tory Party and the country. The Russians themselves saved the day, just before the critical Cabinet meeting in London, by inviting thirty-two nations to meet and discuss a Soviet European Security Plan. It was clear that with this proposal to the fore, they would not consider one for bilateral talks. 'Foreign Secretaries of the World Unite,' Churchill

242

commented contemptuously. 'You have nothing to lose but your jobs.'

In retrospect it seems probable that Churchill's initiative would in any event have been doomed to failure. The mantle of Stalin had by no means fallen on Malenkov whose days of power were numbered and who would have been impotent, even had he so wished, to impose or inspire the dramatic change of heart to which Churchill so eagerly looked forward. With Khrushchev at the helm there might have been a faint glimmer of hope, for he and Churchill had something in common; but Khrushchev, too, was only destined to enjoy a short reign and the dour, implacable Molotov had imprinted an apparently indelible mark of the beast on Russian foreign policy.

So Winston Churchill failed in the last endeavour to which he applied his energy and his will. Yet it was not ignoble for one of Britain's greatest War ministers to end his political life fighting, against overwhelming odds, in the cause of Peace.

43. Improperly Dressed

Winston Churchill was not an admirer of Aneurin Bevan. It was not Bevan's left-wing politics that he minded. Indeed there were extreme Socialists such as James Maxton, Tom Johnston and even the Communist, William Gallacher, whose opinions Churchill detested but for whom he had a personal liking and indeed affection. The reason he could not abide Bevan was that he suspected his patriotism. During the latter stages of the Second World War the Coalition Government suffered in the Commons the stings of several self-appointed gadflies and, in particular, Bevan and Shinwell. The difference between them was that when things were really black Shinwell could always be counted on to rally to his country's cause, and to its Government, whereas the worse the calamity the broader the smile of satisfaction on Bevan's face appeared to grow. So Churchill debated acrimoniously with Shinwell across the floor of the House but spoke well of him behind his back, whereas of Bevan he would admit no praise. It was incidentally apparent that Clement Attlee and Ernest Bevin largely shared Churchill's assessment of the two men.

Bevan was a clever debater and at Question Time in the House he was adept at putting the awkward Supplementary. But Churchill normally won on points, and occasionally on a Napoleonic knock-out. He often did so by contriving to make the House laugh, which was an effective weapon of defence.

At last, however, Churchill met his Waterloo, though it was not in the House of Commons. In June, 1953, there was the Foreign Secretary's Coronation Banquet at Lancaster House, entirely refurbished for the occasion after years of neglect. The guests were the entire Royal Family and the representatives of all the foreign countries who had come to represent their Heads of State at the Coronation. As Anthony Eden was ill, Sir Winston Churchill acted as host, gorgeously bedecked in the full-dress bottle green uniform of the Lord Warden of the Cinq Ports, embellished with the ribbon of the Garter and the pendant badge of the Order of Merit. He felt as magnificent as he looked.

After the banquet, the whole company repaired to Buckingham Palace where there was a State Ball. For the last time in history, the uniforms of former days were generally and officially worn. There were naval officers in pre-war full dress, Bengal Lancers, Hussars, Dragoons and Lancers, the powder-blue coats of Indian Cavalry, the scarlet of the Scots Greys, the old high collared uniform of the RAF, the blue and gold, with white knee-breeches, of the Foreign Service, the dress-coats of Privy Counsellors and, for those few who had no uniform at all, velvet court dress, with sword and ruffles, or at the very least a white tie, tail coat and black knee-breeches. It was the final performance of a splendid Pageant, a last sartorial echo of the Congress of Vienna.

On arriving at the Palace, by the Entrée Door in Buckingham Palace Road, Sir Winston took the wise precaution of asking a Page where he might wash his hands. When a few minutes later he emerged from behind a mahogany door, he came face to face with Aneurin Bevan who alone in that glittering throng was wearing a blue serge suit. 'I think,' said the Prime Minister, 'that at least on this occasion you might have taken the trouble to dress properly'.

Bevan smiled benignly; 'Prime Minister,' he said, 'your fly buttons are undone'.

44. Protocol

In seventeenth-century Naples, the Viceroy once left the Cathedral during Mass because the Archbishop, who was entitled to only one cushion, had been given two. In the same city the burial of a Princess was delayed for weeks because her coffin bore arms to which she had not been entitled in her life-time; and the Cities of Cremona and Padua disputed their precedence for a full century until the Senate of Milan pronounced that the dispute was insoluble.

It should not be thought that passion was only aroused on such matters in 17th-century Italy, or that the experience of two world wars and the growth of democracy made questions of precedence and diplomatic dignity seem an anachronism in the second half of the 20th century.

At the Coronation of Queen Elizabeth II in 1953 it was decided that, in accordance with the 1937 precedent, the Prime Ministers of all the Commonwealth countries should ride in a procession of Clarences. A Clarence is a closed carriage drawn by two horses and driven by a coachman with a footman on the box beside him. For this purpose several of the large and superfluous fleet of Royal Clarences which had been sold to Sir Alexander Korda for use in his films were retrieved and painted anew in the Royal colours. The rest were still in the Mews at Buckingham Palace. As the number of self-governing members of the Commonwealth had grown since 1937, all nine available Clarences were required and in the last the Prime Ministers of Southern Rhodesia and Northern Ireland, accompanied by their wives, were to drive together.

The Prime Minister of the United Kingdom inspected a Clarence on the Horse Guards Parade and viewed it with distaste. It was such an enclosed vehicle that he felt he would neither see nor, which was more important, be seen. However, since no lady, dressed for the Coronation, could possibly drive in an open carriage, and since the Prime Minister was to be accompanied by Lady Churchill, there was no more suitable vehicle available. Accordingly, much against his will Sir Winston Churchill was prevailed upon to drive in the first Clarence, in which special electric lighting was to be installed for the occasion.

Arrangements which were orderly, if not to universal satisfaction, had been completed when at the beginning of May the Prime Minister of Malta announced that he would not come to the Coronation unless he were treated in almost all respects like the Prime Ministers of the self-governing Dominions. One of these respects was that he should drive in a Clarence. The Cabinet, conscious of Malta's position as the George Cross Island and aware that the Queen, who had paid several visits to Malta before her Accession, was anxious to show favour to the island, agreed that this request should be admitted. The Prime Minister of the United Kingdom, whose influence was seen in this decision, at once became a hero in the island of Malta; and the islanders, who had been refusing to sing *God Save the Queen* in the cinemas, and otherwise showing signs of disloyalty, returned with alacrity to their former devotion to the Crown.

At this point discord was unleashed. In order to fit the Prime Minister of Malta and his wife into the procession it was necessary to put him in the last Clarence with the Prime Minister of Northern Ireland and his wife. This meant moving the Southern Rhodesians up one so that they should share a carriage with the bachelor Prime Minister of Ceylon. The Prime Minister of Ceylon was outraged by the suggestion that he should drive with the representatives of a country which was not wholly self-governing. He flatly declined the proposition. The Secretary of State for Commonwealth Relations, Lord Swinton, thereupon approached the new Prime Minister of Pakistan, Mr Mohammed Ali, and asked whether he would object to having his Ceylonese colleague in his carriage. Mr Mohammed Ali, although obviously a gentleman, was no less obviously a tyro in these matters. He accepted the proposition at luncheon in Westminster Hall. When he returned to his quarters his advisers set about him in no uncertain way. It was pointed out that the Indian Prime Minister, Mr Nehru, had a carriage to himself. How could Pakistan accept different treatment? If Mr Mohammed Ali acquiesced in such a proposal, he would be driven out of office and Pakistan might leave the Commonwealth.

At this juncture I tried my hand at the game, most unsuccessfully. Meeting Miss Heather Menzies at a dance I suggested that she should lobby her father to approach the Prime Minister of New Zealand and propose spontaneously (or so it would seem) that Australia and New Zealand should double up. Miss Menzies, to whom I explained that this thought had arisen from my conviction that Australia and New Zealand were the only thoroughly sensible members of the British Community of Nations, appeared to be impressed and promised to telephone her father's reactions the next morning. The fact that in the event she failed to give any indication of her father's views seemed regrettable evidence that Australia and New Zealand had much the same feelings as Pakistan and Ceylon.

By this time the British Cabinet were in a ferment. Buckingham Palace itself was seriously distressed. The Ministers at the Colonial Office, Mr Oliver Lyttelton and Mr Henry Hopkinson, had frequent interviews with the Prime Minister of Malta who refused to budge an inch. Sir Winston Churchill gave his opinion that there would be no harm in the Maltese returning in fury to Malta, since so much had been done to meet their point and so little gratitude had been shown for the British Government's intervention. The Secretary of State for Commonwealth Relations threw a serious spanner into the works by suggesting that the Prime Minister and Lady Churchill should ride in a motor car as an alternative to taking the Prime Minister of Northern Ireland and his wife in their Clarence. The Prime Minister of the United Kingdom jumped at the former idea; Lady Churchill was less enthusiastic, realising that the British populace would consider they had been treated in a manner inferior to the Ceylonese, Pakistanis, Maltese and others. The Queen, when the Prime Minister put the suggestion to her, said bluntly that she thought it was a 'rotten idea'. Moreover, the Earl Marshal pointed out that he had, with the authority of the Coronation Commission (which included not only all the Commonwealth Prime Ministers but members of the Opposition and other notables in this country) and by command of the Queen, pronounced that no mechanically propelled vehicle should drive in the Coronation Procession.

By a superhuman effort the Crown Equerry, at the instigation of the Secretary of State for the Colonies, who had visions of Malta leaving the Empire, threw in his last resources. These were two horses, doubtfully trained to resist the shouts of the mob, which were being kept in reserve in case any of the other horses in the procession were found to be indisposed on the day of the Coronation. A further carriage, of unspecified design, was procured and for several days the harmony of the British Commonwealth and Empire depended on the continued good health of the scores of horses congregated for this historic occasion in the Royal Mews.

45. *Welsh Rarebit*

The Welsh are much less troublesome politically than the Irish, but they usually contrive to present problems to a Prime Minister unless, of course, his name be Lloyd George.

I don't remember what the Welsh grievance was during the 1951 Government. Probably they felt they were not getting enough attention. Somebody had the bright, if absurd, idea that the grievance would be removed or reduced if an Under-Secretary were appointed to the Home Office with a special responsibility for Wales. However improbable this might be, the Prime Minister, who had graver matters on his mind, agreed to the proposal. The Chief Whip suggested a back-bencher, said to be brilliantly clever and impeccably Welsh. His name was Enoch Powell, and he was duly summoned to 10 Downing Street.

While he was with the Prime Minister, Miss Stenhouse rushed into my room. Now Miss Stenhouse was a pillar of 10 Downing Street. She was as faultlessly competent as she was unfailingly friendly and good-humoured. For many years she and Miss Gwen Davies were the ladies to whom everybody looked for the answer to apparently insoluble administrative problems, and they were each a repository of lore, practice and precedent. It was a most efficiently run office for which they might have claimed most of the credit, although they never did.

On this day Miss Stenhouse, for the first and only time in her long career, slipped up. She had, she told me, miscounted. There might, by statute, be no more than seventy members of the House of Commons in the Administration and Miss Stenhouse had believed there were sixty-nine. She had done her sums again and found to her horror that there were seventy. So Mr Enoch Powell could not join the Government.

It was too late to take preventive action. I waited till Enoch

Powell had left and went into the Cabinet Room to tell the Prime Minister. As Principal Private Secretary the responsibility was mine. He was rightly and naturally indignant and complained that he was badly served.

'However,' he said, 'he declined the office. Bring me *Burke's Peerage*. It seems that we must make do with a Welsh nobleman'.

As I was oppressed by guilt I only suggested with diffidence that perhaps the Chief Whip should be asked to search for the requisite nobleman.

'Do as you are told', said Churchill. 'Bring me *Burke's Peerage*'.

So we sat at the Cabinet table and started at A. My own desk was piled high with work and I foresaw this would be a long process. So I sprang into action at the first name, which was Abergavenny. 'Just the man,' I said. 'Good Welsh name, delightful personality, most conscientious, very quick-witted: he was at Cambridge with me.'

'I am not doing this to gratify your Cambridge friends. Besides, his surname is Nevill and he lives in Sussex.'

We plodded on. An hour later we had reached L.

'How about Lloyd George?' said Churchill.

'I don't think he'd do; but he has got a very nice son whom I know well.'

'I have already said I am not doing this to confer favours on your friends. Anyhow his son isn't a peer.'

Lloyd was on the same page. By now it was lunch-time and the morning had been wasted.

'Ah,' I said. 'He has been working hard in the Lords ever since the end of the war. One of the few young peers who helps to run the place. Very good war record. Charming nature. Absolutely admirable.' And then, before I could stop myself, I added: 'I know him well. We were at Cambridge together.'

A menacing sound was audible, but I had the wit to add, just in time: 'What's more he is the son of George Lloyd.'

Churchill calmed down. 'That is different', he said. 'You mean the son of my old friend, George Lloyd? Send for him at once.'

So the 2nd Lord Lloyd of Dolobran, who was busy feeding the pigs when my telephone call came through, went to London and received an office, the duties of which he fulfilled most conscientiously. The Prime Minister was pleased, Lord Lloyd was pleased, and Miss Stenhouse and I were greatly relieved. The only people who showed no obvious gratitude for the trouble taken were the Welsh, but that was not Lord Lloyd's fault.

46. A Game of Bézique

By the late summer of 1954 most of Sir Winston Churchill's colleagues in the Government thought the time had come for him to retire. There was no doubt who his successor should be: Anthony Eden had been the heir apparent and presumptive for nearly ten years. Churchill's stroke in July 1953 had left him temporarily paralysed and he was growing increasingly deaf. His intellect was unimpaired and he could still make a brilliant speech: indeed as late as March, 1955, he delivered two in the House of Commons, on Defence and Foreign Affairs, acclaimed by Government and Opposition alike and worthy to stand comparison with those made in his prime. None the less, with his 80th birthday approaching and the details of administration becoming both a burden and a bore to him, none could deny that retirement, in a blaze of glory and esteem, seemed appropriate.

Nobody was more convinced of this than Lady Churchill who had wanted him to renounce politics in 1945 and had regretted his decision to become Prime Minister once again in 1951. However, like any devoted wife, she resented others criticising her husband or expressing views that it was time for him to go, however much she privately shared them. Mr R.A. Butler, Lord Salisbury, Mr Harold Macmillian and the Chief Whip, Mr Patrick Buchan Hepburn had met to discuss how Churchill might best be induced to resign in favour of Anthony Eden. They had concluded that this delicate operation would best be performed through the agency of Lady Churchill. They delegated Mr Macmillan, whose skilful diplomacy in such matters was undoubted, to make the approach.

Thus it was that Mr Macmillan called on Lady Churchill one morning and presented with great tact the case for Sir Winston's departure. After he had gone, she asked me to go up and see her, recounted the conversation, expressed astonishment and distress and said that she hoped I would have luncheon with Sir Winston and her as she did not wish to be alone when she told him of Mr Macmillan's representations.

So the unsuspecting Prime Minister came down to luncheon in the small white panelled dining-room at No. 10, which lay between the State Dining-Room and the large pillared drawing room. I could see that Lady Churchill was uneasy, but half way through the first course she took a deep breath and unfolded the story. Sir Winston listened attentively but without emotion. When she had finished he said, with mock gravity: 'I think that if the Minister of Housing and Local Government has a message of this kind for me, he should give it to me personally and not burden you, my dear, with such matters'. Then, turning to me, he said: 'When you have finished your fish – but, pray, do not hurry or it may impair your digestion – would you be so kind as to go and ring up the Minister of Housing and Local Government and ask him to come and see me at 4.00 o'clock'. I did so.

Nothing more was said on the subject for the rest of luncheon, but rather to my surprise the Prime Minister, who had abandoned his war-time habit of an hour's sleep in the afternoon, said as he finished his brandy that he proposed to go to sleep for an hour or so. I went downstairs to my desk but at 3.20 precisely the telephone rang and Sir Winston, speaking from his bedroom, said that before continuing his labours, he thought it would be agreeable to have a game of bézique. Would I instruct the servants to have the card table prepared in the Blue Drawing Room and he would be down in a few minutes. I went upstairs to await him.

The Prime Minister had an addiction for six-pack bézique, but seldom in the afternoon. He had discovered that a game normally lasted twenty minutes. He often found this information useful in the early hours of the morning, because if a game ended at about 1.30 a.m. and his opponent was showing obvious signs of fatigue, he could usually inveigle him into playing one more game by assuring him that in twenty minutes he could go to bed.

At exactly half past three we began to play. The cards went my way and I had four béziques three times over – three 'Grand Cops', as Sir Winston called such strokes of fortune. 'Let us have another game,' he said. 'But Mr Macmillan is coming at 4.00', I objected. 'He will probably be late', replied Sir Winston; and at ten to four we began our second game.

At 4.00 precisely a messenger opened the door and announced that Mr Macmillan had arrived. The Prime Minister commanded that he be shown in. 'Ah, my dear Harold, forgive me if we just finish this game. Have a cigar; have a whisky and soda'. Mr Macmillan declined both and sat on the sofa. For the next ten minutes, Sir Winston carried on a running commentary about the game in which, for the second time running, I was holding exceptionally good cards. He complained of my luck; he dilated on the part which chance plays in life; he gave a homily on gambling. Mr Macmillan began, I thought, to look uneasy.

At ten past four the game ended. I had won £1 8s. od. Normally gains and losses were entered in red ink on a scrap of paper, kept in a drawer of the card table, and Sir Winston, who was a constant loser, paid his debts about once a quarter. On this occasion he proclaimed, after further complaints about my luck at cards, that he must pay. So, while Mr Macmillan sat waiting, he sent for one of his 'young ladies' and a cheque book. When the young lady arrived she brought his black pen. He insisted that he could only write cheques with his gold pen. Minutes passed while she went to fetch it and Churchill discoursed gaily on the iniquities of the Opposition. He wrote out the cheque and misdated it. Tearing it up, with comments about the importance, from the Bank's point of view, of cheques being correctly written, he started to write another, pausing for a minute or so to give us a few reflections on the revolution produced by the introduction of credit instead of cash. Mr Macmillan seemed on the verge of fidgeting.

At long last Sir Winston turned to me and said apologetically, as if apprising me of something unexpected, that he believed Mr Macmillan might wish to speak to him of some political matter. Would I mind leaving them alone?

I asked the messenger to let me know when Mr Macmillan left. As soon as he did so, I ran upstairs to the Blue Drawing Room. The Prime Minister was sitting alone at the card table, his lips pursed. 'I really don't know,' he said, 'what Clemmie was making such a fuss about. He was *most* amenable. Let's have another game of bézique.'

47. Churchill College

Winston Churchill's last enterprise culminated in the foundation of a new college at Cambridge University. It happened like this.

One evening after dinner at the Hotel Villa Politi in Syracuse, Churchill, Lord Cherwell (the former Professor Lindemann) and I sat talking of the achievements and failures of Churchill's last Administration which had ended a fortnight previously. We had been looking at some papers, still in Churchill's black box, with which he had omitted to deal before his resignation. Among them was a minute by Cherwell on the comparative failure of the United Kingdom to produce the number of engineers, scientists and technologists of all kinds required to keep pace, even *pro rata* to our population, with the output from institutions in the United States and the Soviet Union. Our quality was good; our quantity was deplorable; and our methods were haphazard. Just because Newton discovered the law of gravity by chancing to notice an apple fall from a tree, it did not follow that British scientists in the 20th century should work on the same pattern.

Churchill said that he had read Cherwell's paper on the subject. He had also read earlier memoranda of a similar kind. He had done nothing about it while he had the power. It was, he continued, the most serious omission of which he was conscious and it left him with a sense of guilt. He should have taken steps to establish in Britain something comparable to the Massachusetts Institute of Technology, which he had several times visited and by which he had been deeply impressed. He had put the matter aside, and now it was too late. Cherwell said it was never too late and I, having drunk enough brandy to be more than usually impetuous, volunteered to raise the money to finance such an enterprise. Churchill turned slowly towards me: 'If you will do that', he said, 'it will be a great relief to me. You may use my name in any way you see fit'.

Back in London I devoted myself to the task. I found that a

number of the largest British companies, including Shell, ICI and
Vickers, had been considering the provision of finance for a smaller
but comparable affair at Birmingham University. Churchill had in
mind a far more ambitious scheme and Lord Salisbury, who as
Lord President of the Council was responsible for scientific and
technological development, put me in touch with the brilliant
Cambridge chemist, Sir Alexander Todd. He, in turn, produced
Sir John Cockcroft, one of the pioneers of nuclear physics, and the
Vice-Chancellor of Cambridge University, Brian Downs. I suggested to Churchill that he should form a Committee of Trustees,
with himself as chairman. We chose a formidable body of industri-
alists: the chairmen of Shell, ICI, Vickers and Associated Electrical
Industries; and they were balanced by distinguished representatives
of the University, Lord Adrian, Master of Trinity and famous Nobel
Prize-winning physicist, Noel Annan, Provost of Kings, Todd,
Cockcroft and Downs. The Trustees met regularly, with Churchill
presiding, at his London house, 28 Hyde Park Gate; and I became
such a bore on the whole subject that Lord Chandos, chairman of
AEI, said to me in bitter-sweet tones, 'If you go on like this, we
shall end by having to call the thing "Colville College".' I had my
own back by persuading Lord Nelson, chairman of AEI's competi-
tor, English Electric, to subscribe £100,000, whereas AEI could
only afford £50,000. Chandos was obliged to ask Nelson to reduce
his subscription by half so that the big electrical companies might
all be seen to give the same.

After an energetic fund-raising campaign, Lord Knollys, chairman of Vickers, and I, with the help of many captains of industry,
found the millions required. As Shell provided, at the company's
own expense, a secretary and all secretarial facilities, the cost of
raising the funds was only 0.3% of the sum subscribed. The Trades
Union Congress, together with the Transport and General Workers
Union, made a substantial gift to build, within Churchill's institution, a library dedicated to their former member, and Churchill's
cherished colleague, Ernest Bevin. Large as was the sum we raised, it
was scarcely sufficient to erect in green fields an entirely new technological university comparable to the Massachusetts Institute of
Technology. That, too, would have meant robbing existing colleges
and universities of their best scientists and engineers. So Cambridge

University, instigated by Downs, Todd and Cockcroft, offered to accept a new college, devoted to science and technology, among its ancient and non-specialist collegiate foundations. They suggested, too, that this new college be called after Churchill and be the national memorial to him.

I was entrusted with the task of laying this offer and proposal before him. He did not, as I had hoped, show immediate gratification; but then he seldom reacted according to expectation. Perhaps he thought it strange that he who, apart from being Chancellor of Bristol and the recipient of a score of honorary degrees, had no connexion at all with universities, should be asked to agree that his own memorial be within one; and no less strange that it should be built in his life-time.

'What memorial', I asked, 'could be more lasting than a great university college?' After a minute or two, he replied: 'It is very nice of them. And I ought certainly to be pleased. After all, it will put me alongside the Trinity'.

48. Ripples

The fate of individuals is, perhaps more often than not, affected by events with which they have no personal connexion. In my case I suppose the event was the Balfour Declaration, made when I was two years old.

In March, 1954, I was offered the post of Head of Chancery in Washington. There was no more coveted opening to a successful career in the Foreign Service. I was just 39, which was young for the post, and I was elated by the prospect. However, as I had a close and valued relationship with Winston Churchill and was profoundly conscious of the debt I owed him, I did not want to disturb his office arrangements as the end of his politically active life approached and I feared that my replacement by an unfamiliar face would indeed disturb him. I decided it would be best to explain my dilemma frankly, asserting that I would not desert him against his wishes for all the gold in Fort Knox but adding that it would, all the same, be a pity not to grasp an opportunity which was unlikely to recur in such an enticing form.

Churchill said that he saw no difficulty. He was in any case contemplating retirement in September and all the Foreign Office had to do was to find a temporary incumbent for six months. I was in no circumstances to miss the opportunity: he would personally arrange the matter with the Foreign Secretary, Anthony Eden.

Anthony Eden must have been delighted. It was the first indication that the Prime Minister had set a date, at least a provisional date, for his retirement; and Eden's right to the succession was uncontested. So arrangements were made for the designated Head of the British Information Services in New York to pause in Washington for six months on his way to his new post and to serve there as acting Head of Chancery. His name was Harold Beeley. He was six years older than me and, entering the Foreign Service after the war, he had established a high reputation as an Arabist with a profound knowledge of the language and culture and a sympathetic under-standing of the Arab cause.

Beeley had not been long in Washington when the Ambassador, Sir Roger Makins, received a call from Mr Sulzberger, the powerful Publisher and Proprietor of the *New York Times*. The reason for his call was to say that if Mr Harold Beeley became Head of the British Information Services in America he would be given no co-operation at all by the American press which was, by and large, dedicated to the Zionist cause.

So the only thing to do was to leave Mr Beeley in Washington, in the safe anonymity of Head of Chancery, and Sir Roger informed me with expressions of regret that the offer to me must be withdrawn. I was gravely disappointed and so when, shortly afterwards, I was offered employment, as soon as Churchill should retire, by Philip Hill, Higginson & Co., a rapidly rising and successful Merchant Bank, I accepted with alacrity, in spite of tempting alternative offers by the Foreign Office. I doubt whether the Foreign Office lost or Philip Hill, Higginson gained very much; and I certainly suffered no disadvantage. The story is only worth telling as an illustration how the smallest ripples from a distant storm, in this case the antagonism of Jew and Arab in Palestine, can change the lives of people who believed themselves totally insulated from the storm centre.

49. Nationalisation

Kwame Nkrumah, first President of the newly independent State of Ghana, had as an adviser Mr Geoffrey Bing, QC, formerly Labour MP for Hornchurch, whose sentiment had been so far to the left in Mr Attlee's 1945 Government that not only the Conservatives but many Labour MPs looked upon him with deep suspicion. Rejected by the Hornchurch electors in 1955, he found solace in the favour of Nkrumah, the Osageyfo or Messiah as he liked to be called locally. As Mr Bing was an advocate of State control he advised the Osageyfo that it would be progressive and advantageous to nationalise the gold mines in deference to which Ghana had previously been known as the Gold Coast.

There were problems. The largest and most lucrative mine was Ashanti which depended for its success on skilled British mining engineers and the import of sophisticated machinery from South Africa, two facts of life which had to be hidden as far as possible from the Ghanaian public. It was much too large a gnat to swallow because the compensation would have been enormous. However, there was a smaller and easily digestible mine which belonged to the Ashanti company and there were four other mines, one of which produced gold at a low cost by dredging sludge instead of the more expensive deep mining. These four companies, all quoted on the London Stock Exchange and owned by a large number of small shareholders, were managed by a mining group with a head office somewhere in Finsbury. At least two of the mines were close to exhaustion and their shares were quoted at a low price which, in the normal course of events, could only be expected to drift lower.

One day the London Manager of the Ghana Commercial Bank called at the office of Philip Hill, Higginson, Erlanger & Co., of which I was a director, and enquired if we were willing to arrange the purchase of all the gold mines, except Ashanti, by the Government of Ghana. The reply was that we should be glad to do so provided that the transaction was effected by an offer to the existing shareholders of all the companies concerned which would be judged fair by the City of London. I was deputed to arrange the transaction and to take with me a young but highly skilled accountant, Peter Kirwan Taylor, who had recently joined Philip Hill. That very night we flew to Accra.

Meanwhile, in the misguided belief that pressure on the mining companies would make them more amenable, Nkrumah and Geoffrey Bing had published a Mines Expropriation bill. It was coupled with a press campaign aimed at the redoubtable Major-General Sir Edward Spears, Chairman of Ashanti, who was temporarily in residence at the company headquarters at Obuasi. The press campaign included offensive and totally undeserved references to the blameless and intelligent Lady Spears, better known as the American authoress, Mary Borden. The infuriated General sent to London for a learned Counsel, Mr David Karmel, QC, in order to seek advice on legal counter-measures.

During our flight to Accra, Peter Kirwan Taylor and I calculated the value of the shares. We must, of course, secure the best bargain for our clients, the Government of Ghana. Equally it must be something which the shareholders and the London Stock Exchange found acceptable. We both felt sure that the Ghanaian negotiators would demand too low a price. So we decided to propose figures threepence, or in some cases sixpence, a share above what we believed to be right in the confident expectation that, after a lot of argument, we should be graciously enabled to reduce our bid to the correct figure. We were pleased with this simple strategy, believing that in the end it would ensure justice for all concerned.

We were met at Accra airport by Mr Geoffrey Bing and the Lord Chief Justice, Sir Arku Korsah, a man who combined legal ability with personal charm and total incorruptibility. Ushered at speed through rows of bowing emigration and Customs officials, we were driven in handsome limousines to Mr Bing's villa where he plied us with well-iced vintage champagne. It was, he said, just the thing after an uncomfortable night's flying. I began to think well of Mr Bing who was intelligent and agreeable in addition to being so hospitable.

At 10.00 o'clock we were driven to Flagstaff House, residence of the Osageyfo. He greeted us courteously and, with his pleasant manner and lively sense of humour, won our instant liking. How much, he asked, would the proposed operation cost? About £10 million in all, we said. We then proceeded to explain the cost per share which we recommended for each mining company. Nkrumah had, he said, come out of a Cabinet Meeting to receive us and must return. He had no time to consider details. What we, representatives of a distinguished Merchant Bank, said was the right price must indeed be the right price. He was glad to accept our offer. Peter and I looked at each other: we were both blushing and before the Osageyfo could vanish into the Cabinet Room, I suggested that we should perhaps discuss the detailed prices with the Minister of Finance, Mr Gbedemah. What, asked Nkrumah, had it got to do with him? He did not even know of the proposal and anyhow it was the Osageyfo who decided: he *had* decided.

Of course, it would have been pleasant for the forty thousand shareholders to receive an unwarranted premium; but the reputation of Philip Hill for fair dealing was more important still. So I begged to see the Minister of Finance and finally Nkrumah, with a shrug of the shoulders, agreed. The unsuspecting Gbedemah was summoned and, much to his credit, secured an immediate grip on the problem without any previous briefing. After half an hour's wrangling he succeeded in beating us down to the prices we had all along considered correct. We mopped our brows.

Nkrumah emerged from the Cabinet and was told that all was settled. 'Good,' he said. 'Now I will send for General Spears'.

'Your Excellency', I replied, 'I have known General Spears since I was a child. He is old enough to be my father. If you send for him to see me, he will be gravely displeased and may decline our offer. I think I should go to Obuasi to see him.'

'But', said Nkrumah, 'it is an eight-hour journey by car and the road is very dangerous. There were four fatal accidents last week'. I must have made a good impression, because my safety was evidently more important than that of General Spears. Suddenly, a thought struck him. 'I tell you what', he said, 'you shall go in my Presidential helicopter. It is a present from Mr Khrushchev. It has a crew of four Russians; and they are just finishing unpacking it at the port. This will be its maiden voyage.'

Footprints in Time

I thought of the *Titanic*, but misgivings were quenched by the impossibility of showing anything but gratification. So I treated the matter lightly.

'How can I be sure your Russian crew will not take the opportunity of dropping a capitalist merchant banker overboard in the middle of the Ashanti jungle, and thus be created Heroes of the Soviet Union?'

'Mr Colville', he replied, 'you have an exaggerated idea of your importance. For that they will only be given the Order of Lenin, 2nd Class.'

We went in search of the helicopter, accompanied by Geoffrey Bing and the Lord Chief Justice with both of whom we were now on such close and affectionate terms that the thought of what the Russians might do to us almost reduced them to tears. We greeted the crew, one of whom spoke a little German. There was, it seemed, a slight hitch in that the only map available lacked an entire corner. The missing corner contained Accra and so the crew had been obliged to draw a flight track to Obuasi based largely on guess-work. Nevertheless we set off and RMS *Titanic*, as Peter and I called the machine, sped faultlessly north-westwards.

An hour later we were gazing down on a vast area of tropical jungle, with no sign of human dwelling, when the German-speaking aeronaut came back into the spacious cabin to say that we were lost. We should be somewhere near Obuasi, but there was no sign of the place. The pilot was therefore eagerly looking for a village where we could descend and ask the way.

A village of mud huts was presently espied; but when we touched gently down, there was not a soul to be seen. The villagers, convinced that an abnormally noxious ju-ju was making a visitation, had seized their children and livestock and vanished into the Bush. Patience and the fact that human curiosity is ubiquitous seemed our best hope. The Presidential ju-ju switched off its engine and the rotors came to a halt.

While we waited I observed the crew unpacking a cardboard box. It contained bronze medallions engraved with a hammer and sickle on one face and on the other a message in English, glorifying the Soviet Union as the only friend and liberator of Colonial peoples. I refrained from enquiring who had in fact liberated the Gold Coast and filled its coffers to the brim a few years earlier. I merely decided to take counter-action, making full use of linguistic advantages. Thus when, at first in twos and threes and at last in a great crowd, the villagers returned, I stood on the steps of the helicopter and informed them, with positively Soviet disregard for the truth, that I was a representative of Her Majesty the Queen and had descended from the clouds to do honour to the village. At that the inhabitants with one accord sang *God Save the King*.

The crew were clearly distraught by this propagandist victory; but when I went on to ask where Obuasi was, the village headman, having first indicated the direction and the distance, showed enthusiasm to guide us and sought to board the helicopter with most of his friends and relations. Then **it was** that British and Soviet Imperialism joined hands. While the pilot started the engine, five strong representatives of Anglo–Soviet Friendship recreated the wartime alliance and successfully repelled boarders.

Ten minutes later we circled the Obuasi football field. Below us was the General, wearing a straw hat and holding a gold-knobbed walking stick. To his right were the fire engine and the ambulance, and behind him serried ranks of Ashanti miners. They had heard that the Presidential helicopter was on its way and they were expecting the Osageyfo in person. However, the General's disappointment was much alleviated when he heard that the Mines Expropriation bill would be withdrawn, that a fair price would be offered for Ashanti's less important subsidiary and that the Osageyfo was sending flowers to Lady Spears. When Mr David Karmel, QC, arrived next day, there was nothing at all for him to do.

50. Sunset

In the late fifties and early sixties the Union Jack was lowered in one colony after another until the British Empire, which had covered almost one third of the world's surface in 1945, consisted of a few islands and two enclaves in the territory of other nations. The transfer of power, invariably amiable, was made with solemn and impressive dignity. Maces copied from that in the House of Commons were presented to legislatures by the Commonwealth Parliamentary Union; Speakers and Judges wore wigs and flowing robes in exact imitation of the British originals; and members of the Opposition were either let out of prison for the occasion or else had not yet been incarcerated. National Anthems were hastily composed, sometimes by musical ladies in Cheltenham or Bournemouth, vivid flags of many colours were unfurled and quite often new names, which few people in other countries could remember, were adopted. The Empire on which the sun never set dissolved in the space of a few years with a gratifying absence of acrimony. The dissolution made few of the former colonials wiser, more prosperous or more contented; but it is agreeable to be independent even if in some cases the price be corruption, maladministration and, at the end of a short and bumpy road, dictatorship.

In 1955 I was honoured to be elected a Director of the Ottoman Bank. It was certainly an honour because this bank, founded after the Crimean war to assist in reviving the fortunes of Turkey, has always had a high reputation for efficiency and integrity. The territories in which it operated spread outwards from those of the former Ottoman Empire and it began to open branches in a number of African countries. One of these was Uganda which, following in the footsteps of Kenya and Tanganyika, became independent in October, 1962. Being a new arrival in Kampala, the Ottoman Bank had not as yet attained the importance which attached to its name in the Middle East, nor was it as well known locally as the British

266

banks already established in the territory. Neither the Chairman nor the Deputy Chairman were free to attend the Independence cere-mony, and so my wife and I were invited to represent the Bank at the Celebrations. We accepted with alacrity.

There can be few more beautiful countries. In Kampala it rains for half an hour every day so that all is green and soft and enchanting to the eye. The town was gay with decorations and there was an almost audible buzz of good-humour, good-manners and goodwill. The Duke and Duchess of Kent represented the Queen and there was to be a succession of military parades, regattas, receptions and balls to all of which the visiting representatives of friendly powers, banks and leading industrial companies were bidden. To all but one, as far as we were concerned: no invitation had been received for the State Ball which was to be held on the night after the Independence Ceremony. We were not in the least distressed, because as it was the last of many entertainments we should certainly be exhausted and we thought it was unlikely to be exceptionally scintillating. The energetic Manager of the Ottoman Bank in Uganda, with whom we were staying, took a different view. Would not Barclays be there, and the Standard Bank and National and Grindlays? The prestige of the Bank in Kampala was at stake. He embarked on a frantic campaign of telephoning and was eventually told, to his immense relief, that our invitation was in the post. Indeed it was alleged to have been there for at least a week. It was sure to arrive before the great event.

The Kabaka of Uganda opened the social bowling. On the first night there was a party in the illuminated garden of his palace. It was crowded with guests and the lights kept on going on and off which added to the fun and originality of the occasion. My enjoy-ment was increased by the discovery that the Kabaka's Royal Anthem, played at his entry, was none other than the hymn, *O Lord on this last Holy Day*, which we had invariably sung at my preparatory school on the last Sunday of term. In one of the brief intervals when the lights came on we discovered the representatives of Her Majesty's Government huddled together in an embrasure of the palace where they hoped to avoid being trampled to death by the throng of variegated guests. They were the First Lord of the Admiralty, Lord Carrington, and the Minister of State, Commonwealth Relations Office, the Duke of Devonshire. They were, they said, giving a dinner party at a restaurant before the State Ball. Would we like to come? We explained that we had not yet been invited to the Ball. Never mind, they said; at least we could dine.

In addition to the Kabaka, there were several monarchs in Uganda, such as the King of Toro and the King of Bunyoro, who had invited guests to stay with them for the Celebrations. Among the King of Toro's guests was Mr Colin Tennant and since Africans are always generously expansive in their notions of hospitality, it is not surprising that when the King and Queen of Toro were invited to a luncheon party given by the outgoing Governor of Uganda in honour of the Duke of Kent, they assumed that they were expected to bring Mr Tennant with them. This was not, alas, the case, for the Governor's dining-room table was limited in size and there were many notables to be invited. So Mr Tennant was turned away with the painful implication that he was gate-crashing. To say that the King of Toro turned ashen white with fury would doubtless be an exaggeration, as well as being physically impossible; but he was not amused.

That night the State Ball was held. We presented ourselves at the restaurant chosen for the Carrington–Devonshire dinner party. I was, I discovered, to sit next to the King of Toro. He had a totally bald head and was dressed in a habit of sack-cloth resembling that of a Franciscan Friar. I bowed low. I addressed him alternately as 'Sir' and 'Your Majesty'. I discoursed on the beauty of the scenery; I lauded the faultless precision of the Independence Ceremony; I asked him what he thought about Mr Obote; I enquired if he had ever been to England. In reply I received nothing but grunts and sideways looks of evident distaste. After dinner I told the Duke of Devonshire that I had not found His Majesty easy going. 'You fool', he said. 'It wasn't the King. It was the Princess Royal. The King was offended about Colin Tennant; so he wouldn't come to dinner and sent his sister instead.'

'Well you might have altered the place-card', I replied with feeling, 'and it is the first time I remember meeting a bald lady dressed as a Franciscan'.

We had all dined well. They told us not to be silly about refusing to go to the Ball just because our invitations had been lost in the post. The Devonshires had been sent two lots of invitations by mistake: we could have their duplicate set. My wife said that nothing would induce her to gate-crash. It was a subject on which she was sensitive because many years before there had been a ball at Bridgewater House, where her father and mother lived, and some gate-crashers had been justifiably ejected by my mother-in-law. It had been head-line news in those distant days and all London Society had taken sides on the issue. I felt, reprehensibly no doubt, that times had changed and that there was all the difference between London and Kampala in such matters; but my wife stuck obstinately to the view that principles were principles and that gate-crashing was the eighth Deadly Sin. Finding no supporters for her righteous indignation, but still protesting strongly, she was finally dragged unwillingly to the Ball.

We had a moment's difficulty getting in. A sharp-eyed man with a beard, scrutinising every invitation, seemed dubious about there being two Dukes of Devonshire; but fortunately he was an ex-naval officer and a stern glance from the First Lord of the Admiralty resolved his doubts.

The Ball was a success. The band was excellent and the company interestingly assorted. Jomo Kenyatta was to be seen dancing with several handsome blondes and the Duke of Kent with a series of Ugandan ladies. We stayed much longer than we intended and when, towards dawn, the band broke into a waltz there were but few remaining guests to see Mr Colin Tennant and Lady Margaret Colville twirling round a deserted dance-floor to a tune which ought unquestionably to have been re-named *The Gate-Crashers Waltz*.

51. Triumph of the Old School Tie

I have long been in love with Spain and the Spaniards, who seem to me to have a greater affinity with the Protestant Anglo–Saxons than with their Latin co-religionists of France, Italy and Portugal. They have the same sense of humour, the same love of sport, the same antipathy to official interference with their daily lives, the same ingrained inability to cook and the same conviction that, although Europeans, they are superior to those unfortunate enough to live north of the Pyrenees or south of the English Channel. It is true that they kill the poor bull in full public view whereas the Portuguese wait to despatch it until, festooned with bandarillas, it has been enticed out of the arena by a herd of mangy cows. All the same it is no more obligatory to watch bull-fights in Spain than it is to hunt foxes in England, shoot kangaroos in Australia or play big-game fish in the Gulfs of Mexico and California.

Until a few years ago Britain was Spain's largest market. Then there were squabbles about Gibraltar and a curious emotional hang-over from the Spanish Civil War, which left British Socialist politicians with such a blinding migraine that they failed to grasp that the worst things going on in Spain under General Franco were mild by comparison with the activities of well over half the régimes in countries with which Her Majesty's Government maintained polite relations. This placed some obstacles in the way of British business-men but the Spaniards, for the most part, had too well developed a sense of proportion to be gravely affected by such folly and it was thus my good fortune to go frequently to Spain in the sixties and seventies in pursuit of banking business and the financing of British exports.

During one of these visits a Basque friend told me about Señor Montoya who lives on the shores of a beautiful bay, shaped like a Coquille St Jacques, near Almeria on the south coast. This bay is called the Bahia dos Genoveses because it was there that the fleet of the Republic of Genoa lay in 1571, awaiting the Spaniards under the Marques de Santa Cruz who were setting forth to meet and destroy the invading Turks at the battle of Lepanto. It is one of the few stretches of the beautiful Spanish coast which has not been irrevocably scarred by high-rise blocks of flats, hotels, casinos and villas built less to the Glory of God than as a sacrifice to the Spanish balance of payments. Here, in some thirty thousand acres of unsullied coastal magnificence, lives Señor Montoya, tilling the land and conserving the last surviving herd of white Andalusian goats. The climate, winter and summer, is delectable and although it only rains once every twenty years or so, it then pours with such vigour that the under-water caverns are filled for another generation and all the land remains green and fertile.

Señor Montoya, I was told, had no children or direct heirs. When he died, it must be feared that the Bay of the Genoese would be sold to speculators so that the task of uglifying the coast line might be completed. Laying temporarily aside my preoccupation with British exports and normal banking business, I pondered how to acquire the land, aided by generous Spanish bank-loans, to develop it with the admirable taste for which those Spanish architects not in search of a quick, heedless profit are renowned, and to sell parcels of it, with rigid conditions to prevent subsequent redevelopment of a loathsome kind, to a number of select and, of course, enormously rich sun lovers. Señor Montoya, they said, only liked Basques and Englishmen. I went to see him with my Basque friend.

He lives in a farmhouse, comfortable, spacious and old-fashioned. He was surrounded by rustic retainers who treated him with respect combined with affectionate familiarity. The white goats browsed on the hill-side, the Andalusian sky was a pure blue, a pre-1914 Rolls-Royce stood at the door, a multitude of red mullet wrapped in paper and caught that morning in the bay were being baked before a huge open fire, and the kitchen was full of shy peasant girls who seemed to play no part in running the house, but had presumably come to eat the red mullet. Señor Montoya, patriarchal lord of everything we could survey, received us with open, hospitable arms. He provided an apolaustic feast; he made our heads reel with heavy Andalusian wines; he showed us the perfect lay-out for a golf-course; and he took us for a walk round the huge semi-circle of the bay, where never a bather's foot had trod on the unpolluted sand. If, he said in his faultless English, he sold this paradise, he would like it to be to an Englishman or a Basque.

I did not enquire about his predilection for the Basques; but 'Why to an Englishman?', I asked. He explained that by some whim of his father he had been sent to school at Charterhouse. Mildly surprised that in the reign of King Edward VII, the strict, cold and doubtless inhibiting régime of an English public-school should have left behind such nostalgia in a hot-blooded Andalusian, I asked him what he had enjoyed about his Carthusian school-days. He was too polite to say what I think he really meant, but his gestures expressed something less than undiluted enthusiasm. 'I learned to speak English and I hated playing cricket', he said. 'The principal advantage came later.'

It seems that in 1936, when the Spanish Civil War broke out, Almeria and the surrounding area was held by the Republicans. They at once put in prison all the priests, landlords, large-scale farmers, retired officers and professional men on whom they could lay hands. They must have been a particularly savage horde of Republicans because they made a habit of taking two class-enemies out into the prison yard every morning and executing them without trial. As the days passed, the ranks of the incarcerated grew thinner and the dire morning came when it was Señor Montoya's turn. He was marched into the yard with a fellow-victim. The leader of the firing-squad was about to tie the bandage round his eyes, when the British Vice-Consul, alerted by nobody knows who, burst into the prison yard. 'Hey', he cried to the head-executioner. 'Dammit man, you *can't* shoot an Old Carthusian'. Britannia ruled the waves; the Royal Navy patrolled the Spanish coasts; and antagonising Great Britain, France or any of the non-aligned European powers would have excited criticism at Republican Headquarters. Señor Montoya was returned to his cell whence, after a less bloodthirsty crew had assumed command, he was finally allowed to go free; for he was not, after all, an obvious enemy of the people.

'So', he said, 'if I ever sold the estate, I should be glad to do so to an Englishman, preferably an Old Carthusian. But, you see, I don't want to sell it'.

52. Reflections

There was a time when books, apart from the Bible, were mainly the preserves of the educated, when education included familiarity with the Classics and when it was therefore unnecessary to translate Latin quotations. In the House of Commons, orators embellished their speeches with Latin tags. I remember Winston Churchill, who was not celebrated as a Latinist, trying one out on the House. There was a gasp of surprise. When he ended the sentence, using the old pronunciation of Latin (for he abhorred the modern one), he continued: 'which I will now proceed to translate for the benefit . . .'; and he paused. The Labour Members sat up and prepared to howl, assuming that he was going to say something like: 'those who have not had the advantage of a public school education.' But it was a trap. 'For the benefit,' he continued, 'of any Old Etonians who may be present.'

Here, after this lengthy prelude, is a quotation from Juvenal, my favourite Latin poet.

> 'Nunc patimur longae pacis mala, saevior armis
> Luxuria incubuit victumque ulciscitur orbem.'

And that, for the benefit of any Old Etonian readers, I will proceed to translate as follows:

> 'Now we suffer from the ills of a long period of peace. Luxury, more destructive than war, has engulfed us and imposes retribution for our conquest of the World'.

Luxury, which spreads like ground-elder as the soil grows richer, is the child of technological progress. It becomes in turn the progenitor of laxity and breeds permissiveness in its own centrally-heated greenhouse, rejecting as outworn what our sterner forbears thought virtuous. Like most of the things that are bad for us, it is exceptionally agreeable.

My mother thought Pride the worst of the Seven Deadly Sins, and I dare say that in the old days of assured dominion over palm and pine it was. In the luxurious society, Envy is ahead by several lengths; and in the same way that nowadays bad news is the only news worth printing or broadcasting, so the Seven Deadly Sins are much preferred to the Seven Cardinal Virtues. Soon, I suppose, people will start calling their children after them, and I must admit that Avarice would be a delightful girl's name, Lust or Anger would do well for a boy and Sloth, like Evelyn or Cecil, would be suitable for both sexes. Greed swims ahead of Luxury, like pilot-fish before a shark, and is effective in driving away Self-Sacrifice which, however, tends to return in times of war and dire necessity. The best antidote to Greed is a surfeit, but unfortunately the results of a surfeit can be repulsive, as we are in the process of discovering. Meanwhile, Greed is running second to Envy in the Deadly Sins Stakes, with the other five still quite well placed; and in case I be accused of mixing metaphors or similes I must assert that even sinful horses can swim.

Those of my parents' generation who were rich were seldom luxurious. There were exceptions, as there are to every rule, and there were hypocrites then as now; but I think the majority of the well-to-do were taught to believe there was virtue in being slightly uncomfortable. They subjected their children, however much they loved them, to an undernourished, over-disciplined monotonous education, and they had a sneaking feeling that Sparta must have been a more wholesome city than Athens. Cold baths, early rising and meticulously enforced punctuality, if not actually keys to the gates of Heaven, were at least letters of introduction; and it was an unpardonable transgression to pry or be inquisitive especially about women's ages or anybody's income. Perhaps all this explains why, if the Victorians were proud of their standards of behaviour, their social inferiors felt little envy.

This code of practice was less imperative to their children, but its influence was still felt by my contemporaries. I remember being one of a team of Harrow boys who went to play cricket against a Borstal XI. The Harrow team was not the best the school could field. Most of the members were, like me, deplorable cricketers; but we had an enjoyable outing. The Borstal boys enquired in detail about our system: the hours of work, quality of food, discipline, accommodation and forms of punishment. We explained and they were aghast. With one accord they thanked their stars they were not at a public school. Whatever the crimes that had landed them in Borstal, it was clear to us that they were innocent of Envy.

Self-righteousness used to be based on the certainty that the standards of morality and the goals of endeavour were unquestionably correct. Historians and some poets tend, by the way, to be particularly self-righteous in their determination to assassinate character. One classic case is Castlereagh, a convinced opponent of slavery and a leading architect of the long peace which followed the Napoleonic Wars. Because it was his misfortune to be in charge of internal security in the lean years after Waterloo, he fell foul of contemporary poets and subsequent historians. Shelley's verse,

> 'I met Murder in the way
> He had a mask like Castlereagh'.

has stuck. Yet Castlereagh's hands were clean compared with those of the French revolutionaries whom Shelley extolled.

There is still self-righteousness, but the modern species seems to grow from uncertainty rather than certainty, and to feed on the plausible theory that the past can be used as a scapegoat for the present. It is intellectually acceptable to look back in anger; it is also comforting to seize on the vices of groups or individuals in days gone by and to assume that those vices were typical of an entire age. The Victorians, in particular, have been most unfairly selected as the arch-hypocrites who covered with a cloak of pious respectability sins which can now be revealed in detail with the utmost enjoyment.

We who throw stones live, alas, in houses built of brittle glass. Perhaps it has always been so; perhaps it is the destiny of mankind both to live in glass houses and to throw stones. I think that as a counter-weight to the many who look back in anger, or even in sorrow, it may be wholesome to make comparisons unflattering to our own generation, nurtured as it has been in comparative affluence, supplied with mechanical conveniences of which our grandparents never dreamed and able not only to communicate with rapidity and ease, but also to receive in our own homes the words of wisdom, cheerful entertainment and pictorial edification which the Good and the Great see fit to offer us.

As a reward for our technological ingenuity, and as a by-product of the luxury which stems from it, we have a world of pessimism instead of sober optimism. It is no longer natural to believe in the gradual but inevitable evolution of human society to peace, justice and unselfishness. That excellent American, Dr Coué, who taught people to say, as they rose from their beds, 'Every day in every way I am getting better and better', is short of disciples. So one of the trilogy of Pauline virtues, Hope, though it does spring eternal and can never be extinguished, is under as great a strain as it has ever been.

Faith too, is unfashionable; not only faith in God and in immortality, but faith in men. All the political parties in all the developed countries proclaim that measures, not men, are the recipe for salvation. More and more complicated legislation is imposed on a bewildered and therefore decreasingly resistant public, until the law becomes discredited and even the temperamentally law-abiding cease to care. As society grows more permissive, the State imposes its own moral code. I personally think that Africans, Asians and women should be treated with courtesy and given equal opportunities to secure good jobs. I also perceive that when driving a car it is wise to wear a seat-belt. It is, however, intolerable to be obliged by law to take a view as to what is morally right or to be ordered by Parliament to do what is for my own good. It is no less intolerable for the State to insist that children be educated, not as their parents wish, but as faceless men in Education Authorities decree. There can only lie ahead a few short, retrograde steps to Sumptuary Laws, such as Peter the Great imposed on his Russian subjects, forbidding them, for instance, to wear beards. Centuries ago Kings and Governments insisted that sins were crimes. Modern State paternalism, replacing the outmoded weapon of social disapproval with sharper swords, moves backwards to medieval philosophy.

Throughout history, great men have abjured the complicated and had the vision to see one clearly sign-posted road on which to lead the people. Indeed, it was beyond the wit even of a Moses, a Julius Caesar, a Napoleon or a Churchill to be anything but simple in his appeal to the masses, nor would they otherwise have been understood or followed. It is therefore unlikely in an age when complicated measures are talismen that great statesmen will again emerge, especially as war, their traditional nursery, would presumably become a world holocaust before their merits were discerned. We have, it seems, resolved that for the future we shall place such faith as we have left not in men, but in measures.

What of Charity? This, the greatest of the three virtues recommended by St Paul, was once easy to define. It is no longer so, for everybody has a different idea of which neighbour he should love, and those he does not choose to love, he thinks it right and logical to hate. We live among people with a selective conscience, people who no longer judge on generally acknowledged grounds of right and wrong, but consciously or unconsciously make heroes of those whom one political group or another find ideologically acceptable, and allow no merit at all to the miscreants on the other side of the fence. The rulers of Chile, Spain or South Africa are detestable to some; those of the Soviet Union, Cuba or Czechoslovakia are no less detestable to others. The outraged denouncers of torture in Chile and Brazil keep silent, or even find excuses, when torture no less vile is used in Eastern Europe. The thousands of students who demonstrated outside every American Embassy during the Vietnam war, stay quietly at home when they read of the atrocious tyranny of the Khmer Rouge in Cambodia. Others who decline to smoke a Havana cigar in case it should help Castro, turn a blind eye to the injustice of Apartheid. And the great mass of the people are like Gallio, the Roman Governor of Corinth: they care for none of these things.

Offences, and even opinions, which were once considered venial are rated as crimes against society; what used to be held unpardonable is excused because the offender was once slapped by his grandmother. The people, or at least those who presume to speak for them, have lost their sense of proportion. Once again I quote Juvenal:

'*Dat veniam corvis, vexat censura columbas,*'

which may be translated: 'The ravens are forgiven; the doves get all the blame.'

Footprints in Time

When the stars of true liberalism were in the ascendant, excessive conformity was regarded with disdain. It was considered the Shibboleth of conservatism. Since then the needle of the compass has swung 180°. Progressives are now conformists, whether it be in education, in Trades Unionism, in architecture or in such matters as metrication. Simple though it be for the retailer, by pressing a few buttons on a pocket calculator, to sell in inches what he has bought in centimetres, the conformists of today believe that idiosyncrasy, even in weights and measures, is a heinous and heretical deviation which should be forbidden by law. It is an attitude of mind much in vogue in Russian and Chinese governing circles. This latter-day conversion of the progressives to conformism does not, however, extend as far as disapproving of impatience with social and educational discipline, nor does it embrace the belief of the old-fashioned conformists that there should be moderation in all things.

Inability to express our meaning clearly and simply is a growing danger to society. Years ago I went to beg money for the foundation of Churchill College from that musical and talented industrialist, Sir Leon Bagrit, then Chairman of Elliot Automation. He gave me a large contribution, but said that he would have given still more if the College, instead of aiming to produce scientists and technologists of the highest quality, had been founded to specialise in semantics. We were, he said, reaching a stage of development at which those working at one end of a computer were unable to understand what those at the other end meant. Language was ceasing to be an efficient means of communication.

I think this is particularly true of English, the language of business and of modern technology. One of the reasons may be the very size of its vocabulary which, if used with discrimination, should increase lucidity and improve intelligibility. Alas, it is no longer used with discrimination. Here Sloth makes up a place or two in the Deadly Sins Stakes. On both sides of the Atlantic words and expressions are created, not adding richness – for the riches are there in abundance for those who seek them – but introducing confusion. The tired and the overworked become verbose, and few have been brought up to value economy of expression.

Laziness and mental exhaustion may be chiefly to blame, but

"8948"

tidn4 goce

Footprints in Time

John Colville

The Colours Change

perhaps some contribution has been made by the departure of Tacitus and Cicero from the school curriculum. Perhaps, too, it is because the poetry of language is no longer cherished or even recognised. Poetry itself, the hall-mark of civilisation and a pleasure once enjoyed as widely as music, has lost its appeal for the majority. Nor is it only the poetry of verse that is of little account. If the Anglo–Saxon peoples once spoke and wrote their language well, it was because they were brought up with a profound knowledge of the Bible, translated by remarkable good fortune in the golden age of English literature. Parts of the Authorised Version were obscure. It may be that the 16th- and 17th-century translators failed to understand all they were trying to translate. Yet the great passages of the Old and New Testament rivalled Shakespeare in language and they provided generation after generation with a model for imaginative thought and expression. When I went to a wedding where the Moderator of the Church of Scotland read the superb Chapter XIII of the First Epistle of the Corinthians, about Faith, Hope and Charity, in the flat, uninspiring words of the New English Bible, I had no Charity. I wanted to ape Jenny Geddes in St Giles Cathedral three hundred years ago and to hurl my stool at the reader; but the service was in the Crypt of the House of Commons and there were nothing but heavy pews.

If the poetry goes out of our lives, if rectangular buildings of dirtying concrete and glass reflect the dingy uniformity of industrial society, if untidiness of dress and disregard of good manners are the fashion of the day, if Liberty is forced to strike her colours to the invading hordes of Equality, and if the legacies of Christianity and the Greek philosophers are denied and derided by the materialists of a new, so-called Civilisation, then the dark results will have been achieved in some part by reinterpreting the past to explain the inadequacies of the present. That has of course been done throughout history, Macaulay being a notorious offender well in advance of the Communists, the Fascists and a host of 20th-century historians; and there is, on the other side of the balance sheet, a long list of equally fallacious white-washers.

Since in fact human beings do not change, however much their environment may do so, we may, as Monsieur Poincaré once said and Sir Winston Churchill never tired of quoting, 'take refuge beneath the impenetrable arch of probability.' We are neither more nor less intelligent or virtuous than the Greeks, the Romans, the ancient Egyptians or the men and women of the Renaissance and the 18th century Age of Enlightenment. It is therefore reasonable to suppose that our ups and downs, our booms and slumps, our intensity of ideological fanaticism, our long periods of animosity and rare interludes of disinterested idealism will not be strikingly different from those that have preceded us, even though we do possess means of destruction which require a higher standard of patience and good temper than past generations have normally displayed.

Whatever our deserts, manna does occasionally fall from heaven. In the future it may take the form of new international groupings, such as the European Community or the Organisation of African Unity, which will damp the still smouldering fires of nationalism and provide human requirements in such a way as to extinguish jealousy and restlessness. Perhaps, too, the undoubted inability of man to live by bread alone will induce Society to substitute for hedonism a religious and moral creed in which superstition departs but faith remains. However dark the clouds (and there is little point in pretending that the sun is shining brightly), I think we can take comfort in looking back even to recent history, not with the object of finding scapegoats and not (like the Irish) to justify present discontents, but to see how it was that others, faced with problems no less grave and apparently intractable than our own, survived because of their courage, endurance and ingenuity.

By the very nature of the society which is developing, it seems that the age of the outstanding individual is unlikely to return, and it remains to be seen whether collective responsibility will prove an effective substitute. In this book I have sketched, for the most part lightly, a few men who did, I think, have true greatness and many others with high qualities. Churchill towers above the rest, less because he was a leader (indeed I doubt if he really had the gift of leadership), but because he had independence of spirit, the courage of a lion, faith in himself and his cause, the capacity and imagination to inspire, an unwavering belief in the triumph of good over evil, a tireless determination to achieve victory at whatever cost, balanced by chivalry to the foe; and, in his soul, the poetry which turned what he was trying to do into romance.

One evening, a few years before Churchill died, he recited this poem to me. I cannot trace it, but I wrote it down because I thought he was applying the words to himself:

> 'All is over: brief career,
> Dash of greyhound, slipping thongs,
> Flight of falcon, leap of deer,
> Cold air rushing up the lungs,
> Sound of many tongues.'

He paused a minute and then he went on:

> 'We tarry on; We're toiling still;
> He's gone and he fares the best,
> He fought against odds and he struggled up hill;
> He has earned his season of rest.'

Index

Index

Index

Index

Index

287